SAINTS
TO
Remember

*Dedicated
to the memory of our Founder
Father Leonard Feeney, MICM*

SAINTS
TO
Remember

Saint Benedict Center
The Slaves of the Immaculate Heart of Mary

DECLARATION

In obedience to the decrees of Pope Urban VIII and other pontiffs, we declare that we submit the entire contents of this book without reserve to the judgment of the Apostolic See of the Holy Roman Catholic Church.

SAINTS TO REMEMBER is published and distributed by *The Slaves of the Immaculate Heart of Mary* at Saint Benedict Center, Post Office Box 1000, 282 Still River Road, Still River, Massachusetts 01467, Phone (978) 456-8296, www.saintbenedict.com

Contents

January

1. The Octave of the Nativity of Jesus. (The Circumcision of Our Lord) (1 A.D.)

This is the day on which Jesus first shed His Precious Blood. It is the day on which Jesus was given His Holy Name. Mary, the virginal Mother of Jesus, held her Divine Child in her arms while His Precious Blood was being shed for the first time. This was in the rite of circumcision, a required religious observance of the Jews. It was the purpose of Jesus to fulfill perfectly all the requirements of the Old Law until the Old Law was abolished and the New Law established in its place. Because of the sacredness of the body of Jesus, and because he was liturgically allowed to do so as head of the family, Saint Joseph circumcised Mary's Child in the cave where He was born. Saint Joseph gave Jesus His Holy Name. This he was told to do by the Angel Gabriel. Circumcision was a rite of the Old Law, but by virtue of shedding the blood of the Lamb of God in this rite, Saint Joseph participated in the priesthood of the New Law.

The feast of the Circumcision was a sorrow to Our Lady, but it was a sorrow mingled with joy. Mary, the Mother of Jesus, knew that all true Christians would see, in the circumcision of Jesus, how incarnate God had become when He could shed blood. One month of the year, the month of July, is wholly dedicated to the Precious Blood of Jesus by the Catholic Church. A special remembrance of the Precious Blood of Jesus occurs on three days of the year: on January 1, the day on which the Precious Blood was first shed; on

The Child Jesus

July 1, the permanent feast of the Precious Blood; and on the fifth Friday of Lent, in a movable feast.

Saint Odilo (1049). He was a saintly Benedictine and a great apostle of the souls in Purgatory. Saint Odilo was the first to celebrate a special feast for All Souls (the souls of the faithful departed). This was in the year 998. The day Saint Odilo chose for this feast was November 2, the day after the feast of All Saints. All priests now have the privilege of saying three Masses for the souls in Purgatory on November 2.

Saint Vincent Mary Strambi (1824). He was a valiant defender of the Catholic Faith against the enemies of the Church during and after the French Revolution, which occurred in 1789. Saint Vincent Mary Strambi offered his life for Pope Leo XII, in 1823, when the Holy Father was in danger of death. God accepted this offering, and Saint Vincent Mary Strambi died in 1824. Pope Leo XII did not die until 1829. Saint Vincent Mary Strambi was a Passionist, and wrote the life of Saint Paul of the Cross, the founder of the Passionist Order, who died in 1775.

2. The Holy Name of Jesus.

This feast was established for the whole Catholic Church in 1721 by Pope Innocent XIII. If there is a Sunday in the interval between January 1 and January 6, this Sunday is the feast of the Holy Name. *Jesus*, is a name which is substantially the same in sound in all the languages of the world. In the early ages of the Church, when Catholics were so persecuted and lived in the catacombs, the beautiful abbreviation of the Holy Name for those who used it was *IHS*. These are the first three letters of the name of Jesus when written in Greek: *IHSOUS*. This symbol Catholics still retain.

No Catholic should ever, under any circumstances, profane the Holy Name of Jesus, nor allow anyone to do so in his presence. The Holy Name of Jesus is written 969 times in the New Testament. Four outstanding apostles of the Holy Name of Jesus have been: Saint Bernard of Clairvaux (August 20), who begged that the Holy Name of Jesus be lovingly kept in everyone's heart and reverently uttered on everyone's lips; Saint Bernardine of Siena (May 20), who carried the Holy Name of Jesus on a banner through the streets of Rome and everywhere he went; Saint John of Capistrano (March 28), who won a battle against the Turks in 1456 by commanding his soldiers to repeat the Holy Name of Jesus with adoration and reverence while they were fighting an army that greatly outnumbered them; and Saint Ignatius of Loyola (July 31), the founder of the Society of Jesus, which has its titular feast on January 1, the day on which Mary's Divine Child received His Holy Name.

Saint Abel (First Age of the world). Abel was the son of Adam. He was the first one ever to die. The first death in the history of all creation was a murder, and the first one to die was a saint. Abel is mentioned every day in the Canon of the Mass in the Catholic Church, and always in the Litany of the Dying. The holy ones of the Old Testament are not usually called saints when they are referred to scripturally or historically. The one day on which they are granted the title of saint is the day on which the Catholic Church especially commemorates them. There are forty-two of these holy ones. In the order in which their feasts occur in the year, they are: Abel (January 2), Malachias (January 14), Micheas and Habacuc (January 15), Amos (March 31), Ezechiel (April 10), Jeremias (May 1), Job (May 10), Eliseus (June 14), Aaron (July 1), Osee and Aggeus (July 4), Isaias (July 6), Joel and Esdras (July 13), Elias (July 20), Daniel (July 21), Samona, the mother of the Machabees, and her seven sons (August 1), Samuel (August 20), Josue and Gedeon (September 1), Moses (September 4), Zacharias (September 6), Jonas (September 21), Abraham (October 9), Abdias (November 19), Nahum (December 1), Sophonias (December 3), Ananias, Azarias and Misael (December 16), Adam and Eve (December 24), Baruch (December 28), and King David (December 29).

Blessed Stephanie (Stephana) (1530).

Blessed Stephana de Quinzanis was born near Brescia and became a Dominican nun at the age of fifteen. Rapt in the love of God she bore the mark of the sacred stigmata, the wounds of Our Lord.

3. Saint Genevieve (512).

Saint Genevieve is the patroness of Paris. At the age of seven, under the protection of her spiritual father, Saint

Saint Genevieve

Germanus of Auxerre, she dedicated herself completely to God. At the age of fifteen, she took the veil of a nun. When she was twenty-nine, in 451, she protected the whole city of Paris from destruction by the pagan army of Attila and the Huns. Saint Genevieve died in her ninetieth year. Her relics were placed in a church dedicated to her name, in Paris. These relics were burned during the French Revolution. The Church of Saint Genevieve was then turned into a temple, called the *Pantheon*, and used as a public burial place for French notables and unbelievers.

4. Saint Dafrosa (363).

She was the beautiful wife of Saint Flavian (December 22), and the mother of Saint Bibiana (Vivian) (December 2), and Saint Demetria (June 21), all of whom were martyred by the apostate Catholic Emperor Julian, who reigned for only two years (361-363), and killed hundreds and hundreds of his fellow Christians. Saint Dafrosa herself was decapitated.

Saint Elizabeth Anne Seton (1821).

Of the many saints named Elizabeth, the one most gloried in by all Americans is Saint Elizabeth Anne Seton who was born in New York City in 1774. After her husband's death she converted to the Catholic Faith from Episcopalianism. She became a nun and founded the Sisters of Charity of Saint Joseph. She died in Emmitsburg, Maryland in 1821, the same year as Napoleon, when she was forty-six years old. She was canonized in 1975.

5. Saint Telesphorus (154). He was the ninth Pope, and a martyr. Saint Telesphorus put the *Gloria in Excelsis Deo* in the Mass. This was the song which the angels in the sky sang to the shepherds of Bethlehem the night Our Lord was born. "Glory to God in the highest, and on earth peace to men of good will," the angels sang to the shepherds, thereby letting us know that anyone who does not believe that Jesus Christ is true God is not a man of good will, and has himself to blame for his own unbelief. Saint Telesphorus gave Catholic priests the privilege of saying three Masses on Christmas Day. The first of these Masses may begin at midnight, the hour when Jesus was born. Jesus was conceived at three o'clock in the afternoon, at the hour when the Angel Gabriel said to Our Lady, "Hail, full of grace, the Lord is with thee; blessed art thou among women." Jesus was conceived at the moment when Our Lady said, "Be it done to me according to thy word." Jesus was conceived on March 25, which is the time of the vernal equinox, when day and night are of equal length, and the days are going to get longer. Jesus was born on December 25, which is the time of the winter solstice, when the night is the longest and the day shortest, but the days are going to increase. The summer solstice, June 24, and the autumnal equinox, September 24, relate respectively to the birth and conception of Saint John the Baptist, the precursor of Our Lord. This lets us know how beautifully liturgical God's seasons are.

Saint Simeon Stylites (459). At the age of thirteen he was watching his father's sheep when he heard this verse of the Gospel: "Woe to you that now laugh; for you shall mourn and weep." (Luke 6;25) He asked an old man the meaning of these words, and it was explained to him that eternal happiness is obtained by suffering, and that it is in solitude that it is most surely gained.

Stylites comes from a Greek word, *stulos*, meaning column or pillar. He spent some time as a hermit and then as a monk. To better show his complete and absolute dedication to Jesus in separation from the world, he spent thirty-seven years on top of a pillar, exposed to heat and cold, adoring Jesus night and day. He was seventy-one years old when he died. He cured many spiritual and bodily illnesses. He was a perfectly humble soul.

Saint John Neumann (1860). He was born in Bohemia in 1811 and came to the United States in 1836. After being ordained he worked among the immigrants around Buffalo. He joined the Redemptorist Order and became the superior in America. In 1851 he was made Bishop of Philadelphia where he started the Catholic parochial school system and inaugurated the Forty Hours Devotion in this country. He spent many hours in the confessional. At the age of forty-nine he died. He was simple, poor and unassuming, but he performed all his duties extraordinarily well, and for this he was canonized in 1977.

6. The Epiphany (1 A.D.). This was the showing of Our Lord as a Child to the Gentile Kings. The Epiphany occurred twelve days after the birth of Jesus. The English call it Twelfth Night. It is one of the most important feasts in the Catholic Church. The Epiphany is God letting us know simply and dramatically that though He was born of the Jews, He was destined for the Gentiles. The Jews rejected Jesus. Their Temple was crashed to the ground in the year 70, and has never been built up since. Gentile Kings came over a thousand miles from the East to greet Jesus at His birth.

The Baptism of Jesus (30). Jesus was baptized when He was thirty years old and about to begin His public life. A special feast of the Baptism of Jesus is kept on the octave of the Epiphany, January 13.

The Marriage Feast at Cana (30).

This marriage feast occurred at the end of January, in the year 30, but it is celebrated today because it is, in its way, an epiphany—a showing of the power of Jesus—because it was His first miracle. This marriage feast is spoken about in the second chapter of Saint John. It was held in the little town of Cana, north of Nazareth, in Galilee, in the first year of Our Lord's public life. At the Blessed Virgin's request, Jesus changed six jars (120 gallons) of water into wine. This miracle, in addition to showing God's generosity and His eagerness to grant Our Lady any favor, is by way of giving us the type and symbol of the fact that the water poured upon every Catholic at Baptism is to give him the right to another sacrament, which he receives at Holy Communion.

Saints Gaspar, Melchior & Balthasar

Saint Gaspar, Saint Melchior and Saint Balthasar (First Century).

January 6 is the feast of these three Magi, who brought Jesus gifts of gold, frankincense and myrrh. The Magi brought Jesus gold to show that He was a king; frankincense to honor Him as God; and myrrh to greet Him as man. These Magi first saw the star which led them to Bethlehem on the previous March 25, the day, and at the moment, that Jesus was conceived in Mary's womb. It took the Magi nine months and twelve days to reach Bethlehem, guided by the star. The star left them when they were in Jerusalem. But it shone again after the Magi left Jerusalem, and led them to the cave of Bethlehem. Our Lady let each of the Magi hold Jesus in his arms. They were given some of His baby clothes to bring back to the East by way of relics. The Magi returned to the East, to Persia, and later were baptized there by Saint Thomas the Apostle, in the year 40. All three of the Magi were martyred for the Catholic Faith. Their names are now, and should always be called, Saint Gaspar, Saint Melchior and Saint Balthasar. The bodies of Saint Gaspar, Saint Melchior and Saint Balthasar were first brought to Constantinople, and then to Milan, and in the twelfth century they were placed in the Cathedral of Cologne, in Germany, where they are venerated with much love by the Christians who worship there.

The Sunday within the octave of the Epiphany is the feast of the **Holy Family**. This Holy Family is now in Heaven, all three, in body and in soul. Saint Joseph's grave was opened on Good Friday, the day that Jesus died. Saint Joseph ascended into Heaven, in body and in soul, with Jesus, forty days after Easter. Twenty-five years later, in the year 58, Mary, when she was seventy-two years old, died, and three days later she was assumed into Heaven, in body and in soul. The Holy Family,

Jesus, Mary and Joseph, is in Heaven, anxious to help us when we pray, waiting to receive us when we die.

The octave of the Epiphany, January 13, is the day on which a special Mass is said in the Catholic Church to commemorate the Baptism of Jesus by John the Baptist in the River Jordan. Under recent liturgical changes, if the octave of the Epiphany falls on a Sunday, then the feast of the Holy Family is celebrated on that day and there is no commemoration made of the Baptism of Jesus that year.

Blessed André Bessette (1937). Brother André was a simple lay brother of the Congregation of the Holy Cross at Montreal in Quebec. He had a consuming love for Saint Joseph and spent his life in spreading devotion to him. He is responsible for the famed Oratory of Saint Joseph at Montreal. Through Brother André's prayers to Saint Joseph countless cures took place even during his lifetime. Nearly a million people came to pay him their last respects when he died in 1937, at the age of ninety-one.

7. The Bringing Back of the Child Jesus from Egypt (3 A.D.). This

was when Jesus was three years old. The Holy Family fled into Egypt, a land of the Gentiles, on February 17, 1 A.D. They lived in Egypt, in a town called Fostat, near

Saint Apollinaris

Heliopolis and not far from Cairo. The Holy Family had to leave Bethlehem because of the wickedness and cruelty of the Jews, and had been warned to do so by the Angel Gabriel appearing to Saint Joseph. Herod, the King of the Jews, who tried to slaughter Jesus as an innocent Child, died in 3 A.D. Joseph and Mary then returned to Jerusalem with the Divine Child. But they had no trust in Herod's successor, whose name was Archelaus and who was one of his sons. They were warned again by an angel to avoid him, and so, on their return to the Holy Land, they traveled north of Judea, to Galilee, to the town called Nazareth, where Jesus was conceived. There they lived for twenty-seven years in the little house where Mary also was conceived and where she was born. This little house, miraculously transported, first to Dalmatia in 1291, and then to Loreto, in Italy, in 1294, is known as the Holy House of Loreto.

8. Saint Apollinaris (180). He was Bishop of Hierapolis, in Phrygia, and one of the great Fathers of the early Church.

Our Lady of Prompt Succor. This feast is celebrated especially in New Orleans. The miraculous statue of Our Lady of Prompt Succor was brought there from France by the Ursuline Nuns. It is still in their New Orleans convent. In 1815 when the British Army attacked New Orleans, the Ursulines and many others prayed to Our Lady of Prompt Succor. The greatly outnumbered American Army drove off the British, and General Andrew Jackson thanked the Sisters, saying, "The unerring hand of Providence shielded my men." The Pope designated Our Lady of Prompt Succor the patroness of Louisiana.

9. Saint Julian of Antioch (313). He was a martyr, the husband of a beautiful virginal wife, Saint Basilissa, who died before him, but whose feast day is also celebrated on January 9. Saint Julian of Antioch converted great numbers to the Catholic Faith. He was noted for miracles and raised a dead man to life.

10. Saint Nicanor (76). He was one of the Seven Deacons chosen by the Twelve Apostles, as we are told in Chapter 6 of the Acts of the Apostles. One of these deacons was Saint Stephen, the protomartyr of the Church, whose feast day is December 26, the day after Christmas. Six of these Seven Deacons are saints. They are: Saint Nicanor (January 10), Saint Parmenas (January 23), Saint Prochorus (April 9), Saint Timon (April 19), Saint Philip (June 6), and Saint Stephen (December 26). One of the Seven Deacons is not listed among the saints. His name was Nicholas. One of the Twelve Apostles was a traitor. His name was Judas. A vocation and sanctity are not one and the same thing. A vocation is a call to sanctity to which one must fully respond in order to be a saint.

11. Saint Hyginus (158). He was the tenth Pope. He fought vigorously against the heretics of his time, known as the Gnostics, who claimed that from reason and not from Revelation we could know all about God. He made beautiful regulations for the grades of rank among the clergy.

The clerics of the Catholic Church include four minor orders: porter, lector, exorcist and acolyte. Then come the three major orders: subdeacon, deacon and priest.

For monastic orders there are priors and abbots; for other religious orders, superiors, provincials and generals. After this there are such hierarchical titles as monsignor, protonotary apostolic, chancellor and vicar-general. Then come auxiliary bishop, coadjutor bishop, and then bishop, archbishop, apostolic delegate, primate, cardinal, patriarch, and, at the top, singularly and uniquely as the successor of Saint Peter, is the Pope.

The body of Saint Hyginus is buried near that of Saint Peter, the first Pope.

12. Saint Benedict Biscop (690). He was abbot of Saint Augustine's monastery at Canterbury in England. He founded the monasteries of Wearmouth and of Jarrow. "Biscop" is the old English form of bishop, and is taken from the Latin word *episcopus*, which means bishop.

Saint Marguerite Bourgeoys (1700). She came from France to Montreal in Quebec in 1653 and established the first school there. She founded the Congregation of Notre Dame, the first uncloistered congregation of Sisters in the New World. The French settlers in Quebec called her the "Mother of the Colony."

Saint Anthony the Abbot

13. The Commemoration of the Baptism of Our Lord Jesus Christ. On this day a special Mass is said in the Catholic Church to commemorate the Baptism of Jesus by John the Baptist in the River Jordan. This was when the heavens opened and the Eternal Father's voice was heard to say, "This is My Beloved Son, in Whom I am well pleased." In dramatic simplicity and clear revelation, the voice of God the Father let us know that the Child of Mary the Virgin is both true God and true Man. No one who does not believe this can be saved. The Baptism of Jesus also commemorates the institution of the sacrament of Baptism—of Baptism by water, essentially necessary for salvation. The presence of Jesus in the River Jordan sanctified, on this day, all the water of the world for this purpose.

14. Saint Hilary of Poitiers (368). He was a bishop and a Doctor of the Church. He was the first Doctor of the Church to die, and suffered many things for the truth of the Catholic Faith, including banishment from his own diocese. There are thirty-three Doctors of the Church, and the list of their names and feasts is given under the date of February 9.

Saint Malachias (Fifth Century B.C.). He was a glorious prophet of the Old Testament. There are seventeen of these writing prophets who wrote books of the Bible, and all of them are commemorated by the Catholic Church as saints. The four major prophets are: Isaias, Jeremias, Ezechiel and Daniel. And along with them, Baruch. And the twelve minor prophets are Osee, Joel, Amos, Abdias, Jonas, Micheas, Nahum, Habacuc, Sophonias, Aggeus, Zacharias, Malachias.

15. Saint Paul, the First Hermit (342). This was the first notable Catholic saint who went apart completely and absolutely from the world to live a life of perfect contemplation of God. His glorious life was written by Saint Jerome. Saint Paul the Hermit was one hundred and twelve years old when he died.

16. Saint Marcellus (309). He was the thirty-first Pope, and a martyr. The

Catholic Faith was completely spread in the early ages by the shedding of the blood of martyrs. From the year 36 to the year 306, there were eleven million Catholics martyred for the Faith.

The Five Protomartyrs of the Franciscan Order (1220). The Franciscan Order was officially approved in 1215. Five years later, and six years before Saint Francis of Assisi died, five members of his Order were killed by the Mohammedans. The names of these glorious Franciscan martyrs are: Saint Berard, Saint Peter, Saint Otho, Saint Accursius and Saint Adjutus. Their death was the inspiration which led Saint Anthony of Padua, the most notable Franciscan saint after Saint Francis, to join the Franciscan Order.

Saint Priscilla (First Century). Saint Priscilla was the hostess of Saint Peter when he went to Rome in the year 42. It was at her house that the Chair of Saint Peter was first set up in Rome. She is a glorious woman, now in Heaven, whom no true Catholic should ever forget. She was the mother of Saint Pudens, a Roman senator, whose wife, Saint Claudia, an English girl, was also heroic in her holiness. Their children, four of them, are saints: Saint Pudentiana, Saint Praxedes, Saint Novatus and Saint Timothy—two daughters and two sons—all grandchildren of Saint Priscilla.

17. Saint Anthony the Abbot (356). This was the first great Saint Anthony. His name is mentioned in the Litany of the Saints. His life was written by Saint Athanasius. It was the story of this life, told to Saint Augustine, that helped to lead to his conversion and Baptism. Saint Anthony the Abbot was greatly loved and admired by Saint Hilarion. Saint Anthony the Abbot was one hundred and five years old when he died. He is the father of all monks.

Our Lady of Pontmain (1871). During the Franco-Prussian war when the German army was about to overrun the French village of Pontmain, Our Lady appeared in the sky to six children. She gave them a message of hope: "…pray my children. God will hear you in a short time. My Son permits Himself to be moved." Pontmain was saved and within ten days the armistice was signed and the bloodshed was over.

Saint Sebastian

18. This is the earliest day that **Septuagesima Sunday,** the first approach-Sunday to Lent, can occur. The latest day on which it can fall is February 21, or, in leap year, February 22.

Saint Prisca (270). This was a lovely virgin martyr killed in Rome for the Catholic Faith. There is a church dedicated to her there. Saint Prisca is one of the eleven million Catholics, men, women and children, who were martyred and shed their blood for the one true Faith from the year 36 to 306. Saint

Saint Paula

Prisca was only thirteen years old when she was martyred.

19. Saint Marius and Saint Martha, his wife, and their sons, **Saint Audifax and Saint Abachum (270).** This was a family of noble Persians, all martyred together for the Catholic Faith.

Saint Canute (1086). He was a king of Denmark, and a martyr for the truths of the Catholic Faith.

20. Saint Fabian (250). He was the twenty-first Pope, and a martyr. The first thirty-one Popes of the Catholic Church were martyred for the Faith that Catholics now possess.

Saint Sebastian (288). He was a noble young soldier, one of the earliest martyrs under the cruel Emperor Diocletian, whose reign lasted from 284 to 305. Saint Sebastian was first shot with arrows, and later scourged to death. Saints Fabian and Sebastian are mentioned together in the Litany of the Saints.

21. Saint Agnes (304). Saint Agnes was a glorious virgin and martyr slain with the sword at the age of thirteen. Her name is mentioned every day in the Canon of the Mass, and always in the Litany of the Saints. Saint Agnes is one of the most beloved saints in the Catholic Church, and every age has venerated her. Her name has been given to thousands of Catholic churches, and to hundreds of thousands of Catholic girls.

22. Saint Vincent (304). He was a Spanish deacon, tortured to death for the Catholic Faith under the diabolical Emperor Diocletian. He is greatly loved and remembered in the Catholic Church. His name is in the Litany of the Saints, the third name mentioned among the martyrs.

Blessed Laura Vicuna (1904). Blessed Laura, a little Chilean girl who lived in Argentina, was martyred for purity when she was twelve years old. Her mother, Mercedes, had become the mistress of a rich man, so Laura offered her life to God for her mother's conversion. Mercedes, alarmed at the man's growing interest in Laura, left him. Eventually he followed them and, upon their refusal to return to him, he beat Laura so severely that she died a week later. The evening Laura died her mother returned to the sacraments.

23. The Solemn Espousals of Our Lady and Saint Joseph (1 B.C.). This marriage of Our Blessed Lady and her virginal spouse took place when he was thirty and when she was fourteen years, four months and fifteen days old. Their first espousals (their engagement) took place on the previous September 8, Our Lady's birthday. These espousals were arranged by the providence of God so that the virginal Mother of the Eternal God might have a virginal husband who would care for her and protect her Divine Child. Saint Joseph died when he was sixty years old, in the year 29 A.D. Our Lady died when she was seventy-two years old, in the year 58 A.D. Both of them are now, in soul and in body, in Heaven, along with Jesus, the third member of the Holy Family.

Saint Raymond of Pennafort (1275). Saint Raymond was the third General of the Dominican Order. He was also the cofounder, with Saint Peter Nolasco, in 1218, of the Order of the Mercedarians, for the redemption of Catholic captives from the Mohammedans. Saint Raymond of Pennafort was one hundred years old when he died.

24. Saint Timothy (97). He was a disciple of Saint Paul. To him Saint Paul wrote two Epistles. Saint Timothy was the first Bishop of Ephesus, where Saint John the Evangelist died and where Our Lady visited, and where the Third Ecumenical Council of the Church took place. This was the Council that defended the Divine Maternity of Mary. Saint Timothy was stoned to death for defending Our Lady's virginity and for attacking the Greek goddess, Diana of the Ephesians.

25. The Conversion of Saint Paul (36). Saint Paul the Apostle, whose name before his conversion was Saul, on the road to Damascus heard the voice of Jesus speaking to him from the sky and saying, "Saul, Saul, why persecutest thou Me?" He then went on to Damascus, and was baptized in the Catholic Faith by Saint Ananias. Later on, because he was meant to be the Apostle to the Gentiles, and after seeing how much the Jews as a nation despised and rejected Jesus, he changed his name from Saul, which is Jewish, to Paul, which is Gentile. This was in admiration of a Roman named Sergius Paulus (Saint Paul of Narbonne, feast day March 22), whom he met and converted.

26. Saint Polycarp (166). He was a bishop and a martyr, a disciple of Saint John the Evangelist. He was also the spiritual father of Saint Irenaeus, one of the greatest of the early saints of the Church, whose feast day is July 3.

Saint Paula (404). She was a noblewoman of Rome,

Saint Francis de Sales

and a widow, who, with her virginal daughter Saint Eustochium, went to live in Bethlehem near the crib where Our Lord was born. Her life was written by Saint Jerome, great Doctor of the Church. Lives of the saints are best written by saints themselves. Among such lives of saints written by saints, we may mention:

Saint Jerome, Doctor of the Church, wrote the life of Saint Paul the Hermit and of Saint Paula.

Saint Athanasius, Doctor of the Church, wrote the life of Saint Anthony the Abbot, the life which led to the conversion of Saint Augustine.

Saint Ephrem, Doctor of the Church, wrote the life of Saint Abraham the Hermit.

Saint Gregory, Pope and Doctor of the Church, wrote the life of Saint Benedict, founder of the Benedictine Order.

Saint Bernard, Doctor of the Church, wrote the life of Saint Malachy O'More, the Primate of Armagh, in Ireland, who died in Saint Bernard's arms and who was buried with him.

Saint Peter Damian, Doctor of the Church, wrote the life of Saint Romuald, founder of the Camaldolese monks.

Saint Bonaventure, Doctor of the Church, wrote the life of Saint Francis of Assisi, founder of the Franciscan Order.

Saint Bede, Doctor of the Church, wrote the life of Saint John of Beverley, Archbishop of York.

Saint Robert Bellarmine, Doctor of the Church, wrote the life, by way of eulogy, of Saint Aloysius, angelic young saint of the Society of Jesus.

Saint Gregory of Nyssa, brother of Saint Basil the Great, wrote the life of Saint Ephrem, Doctor of the Church.

Saint Pontius wrote the life of Saint Cyprian, Father of the Church.

Saint Zosimus gave the details for the life of Saint Mary of Egypt, who spent forty-seven years in the desert.

Saint Willibald, his disciple, wrote the life of Saint Boniface, the great apostle to Germany.

Saint Rembert wrote the life of Saint Ansgar, the first great apostle to the Scandinavian countries.

Saint Ansgar wrote the life of Saint Willehad.

Saint Braulio wrote the life of Saint Aemilian.

Saint Adamnan wrote the life of Saint Columbkille, glorious Irish saint.

Saint Paphnutius wrote the life of Saint Humphrey (Saint Onuphrius).

Saint Possidius wrote the life of Saint Augustine, Doctor of the Church.

Saint Ludger, first Bishop of Münster, wrote the life of Saint Gregory of Utrecht.

Saint Ennodius wrote the life of Saint Anthony of Lerins and of Saint Epiphanius.

Saint Venantius Fortunatus wrote the life of Saint Radegunde.

Saint Hildegarde wrote the life of Saint Rupert and of Saint Disibode.

Saint Antoninus wrote the life of Blessed John the Good.

Blessed Raymond of Capua wrote the life of Saint Agnes of Montepulciano and the life of Saint Catherine of Siena.

Saint Vincent Mary Strambi wrote the life of Saint Paul of the Cross, founder of the Passionist Order.

Saint Killian wrote the life of Saint Bridget of Kildare, the "Mary of the Gael."

Saint John Bosco wrote the life of Saint Dominic Savio, who died when he was fifteen years old, in 1857, and whose great motto was, "Death rather than sin!"

Saint John Bosco

27. Saint John Chrysostom (407).
He was Patriarch of Constantinople and a Doctor of the Universal Church. He suffered terribly for his orthodoxy and his defense of the Catholic Faith, and was even exiled from his diocese. But he was beautifully supported by the holy Pope, Saint Innocent I. Saint John Chrysostom's relic's were given to the Orthodox Church by Pope John Paul II, in November of 2004.

28. Saint Peter Nolasco (1256).
He was cofounder with Saint Raymond of Pennafort, in 1218, of the Order of Our Lady of Ransom (the Mercedarians) for the redemption of Catholic captives from the Mohammedans.

29. Saint Francis de Sales (1622).
He was Bishop of Geneva and a Doctor of the Universal Church. He was only fifty-five years old when he died. He was cofounder, with Saint Jane Frances de Chantal, in 1610, of the Order of Visitation nuns, the Order to which Saint Margaret Mary, the great apostle of the Sacred Heart of Jesus, would one day belong. He converted 72,000 Calvinists to the Catholic Faith.

30. Saint Martina (228).
This was a lovely virgin and martyr who died at Rome, killed for what she believed.

Saint Hyacintha Mariscotti (1640).
She was a Third Order Franciscan nun who gave the last twenty-four years of her life completely to God, and is now the patron saint of Viterbo.

31. Saint John Bosco (1888).
He was one of the glories of the Catholic Church in the 19th century. He was the founder of the Salesians, a Religious Order for men under the protection of Saint Francis de Sales, and of a Religious Order for women called the Daughters of Mary, Help of Christians. Saint John Bosco was the spiritual father of that glorious young boy, Saint Dominic Savio, whose life he wrote.

February

The Month of the Passion of Our Lord

1. Saint Ignatius of Antioch (107). He was the third Bishop of Antioch and governed the Church there for forty years. Because of the courage and clarity with which he declared the truths of the Catholic Faith and its necessity for salvation, he was taken to Rome and thrown to wild beasts in the amphitheater before 87,000 people. The beast tore him to pieces. He is one of the Fathers of the Church.

Saint Brigid of Kildare (525). She is called "the Mary of the Gael." She was so beautiful that many thought she might be the Blessed Virgin in an apparition. She was the spiritual daughter of Saint Patrick. She died at the age of seventy-two, the same age at which Our Lady died. Saint Brigid of Kildare is buried in the same grave with Saint Patrick and Saint Columbkille.

2. The Purification of the Blessed Virgin Mary (1 A.D.). The Presentation of the Child Jesus in the Temple. Forty days after the birth of Jesus, His virginal Mother went to the Temple to fulfill the rite of purification, for which she had no need, but to which, in her humility, she submitted because it was

Saint Blaise

one of the requirements of the Jews. This was the first day Jesus ever entered a church. He was carried there by His Blessed Mother and Saint Joseph, and presented to His Eternal Father in the Temple. Most of the Jews, men and women, in the Temple in those days were wicked and faithless people. There was one old man named Simeon whose faith and belief in the coming of the Messias was still true. He took the Child Jesus in his arms and uttered the beautiful canticle: *"Now Thou dost dismiss Thy servant, O Lord, according to Thy word in peace, because my eyes have seen Thy salvation which Thou hast prepared before the face of all peoples; a light to the revelation of the Gentiles and the glory of Thy people, Israel."* This prayer of Simeon is one of the three canticles in the New Testament. The other two are: the *Magnificat* of Mary, the Mother of Jesus, and the *Benedictus* of Zachary, the father of John the Baptist.

There was also in the Temple when Mary went there with Joseph to present Jesus to His Eternal Father as God made man, a saintly old woman, a widow, named Anna, a prophetess, who was eighty-four years old. She went around the Temple and told all the Jewish women there what had happened, and Who had come to the Temple, at last.

Saint Cornelius the Centurion (First Century).
He was baptized by Saint Peter the Apostle, as we are told in the Acts of the Apostles, Chapter 10. He was later made Bishop of Caesarea in Palestine. He was a Gentile, and his Baptism is commemorated in Holy Scripture because it is the clear message of the Bible that the Faith was to go to the Gentiles by way of preservation to the end of the world.

3. Saint Blaise (316).
He was a doctor, a physician, who became a priest, and later was appointed Bishop of Sebaste in Armenia. He was a martyr for the Faith. At one time there were thirty churches dedicated to him in Rome. He is one of the fourteen Holy Helpers and is the protector against diseases of the throat.

This, in feast days, is the first of the fourteen Holy Helpers. Three of these Holy Helpers are women, eleven are men. Here is their list and the special needs for which we invoke them.

Saint Agatha

Saint Aegidius (Giles), September 1, patron of cripples.

Saint Acacius, May 8, invoked against headaches.

Saint Eustace, September 20, protector against fire, temporal or eternal.

Saint Erasmus, June 2, invoked against diseases of the stomach.

Saint Cyriacus, August 8, protector against eye diseases.

Saint Denis, October 9, prayed to for protection against demons.

Saint Christopher, July 25, patron of travelers.

Saint Blaise, February 3, invoked against diseases of the throat.

Saint Vitus (Guy), June 15, prayed to for protection against nervous diseases, epilepsy and paralysis.

Saint Pantaleon, July 27, invoked against lung diseases.

Saint George, April 23, invoked against diseases of the skin.

Saint Barbara, December 4, protects against lightning.

Saint Catherine, November 25, patroness of philosophers and invoked in law suits.

Saint Margaret, July 20, invoked against kidney diseases.

4. This is the earliest day on which **Ash Wednesday** can occur. The latest day on which it can occur is March 10.

Saint Andrew Corsini (1373). He was a Carmelite friar, and later the Bishop of Fiesole, a small town near Florence in Italy.

5. Saint Agatha (251). She is the beautiful little virgin martyr of Catania, in Sicily, who was killed for the Catholic Faith. Her name is mentioned every day by every Catholic priest in the Canon of the Mass. She is also one of the seven girls named in the Litany of the Saints.

Saint Paul Miki, Saint James Kisai and Saint John de Goto (1597). These were three Japanese, members of the Society of Jesus, crucified for the Catholic Faith at Nagasaki in Japan. Saint Paul Miki was thirty-three when he was martyred. Saint James Kisai, a lay brother, was sixty-four and Saint John de Goto was nineteen. With them suffered a Spaniard, Saint Philip of Jesus, a Franciscan born in Mexico City. He was also crucified. With them also were martyred twenty-two other heroic Franciscans. When Saint Paul Miki was dying on the cross, at the age, as we have said, of thirty-three, these were his last words: "I pray that all Japa-

nese people may walk on the only true road that leads to God. How happy I am, like my Saviour, at His own age to die for Him, and like Him, on the cross." His last two words were, "Jesus! Mary!"

6. Saint Titus (96). He was the beloved disciple of Saint Paul and the first Bishop of Crete. To him, Saint Paul wrote one of his Epistles.

Saint Dorothy (311). She was a radiant little Catholic virgin martyred for her Faith and her purity in Asia Minor. Her name, Dorothy, means *gift of God*. She was also a gift *to God* from the Catholic Faith.

Saint Warren (Guarinus) (1159). Saint Warren was an illustrious cardinal, Bishop of Palestrina, and a member of the Order of Saint Augustine.

7. Saint Theodore the General (306). Was a general in the area of Heraclea in Pontus under the Emperor Licinius. It was discovered that he was a Christian when he refused to participate in pagan rites unlike the the rest of his comrades. He was tortured and then beheaded by order of the Emperor.

Saint Dorothy

Saint Romuald (1027). He was a Benedictine monk, and later an abbot. He was the founder of the Camaldolese Order of the Benedictines in 1024. His life was written by Saint Peter Damian, Doctor of the Church.

Blessed Pope Pius IX (1878). Pope Pius IX was born Giovanni Maria Mastai-Ferretti on May 13, 1792. While in Rome studying for the priesthood, he suffered from epilepsy. At this time Saint Vincent Mary Palotti predicted that Giovanni would be cured by the Virgin of Loreto and eventually become pope. After ordination he fulfilled his pastoral duties while always maintaining a marvelous interior recollection centered on the Eucharist and Our Lady. In 1840 he received the Cardinal's hat, and was elected pope in 1846. His reign of 32 years was the second longest, but perhaps the most troubled, in history. The anti-Catholic revolution in Italy forced him into exile from 1847-1850. His astounding accomplishments include defining the dogma of the Immaculate Conception on December 8, 1854; publishing the Syllabus of Errors which condemned secret societies, freemasonry, communism and modernism, which teaches that one religion is as good as another; and convoking the First Vatican Council, which defined Papal Infallibility.

Saint Theodore the General

8. Saint John of Matha (1213).

He was the cofounder with Saint Felix of Valois, in 1198, of the Order of Trinitarians for the redemption of Catholic captives who were taken by the Mohammedans.

Blessed Josephine Bakhita (1947). Josephine Bakhita was born in Central Africa in 1869. As a child she was kidnapped by slave traders and sold into slavery in her own country. She was terribly mistreated until an Italian couple purchased her. They were kind to Bakhita and took her with them to Italy. Eventually Bakhita was sent as their little daughter's companion to the Canossian Sisters' school in Venice. Here she learned the Catholic Faith and pleaded to remain with the Sisters when the family decided to return to Africa. The authorities intervened on Bakhita's behalf stating that slavery was illegal in Italy. She joined the Canossian Sisters in 1895 where she was known as Mother Josephine. She was described as "pure as an angel, meek as a lamb." She often said, "Mary protected me even before I knew her," and "O Lord, if I could fly to my people and tell them of Your goodness at the top of my voice, O how many souls would be won."

9. Saint Cyril of Alexandria (444). He is a Doctor of the Church, and was "the soul of the Council of Ephesus" in 431. This was an Ecumenical Council, the third one, and it defended the Divine Maternity of the Blessed Virgin Mary against a diabolical heretic, a bishop named Nestorius. It was this Council, and largely due to Saint Cyril's inspiration, which gave us the last half of the *Hail Mary*: "Holy Mary, Mother of God, pray for us sinners," to which was later added, "now and at the hour of our death. Amen."

There are thirty-three Doctors of the Church, and their feast days, are in the following monthly order: Saint Hilary of Poitiers (January 14), Saint John Chrysostom (January 27), Saint Francis de Sales (January 29), Saint Cyril of Alexandria (February 9), Saint Peter Damian (February 23), Saint Thomas Aquinas (March 7), Saint Gregory the Great (March 12), Saint Cyril of Jerusalem (March 18), Saint John Damascene (March 27), Saint Isidore of Seville (April 4), Saint Leo the Great (April 11), Saint Anselm (April 21), Saint Peter Canisius (April 27), Saint Catherine of Siena (April 30), Saint Athanasius (May 2), Saint Gregory Nazianzen (May 9), Saint Robert Bellarmine (May 13), Saint Bede (May 27), Saint Anthony of Padua (June 13), Saint Basil (June 14), Saint Ephrem (June 18), Saint Bonaventure (July 14), Saint Laurence of Brindisi (July 21), Saint Alphonsus Maria de Liguori (August 2),

Saint Apollonia

Saint Bernard (August 20,) Saint Augustine (August 28), Saint Jerome (September 30), Saint Thèrése of Lisieux (October 3), Saint Teresa of Avila (October 15), Saint Albert the Great (November 15), Saint John of the Cross (November 24), Saint Peter Chrysologus (December 4), Saint Ambrose (December 7).

Saint Apollonia (249). She was a noble and valiant Catholic woman of Alexandria in Egypt. She was burned to death for professing the Catholic Faith, after all her teeth were torn out. Saint Apollonia is the patroness of Catholic dentists.

10. Saint Scholastica (543). She was the twin sister of Saint Benedict, the great founder of the Benedictine Order. She became a nun when her brother became a monk. She lived a life of radiant holiness. Saint Scholastica died forty days before her brother, Saint Benedict. They were both buried in the same grave. Other noted twins among the saints are: Saint Cosmas and Saint Damian, Saint Gervase and Saint Protase, Saint Mark and Saint Marcellian, Saint Medard and Saint Gildard.

11. Our Lady of Lourdes (1858). This is the feast of the first of the eighteen apparitions of the Blessed Virgin Mary to a little fourteen-year-old French girl in southern France, in 1858. The name of the little girl was Marie Bernadette Soubirous.

The first of Our Lady's apparitions to her was on February 11. The last was on July 16, the feast of Our Lady of Mount Carmel. The greatest was on March 25, the feast of the Annunciation. The Mother of God, on March 25, said to Saint Bernadette, in keeping with the doctrine defined four years before by Pope Pius IX, affirming that she had been immaculately conceived, not "I was immaculately conceived," but "I AM THE IMMACULATE CONCEPTION," thereby letting us know that she was God's very notion of this grace from all eternity.

12. The Seven Holy Founders of the Servants of the Blessed Virgin Mary (1233).
This Order was dedicated to the virginal Mother of God in complete love and loyalty, and is known as the Servites. Their founders were seven noblemen of Florence who dedicated their whole lives to the cult and honor of the Immaculate Mother of God, and who believed that no revealed truth of God can be understood without reference to the Blessed Virgin Mary. The great devotion of these seven Holy Servites was to Our Lady's Seven Sorrows, a devotion commemorated by the Catholic Church on two special feasts, one on the sixth Friday of Lent and the other on September 15. The seven Holy Servites have separate feast days because all are saints, but February 12 is their joint feast. Their names are: Saint Bonfilius Monaldius, Saint Bonajuncta Manettus, Saint Manettus Antellensis, Saint Amideus de Amadeis, Saint Uguccio Uguccionum, Saint Sosteneus de Sosteneis and Saint Alexis Falconieri. They were all canonized together in 1887. Saint Alexis was one hundred and ten years old when he died.

13. Saint Polyeucte (259).
He was a Roman officer martyred for the Catholic Faith by the Emperor Valerian. The story of his martyrdom is so dramatic that it was put into a classical play by Corneille, one of the famous French dramatists.

14. Saint Valentine (269).
He was a priest at Rome, beheaded for the Catholic Faith. Because this day is considered by many to be the first approach of Spring, and so connected with romance, Saint Valentine's Day is celebrated for other than a religious reason.

15. Saint Claude de la Colombiére (1682).
This was the brilliant and saintly priest of the Society of Jesus who was the spiritual director and complete supporter of Saint Margaret Mary in establishing devotion to the Sacred Heart of Jesus. He died eight years before Saint Margaret Mary, when he was only forty-one years old, but he let her know how pleasing to God was her work, to propagate devotion to the Sacred Heart, and also told her how welcome she would be in Heaven. In one of the apparitions of Jesus to Saint Margaret Mary, Our Lord referred to Saint Claude de la Colombiére as "My faithful servant and perfect friend."

The Finding of the Tongue of Saint Anthony of Padua (1263).
Saint Anthony died in 1231, when he was thirty-six years old. His body was exhumed thirty-two years later and examined, and it was found all corrupt except his tongue, which was as fresh as the day he died. This favor was given to Saint Anthony of Padua because by his tongue he was "a hammer of heretics." Four notable tongues we remember among the saints: first, the tongue of Saint John the Baptist, which was stabbed with a knife by Herodias, after his head had been served on a platter at the order of Herod Antipas, in payment of a promise to Salome, the daughter of Herodias, his wicked wife, whom John the Baptist had rebuked; second, the tongue of Saint Anthony, the feast of the finding of which is this day; third, the tongue of Saint

John Nepomucene, which was found incorrupt 336 years after his death, because he had laid down his life as a Catholic priest, choosing to be thrown into a river and drowned rather than violate the seal of the confessional; and fourth, the tongue of Saint Christina of Lake Bolsena, in Italy, who had her tongue cut out because she sang beautiful hymns to Jesus and Mary. She went right on miraculously singing, with no tongue, until she was shot down with arrows, in the persecution of the Christians by the Emperor Diocletian.

16. Saint Onesimus (95).
He was a slave of Philemon, to whom Saint Paul wrote an Epistle. He ran away from Saint Philemon and met Saint Paul, who sent him back to Saint Philemon, carrying the Epistle. Saint Onesimus was converted to the Catholic Faith by Saint Paul, who baptized him. Later, he became Bishop of Ephesus. Still later, he shed his blood in Rome for the dogmatic truths of the Catholic Faith.

17. The Flight into Egypt (1 A.D.).
It was on the seventeenth of February, fifty-five days after the birth of Jesus (Note: the term 1 A.D. is applied to the last seven days of the calendar year when Our Lord was born, and to the twelve months of the calendar year that followed them), when King Herod's soldiers—sent to slaughter all little boys in Bethlehem and its neighborhood who were two years old or under, in order to get rid of Jesus—were getting perilously near the cave at Bethlehem, where at first they little expected Our Lord to be, that Saint Joseph and Our Lady set off with their Divine Child, left the land of the Jews and went off to a land of the Gentiles. They took no one with them, by way of servants or friends, as Saint Peter Chrysologus tells us. The town to which the Holy Family fled was called Fostat. It was three hundred miles from Bethlehem. A church has been erected there, on the site of the house where the Holy Family lived during their exile.

The little town where the Holy Family stayed in Egypt was not far from Heliopolis, a city in which—when Jesus, Mary and Joseph passed through it—statues of pagan gods crashed to the ground. Both Fostat and Heliopolis are not far from Cairo in Egypt.

18. Saint Bernadette (1879).
Marie Bernadette Soubirous was a little girl who lived in southern France, in the town of Lourdes. When she was fourteen years old, Our Lady appeared to her eighteen times, in the year 1858. Marie Bernadette later became a Sister of Charity at Nevers. She died when she was thirty-five years old. Her name is known and loved and reverenced everywhere in the Catholic world.

Blessed Fra Angelico (1455).
He is the greatest painter of the fifteenth century and one of the greatest artists of all time. When he entered the Dominicans in 1407, he was given the name Fra Giovanni (Brother John), but because of his holy life, he came to be called Fra Angelico (Angelic Brother). Fra Angelico was convinced that "to picture Christ, one must strive to be Christ-like." He always began his work with a silent prayer. The holiness of his life is reflected in his paintings.

19. Saint Gabinus (296).
He was the brother of Saint Caius, the twenty-ninth Pope. He was the father of the beautiful little virgin martyr, Saint Susanna, whose feast is August 11, and who was martyred for her Faith and for her purity, because she would not marry the son-in-law of the pagan Emperor Diocletian. Saint Susanna was martyred in 295, and one year later, in 296, her father, Saint Gabinus, shed his blood for the Faith for which his daughter had died.

Saint Odran (452). Saint Odran was the charioteer of Saint Patrick, the great apostle of Ireland. Saint Odran was martyred in place of Saint Patrick, by giving his life to some pagans who wanted to kill Saint Patrick. Saint Odran died forty-one years before Saint Patrick, who died in 493.

20. Saint Leo Thaumaturgus (Wonderworker) (787). Thaumaturgus means wonder-worker. This was the name given to the Bishop of Catania, in Sicily, the town of Saint Agatha. Saint Leo Thaumaturgus professed and taught the Catholic Faith there, in the eighth century.

Saint Amy (Amata) (1250). She was a Poor Clare nun and a niece of Saint Clare of Assisi.

Blessed Francisco and Jacinta Marto (1919 & 1920). These two modern day saints were born in Portugal in the early twentieth century. The young shepherd children were brother and sister who, together with their cousin Lucia dos Santos, were privileged with three appearances by an angel and six by Mary, the Mother of God. The children's sole desire henceforth was to offer reparation to the Immaculate Heart of Mary for all the sins of the world. After a short life filled with much penitence and sacrifice they were taken to Heaven: Francisco died at the age of 11 in 1919 and Jacinta at the age of 10 in 1920. Francisco announced shortly before he died, "In Heaven I'm going to console Our Lord and Our Lady very much." Jacinta likewise said, "In Heaven, I'm going to love Jesus very much, and the Immaculate Heart of Mary.

21. This is the latest day (except leap year) when the feast of **Septuagesima Sunday** can fall. The earliest day on which it can fall is January 18.

Saint Peter Mavimenus (743). He was killed by the Arabs at Damascus, the city where Saint Paul was baptized, when he said to these Arabs, "Every man who does not hold the Catholic Christian Faith is damned like Mohammed, your false prophet."

22. The Chair of Saint Peter (36) (42).
Antioch, in Syria, was the city where the first Pope of the Catholic Church, Saint Peter, set up his Chair after his departure from Jerusalem. This was at the house of a noble Gentile Christian named Theophilus, the one to whom Saint Luke dedicates his two books: the Third Gospel and the Acts of the Apostles. Nearly seven years later, in the year 42, Saint Peter set up his Chair at Rome, at the home of Saint Pudens, a senator, and his mother, Saint Priscilla. Saint Peter occupied his Chair at Rome for twenty-five years, from the year 42 to the year 67, when he was crucified for the Faith.

Saint Matthias

23. Saint Peter Damian (1072). He was a Camaldolese monk, a cardinal, and is one of the thirty-three Doctors of the Church. He was illustrious and brilliant, simple and outspoken in his denunciation of all heresies and evils. He wrote the life of Saint Romuald, the founder of his Order.

24. Saint Matthias (65). Saint Matthias was the Apostle chosen in place of Judas Iscariot, the traitor who commited suicide. Saint Matthias was beheaded by the Jews in Jerusalem. His body is kept in the Church of Saint Mary Major in Rome.

25. Saint Walburga (779). She was an English girl who went to Germany and died there as an abbess. She is the sister of Saint Willibald and Saint Winibald, and the daughter of Saint Richard, an English king.

Saint Walburga

26. Saint Porphyry (420).
He was a noble and wealthy Greek. He was first a hermit, and then a bishop, at Gaza in Palestine. He died the same year as Saint Jerome. Saint Porphyry's life was written by one of his disciples named Mark.

Saint Alexander of Alexandria (326).
He was the courageous Catholic bishop who discovered the heresy of Arius, a priest, who was going about denying the divinity of Our Lord Jesus Christ. Saint Alexander was the spiritual father and supporter of the great Saint Athanasius.

27. Saint Gabriel of the Most Sorrowful Virgin (1862).
This was an angelic young Passionist brother who, consumed with love and veneration for the Seven Sorrows of Our Lady, after extreme sufferings and weakened by tuberculosis, died of sheer love at the age of twenty-four, at Isola in Italy. He had been a religious six years. He died at the same age as the Little Flower of Jesus, Saint Elizabeth of Hungary and Saint Casimir of Poland.

28. Saint Hilary (468). He was the forty-eighth Pope. He was born on the Island of Sardinia. He fought tirelessly against the heretics who denied the Divine Maternity of Mary and the abiding humanity of Jesus.

March

The Month of Saint Joseph

1. Saint David of Wales (601). He was the disciple of Saint Paulinus, an apostle to England. Saint David is the patron of Wales, where thousands and thousands of noble Catholics have lived and where many saints have been given to God. Saint David was a most militant adversary of all heresy, especially that of Pelagius, a Briton, who held that grace is not necessary for the performance of good works and that mere natural virtues can lead one to salvation. Saint David of Wales died when he was one hundred and forty-seven years old.

2. Blessed Charles the Good (1124). He was the son of Saint Canute, King of Denmark, and was called "the Good" because of his outstanding Catholic virtues. He was martyred in a Catholic church in Bruges. Noted Catholic saints killed in Catholic churches by enemies of the Faith include:

Saint Canute, father of Blessed Charles the Good, martyred at the foot of the altar, just after he received Holy Communion.

Saint Matthew the Apostle, who was martyred at the altar in Ethiopia for supporting Saint Iphigenia, when she refused to marry her father's successor, King Hirtacus, after Saint Matthew had raised her from the dead and dedicated her, with a group of young virgins, to live the life of a nun.

Saint Boniface, the apostle of Germany, martyred as he started Mass.

Saint Thomas à Becket, the Archbishop of Canterbury, in England, who was murdered in his cathedral as he knelt at prayer.

Saint Anthony Daniel, one of the eight North American martyrs, who was tomahawked by Indians after he had received from his chalice the Precious Blood of Jesus.

Saint Stephen I, Pope, who was killed in the catacombs as he went to sit on his chair at the end of the Mass he had just said.

3. Saint Cunegunda (1040). She was the virginal wife of Saint Henry II, Emperor of Germany, who dedicated her to God as soon as he married her. Saint Henry's feast is on July 15. After Saint Henry's death, Saint Cunegunda, the virgin, became a Benedictine nun. Her relics, and those of her saintly husband, are kept together in the Cathedral of Bamberg.

Saint Katharine Drexel (1955). Katharine was born in Philadelphia in 1858, an heiress to millions of dollars. Even while enjoying the balls and festivities of Philadelphia society she felt attracted to a life of contemplative prayer. She had always taken an interest in the Indians of the West, and when in Rome had asked the Holy Father, Pope Leo XIII, to send missionaries to them and to the recently emancipated Black people. Pope Leo replied, "But why not be a missionary yourself, my child?" So in 1891 she founded an Order for this work, the Sisters of the Blessed Sacrament for Indians and Colored People. Mother Drexel lived a life of hard work and personal poverty spending her entire fortune for the education, welfare and spiritual good of her beloved people.

4. Saint Casimir of Poland (1483). He was the son of a king of Poland, and a most saintly prince. He refused the crown of Hungary, and died when he was only twenty-four years old, of tuberculosis. His great love was for the virginal Mother of God. The only royalty he desired was to be her son. He recited every day on his knees Saint Anselm's lovely hymn, "Daily, daily sing to Mary" *(Omni die dic Mariae)*. He asked that this hymn be buried with him in his grave. One hundred and twenty years after his death, saint Casimir's body was found incorrupt; thanks to the protection of the Blessed Virgin Mary and the little hymn he kept beside him.

5. Saint John Joseph of the Cross (1734). He was a Franciscan who died after a life of heroic mortification and sanctity in Naples, in Italy. He was eighty years old when he died. He died with his eyes fixed on a statue of the Blessed Virgin Mary, which he always wanted kept before him.

6. Saint Perpetua and Saint Felicitas (203). Saint Perpetua was a noble young matron, twenty-two years old, who lived in Carthage, in Africa, and was taking instructions to be a Catholic when she was seized by the pagans there and thrown into prison. She was a mother of a very young child. Arrested with her was her servant, Saint Felicitas, who was with child, soon to be born. Both these saints were baptized with water between their arrest and their imprisonment. After the birth of the child of Saint Felicitas, these two heroic and saintly African women were brought to the amphitheater in Carthage, and gored by a wild cow. Finally, after embracing each other for the last time, they were both martyred by the sword. Their children were taken and reared by Christian women. Saint Perpetua and Saint

Saint Colette

Saint Frances of Rome

Felicitas are mentioned every day in the Canon of the Mass. They are two of the seven women to whom this honor is given. These are the seven: Saint Felicitas, Saint Perpetua, Saint Agatha, Saint Lucy, Saint Agnes, Saint Cecilia, Saint Anastasia.

Saint Colette (1447). She was a Poor Clare nun who was born in 1381. Her special devotions were to the Passion of Our Lord and to the practice of holy poverty. She was a loyal friend of the great Dominican, Saint Vincent Ferrer. Along with him, she was responsible for the end of the Great Western Schism, which lasted from 1378 to 1417.

7. Saint Thomas Aquinas (1274).

He was an Angelic Doctor of the Church, a member of the Dominican Order, admired for the brilliance of his mind in writing such great works as the *Summa Theologica*, but loved for the warmth and devotion his heart had for the Blessed Sacrament. Saint Thomas said, "I found more wisdom in prayer at the feet of the Crucified than in all the books I ever read." When Saint Thomas Aquinas was thirty-nine years old, at the request of Pope Urban IV, he wrote the Mass and the Office for the feast of Corpus Christi. This was in the year 1264. The Catholic hymns, *Tantum Ergo* and *O Salutaris*, and the *Panis Angelicus* and *Adoro Te Devote*, and the beautiful sequence in the Mass of Corpus Christi, read after the Epistle in that Mass and known as the *Lauda Sion Salvatorem*, are all the works of Saint Thomas Aquinas. Every time a Catholic priest gives Benediction of the Blessed Sacrament, he chants a prayer of Saint Thomas Aquinas and the choir sings a hymn he composed. Saint Thomas died when he was only forty-nine years old, on his way to the Second Council of Lyons. Although a Dominican, he died in a Benedictine Monastery, of Fossa-Nuova, and the monks of this monastery thought his death there one of the greatest honors their house had ever been given.

8. Saint John of God (1550).

He was born in Portugal. He lived in Spain and, for a time, in Hungary. He was a poor shepherd. Saint John of God had a great devotion to sacred images. He founded the Order of Brothers Hospitallers. They are often called "the Brothers of Saint John of God." Saint John of God died when he was fifty-five years old.

9. Saint Dominic Savio (1857).

He was the young disciple of Saint John Bosco, who wrote his life. Saint Dominic was only fifteen years old when he died. He was one of the glories of the 19th Century by way of a heroic young Catholic boy. He was totally given in all his thoughts and deeds to Jesus and Mary.

Saint Frances of Rome (1440). She was a noble matron who lived a life of heroic charity. She had such a great devotion to her Guardian Angel that she was given an almost constant vision of him walking at her side. She was fifty-six years old when she died.

10. This is the latest day on which **Ash Wednesday** can occur.

The Forty Holy Martyrs of Sebaste (320). These were forty soldiers who, under the Emperor Licinius, in Armenia, were all frozen to death on an icy lake because they would not apostatize from the Catholic Faith. One of the forty *did* give in, but his place was taken by one of the guards. The youngest and last of these forty soldiers to die was named Melitho. His mother, who was standing by, took him in her arms and carried him to the place where the other martyrs were being burned. He died in her arms. She then laid him with the other martyrs, to be thrown into the fire.

11. Saint Sophronius (639). He was born at Damascus, in Syria, where Saint Paul was baptized. He was the great defender in the East of the full humanity of Jesus Christ against those horrid heretics, the Monothelites, who denied that Our Lord had a human will, and therefore that He truly became man for love of us.

12. Saint Gregory the Great (604). He was a Pope and Doctor of the Church. He was the sixty-sixth Pope, and one of the greatest leaders the Catholic Faith has ever had. He reigned as Roman Pontiff for fourteen years. His mother, Sylvia, was a saint, as were his aunts, Saint Aemiliana and Saint Tarsilla. Saint Gregory revived for the Catholic Church its great love for liturgical chant and music. Saint Gregory sent Saint Augustine of Canterbury to be the apostle of England, in 597.

Saint Nicholas Owen (1606). At the time of the Reformation in England Saint Nicholas was a carpenter who devoted his life to building hiding places for Catholic priests who, at the peril of their lives, were ministering to the persecuted English Catholics. He died in the Tower of London under torture, taking his secrets into eternity with him.

Blessed Louis (Luigi) Orione (1940). Blessed Louis, *Don Orione,* lived in Italy and studied with the Salesians in Turin for three years. Here he met the aging Saint John Bosco who told him. "We shall always be friends." Blessed Louis entered the diocesan seminary and was ordained in 1895. Even while he was a seminarian he began a boarding school for poor boys which became the foundation of his Little Work of Divine Providence. They serve especially the poor, the orphaned, the elderly, and the handicapped. This work includes the Sons of Divine Providence and the Little Missionary Sisters of Charity, who work in countries all over the world as missionaries. Don Orione counseled his spiritual children, "Serve God with joy and simplicity of heart."

13. Saint Euphrasia (410). She was the daughter of a Roman senator. She became a Catholic nun at the age of seven. She refused all offers to leave the convent and marry a member of the nobility. She gave all her goods to the poor and died at the age of thirty.

14. Saint Matilda (Maud) (968). She was a German queen, the mother of a

German emperor, Otto the Great, and of Henry, Duke of Bavaria, and of Saint Bruno, Archbishop of Cologne. She was an Oblate of the Benedictine Order.

15. Saint Clement Mary Hofbauer (1820). He is one of the Three Canonized saints of the Redemptorist order. (The other two are: Saint Alphonsus Maria de Liguori and Saint Gerard Majella.) Saint Clement Mary Hofbauer, in the midst of the aftermath of the Masonic French Revolution, gloriously and courageously preached the necessity of the Catholic Faith for the salvation of all men.

Saint Longinus (First Century). He was the centurion who pierced the side of Our Lord when He was hanging on the Cross after his death. It was Longinus who exclaimed on Mount Calvary, on the first Good Friday, "Indeed, this was the Son of God!" Longinus was converted to the Catholic Faith. He later went to Cappadocia, and shed his own blood there for the teaching of the crucified Jesus. The relics of Saint Longinus are now in the beautiful church of Saint Augustine, in Rome, not far from the body of Saint Monica.

Saint Patrick

Saint Louise de Maurillac (1660). She was a French girl, born in Paris. After her husband's death she became a nun and cooperated with Saint Vincent de Paul in establishing the Sisters of Charity. This order was started in 1634. Saint Louise was canonized by Pope Pius XI in 1934.

16. Saint Abraham (360). He was a holy hermit of Mesopotamia whose life was brilliantly written by Saint Ephrem, Doctor of the Church. Saint Abraham's niece named Mary was reconverted by him to a life of mortification and self-sacrifice for the sake of Jesus. She too became a saint.

17. Saint Patrick (493). Saint Patrick, the glorious apostle of Ireland, was born in France, in the year 387. His father was an official of the Roman government. His mother's brother was Saint Martin, Bishop of Tours. When Saint Patrick was almost sixteen years old, he was captured by pirates and brought to Ireland, where he met the people who would one day be his spiritual children. Saint Patrick was miraculously freed, and returned to France. He was sent back to Ireland in 432 as a bishop by Saint Celestine, the Pope. Saint Patrick's most noted spiritual daughter in Ireland was Saint Brigid, called "the Mary of the Gael." Saint Patrick drove all the snakes—symbols of the devil—out of Ireland. He raised thirty-three persons from the dead. By making the sign of the cross, he caused the earth to swallow up a heathen who mocked the virginity of the Blessed Virgin Mary. Saint Patrick's charioteer, Saint Odran, was martyred in place of him by some Celtic heathens. Saint Patrick was one hundred and six years old when he died. Saint Patrick, Saint Brigid and Saint Columbkille are all buried together. Saint Patrick, Saint Brigid and Saint Columbkille are the patron saints of Ireland.

Saint Joseph of Arimathea (First Century). He was a noble counselor (a lawyer) who became a disciple of Our Lord. He took care of the burial of Jesus in a grave that he owned, and which never had been used by another. Our Lord's two pallbearers were Saint Joseph of Arimathea and Saint Nicodemus. Saint Joseph of Arimathea was the first apostle to Britain, and founded the church at Glastonbury. It was he who brought the Holy Grail—the Cup, which Jesus used for His Precious Blood at the Last Supper—to England. Saint Joseph of Arimathea was more than eighty years old when he died.

18. Saint Cyril of Jerusalem (386). He is a Doctor of the Church, born in Palestine, near Jerusalem. His simple and clear explanations of the Catholic Faith, which an innocent child can understand, have been responsible for his being truly and properly proclaimed a Doctor of the universal Church. Here is the way he speaks: "Believe in the Son of God, the one and only, Our Lord Jesus Christ, begotten as God from God, begotten as Light from Light, begotten as Life from Life, like in all thing to the Father, not receiving His existence in time, but begotten of the father eternally and incomprehensibly before all ages…"

Saint Joseph

19. Saint Joseph (29). He was the royal and divinely-trusted man to whom the Blessed Virgin Mary was given as a bride, and whom God knew would guard her innocence as a virgin and protect her Divine Child. Saint Joseph is the foster father of Jesus. The Litany of the Saints refers to him as the last of the patriarchs. Saint Joseph was espoused to Our Blessed Lady by divine arrangement on September 8, in the year 2 B.C., when she was just fourteen years old. Saint Joseph was thirty years old at the time. His solemn espousals to Our Lady took place on the following January 23. Saint Joseph died when he was sixty years old, just before the public life of Our Lord began. The whole month of March is dedicated to Saint Joseph. Saint Joseph's body arose from the grave when Our

Lord died, on Good Friday. Saint Joseph ascended with Jesus into heaven, in soul and in body, forty days later, to await there the coming of Mary on the great feast of the Assumption, on August 15, in the year 58. Saint Joseph has now two special feast days, one for his royalty on March 19, and one for his humility as a workman, on May 1. It was told to the Israelites in the Old Testament, "Go to Joseph," if they wanted a favor or benefit. "Go to Joseph," is the advice and counsel given to every Catholic who wants a favor and who believes in the sanctity of the Holy Family and in the simple and innocent hierarchy. Anything Saint Joseph asks of Mary and of Jesus in eternity, he will get. He is still the head of the Holy Family. One of his greatest admirers and lovers among the saints was Saint Teresa of Avila.

20. This day commemorates the **First Day of Creation**, when God said, "Let there be light."

Saint Photina (First Century).

It is fitting that on this day should be celebrated the feast of a radiant saint named Photina, which means *light*. She was the Samaritan woman whom Jesus met at the well of Jacob. She was martyred at Carthage, in Africa, and was thrown into a well. Martyred with her were her two sons, Saint Victor and Saint Joseph.

Saint Benedict

21. Saint Benedict (543). This is the great Saint Benedict of Nursia, father of all Western monks. Saint Benedict was born in Italy, in 480. In 529, on a mountain called Monte Cassino, he built the first great abbey of the Benedictines. His twin sister Saint Scholastica became a nun and a saint. She died forty days before him, on February 10, and they were both buried in the same grave. Saint Benedict died, standing before the altar, just after he had received Holy Communion. In his humility, he never became a priest. His life was written by the Pope, Saint Gregory the Great. The Benedictine order, as we are told in the martyrologies of its monasteries, has given the Catholic Church 57,000 known saints. This great Order has also given the Catholic Church thirty-five Popes, of whom seventeen have been declared either Saints or Blesseds.

22. This is the earliest day on which **Easter Sunday** can occur. The latest day on which it can fall is April 25, the feast of Saint Mark.

Saint Catherine of Sweden (1381).

She was the daughter of Saint Bridget of Sweden. She persuaded the man whom she married to make a vow of chastity and live with her the life of a religious. She became an abbess. She died when she was fifty years old. She is also commemorated on March 24.

23. Our Lady of Victories. This is the name given to a beautiful image of the Blessed Virgin, which the French took from the Greeks at Constantinople in 1204 in a battle in which they scored a victory. There is also a famous and much-loved church called Our Lady of Victories in Paris. This church was desecrated during the French Revolution, but Our Lady miraculously restored it with the help of a simple French priest named Father Desgenettes, in 1836. "Consecrate your parish to the most holy and Immaculate Heart of Mary," he heard a voice say to him at morning Mass, when only ten were present. One evening at vespers, after he had obeyed Our Lady's orders, the hitherto empty church was filled for the first time in many, many years. It was one of the favorite churches of the Little Flower of Jesus. She visited it ten years before her death.

Saint Turibius (1606).
Saint Turibius was born at Mayorga, Spain of a noble family and was highly educated. He became a professor of law at the University of Salamanca and was renowned for his learning and practice of virtue. King Philip II appointed him the Grand Inquisitor of Spain because of his prudence and justice. Later the Pope selected Turibius as Archbishop of Peru. Arriving in Peru he immediately began his mission work, baptizing, teaching and confirming. Three times he traveled eighteen thousand miles of his diocese, generally on foot. He built the first seminary in the new world in Lima in 1591. His favorite saying was "Time is not our own, and we must give a strict account of it." Among the many souls that Saint Turibius was responsible for there were among them Saint Rose of Lima, Saint Francis Solano, Saint Martin de Porres and Saint John Massias. Years before Saint Turibius died, he predicted the day and hour of his death.

24. Saint Gabriel. Saint Gabriel is one of the Seven Angels who stand before the throne of God. The name Gabriel means *strength of God.* Saint Gabriel is the special angel of the Annunciation. He is the Guardian Angel of the Blessed Virgin Mary. It was he who brought the news of the Annunciation to her. He came in the guise of a man, though he was always an angel, because his was the message of the Incarnation, to let it be known that God was ready to become man. It was Saint Gabriel who gave us the first greeting of the *Hail Mary,* "Hail (Mary), full of grace, the Lord is with thee. Blessed art thou among women."

Saint Simon of Trent (1475).
He was a little Italian boy, two years old, crowned with thorns and crucified by the Jews on Good Friday, in mockery of Jesus.

Saint William of Norwich (1144).
He was an English boy, crucified by the Jews in England when he was twelve years old. It was just before the feast, that year, of the day on which Our Lord died. Among other Catholic boys martyred by the Jews, usually by way of crucifixion and often crowned with thorns, the Catholic Church lovingly remembers: Little Saint Hugh of Lincoln (1255), Saint Dominic del Val (1250), Saint Richard of Pontoise (1182), Saint Christopher de la Guardia (1490), Saint Harold of Gloucester (1168), and Saint Robert of Bury Saint Edmund's (1181).

25. This is the Greatest of All Days in the History of the World. It was on March 25 that Adam and Eve were created. It was on March 25 that Our Lord was conceived in the womb of the Blessed Virgin Mary. It was on March 25 that Jesus died on the Cross for us, on Mount Calvary. All these events occurred in the simple innocence and charm of God's liturgical love at three o'clock in the afternoon. Saint John the Baptist was beheaded on March 25, one year before the death of Our Lord. By way of title, March 25 is called the Feast of the **Annunciation**. To show how much Our Lady still loves this day in the calendar of her affection and remembrance, it was on March 25, 1858, that the Blessed Virgin Mary said to Marie Bernadette at Lourdes, "I AM THE IMMACULATE CONCEPTION."

Saint Dismas (33). He was the penitent thief crucified with Jesus. He died shortly after Our Lord, when the Roman soldiers broke his legs. Dismas said to Jesus, while hanging beside Him on the Cross, "Lord, remember me when Thou comest into Thy Kingdom." Jesus replied to Dismas, "Amen I say to thee, this day thou shalt be with Me in paradise." He is also commemorated on October 13.

Saint Ludger

26. Saint Ludger (809). He was the great apostle of Saxony, and the first Bishop of Munster. He supported the Emperor Charlemagne in his appreciation and realization of the sanctity and the necessity of the Catholic Faith. Saint Ludger wrote Saint Gregory of Utrecht's life.

27. The Apparition of Our Lord to the Blessed Virgin Mary on the day of his Resurrection. It was on March 27, in the year 33, that Jesus rose from the dead. This was the first Easter Sunday. Our Lord died at three o'clock in the afternoon, on March 25, in the year 33, and was three days in the tomb. Our Lord arose from the dead on March 27, at seven o'clock in the morning. Our Lord was forty hours dead. Our Lord then spent forty days on earth before He ascended into heaven. During these days, Jesus appeared to many. The best known apparitions of Our Lord after His Resurrection, and before His Ascension, are twelve. They are these:

To Our Lady, the first of His apparitions to anyone. So great was Mary's grief from having seen Jesus die on the Cross that Our Lord was obliged to stay a long time with Our Lady in order to comfort her.

To Saint Mary Magdalen, the greatest of all penitents, on Easter Sunday.

To Saint Mary of Cleophas and Saint Mary Salome, the former of whom was the mother of the Apostles Saint Simon, Saint James and Saint Jude, and the latter, her daughter, the mother of the Apostles Saint John and Saint James. This apparition was on Easter Sunday.

To Saint Peter, on Easter Sunday.

To the disciples on the road to Emmaus, on Easter Sunday. One of these disciples was

Saint Cleophas, the husband of Saint Mary of Cleophas and the brother of Saint Joseph.

To all the Apostles, except Saint Thomas, in the Supper Room, on Easter Sunday.

Besides these well-known apparitions on Easter Sunday, Our Lord appeared before His Ascension, (a) to all the Apostles, including Saint Thomas, assembled in the Supper Room one week after Easter Sunday; (b) to seven Apostles by the Lake of Genesareth; (c) to a multitude on a mountain in Galilee; (d) to Saint James the Less, the first Bishop of Jerusalem; (e) to Saint Joseph of Arimathea, the kindly man who gave Jesus a grave in which to be buried for three days; (f) to all the Apostles and many others on the Mount of Olives on the day of his Ascension into Heaven, on May 5, forty days after His Resurrection, at which great event Our Lady assisted as the Mother of Jesus and our Queen.

Saint John Damascene (749). He was the last of the Greek Fathers and a great Doctor of the Church. His veneration for holy pictures and images caused him to have his right hand cut off by order of the Emperor Leo the Isaurian. The Blessed Virgin Mary miraculously restored his right hand to him when he knelt before one of her images. Saint John Damascene was seventy-three years old when he died.

28. Saint John of Capistrano (1456). He was one of the great apostles of the Holy Name of Jesus. Three other great apostles of the Holy Name of Jesus are: Saint Bernard of Clairvaux, Saint Bernardine of Siena and Saint Ignatius of Loyola. Saint John of Capistrano was a Franciscan. It was through his devotion to the Holy Name of Jesus that the Catholics were able to beat the Turks in the Battle of Belgrade, in 1456. Led by Saint John of Capistrano, every soldier in the Catholic army kept saying, "Jesus! Jesus!" as he fought. The Lutherans threw the relics of Saint John of Capistrano into the River Danube in the sixteenth century, but the Catholics were able to recover them.

29. Saint Jonas and Saint Barachisius (327). These were Persian brothers who, with nine companions, were martyred for the Catholic Faith.

30. Saint John Climacus (605). He was a monk on Mount Sinai, who went there to live at the age of sixteen. He became an abbot, but after four years returned to his life as a hermit on this sacred mountain. It was on Mount Sinai that God gave Moses the Ten Commandments. It is on Mount Sinai that Saint Catherine of Alexandria is buried. Angels carried her there after her death in Egypt. Mount Sinai is about one hundred and ninety miles south of Jerusalem.

31. Our Lady of the Holy Cross in Jerusalem. This is one of the churches called the "Seven Churches" of Rome. These seven churches of Rome are:
1. Saint Peter's, which is called the Vatican.
2. Saint John Lateran. It contains the heads of the Apostles Saints Peter and Paul.
3. Saint Mary Major, where the crib of the Infant Jesus is kept.
4. Saint Paul-outside-the-Walls.
5. The Church of the Holy Cross in Jerusalem.
6. Saint Laurence-outside-the-Walls.
7. Saint Sebastian-outside-the-Walls.

April

The Month of the Holy Eucharist

1. Saint Hugh of Grenoble (1132). He was a Benedictine, and was for fifty-two years Bishop of Grenoble. He was made a bishop despite his humility in not wanting to be elevated to that dignity, and in spite of his efforts to retire and become a monk. He was one of the great supporters of Saint Gregory VII, Pope. It was in the diocese of Grenoble, with Saint Hugh's permission, that Saint Bruno founded the Carthusian Order, in 1084.

2. Saint Francis of Paula (1507). He was the founder of the Order of the Hermits of Saint Francis, called the Minims, which means the *Least*. He died on Good Friday, when he was ninety-one years old. He was canonized twelve years after his death. The French Calvinists opened his tomb in 1562. They found his body incorrupt, and, destroyed and burned it.

Saint Mary of Egypt (421). She was a beautiful penitent who was converted to a good life in the Catholic Faith at the tomb of Our Lord, in Jerusalem. She then fled into the desert by the Jordan River and spent forty-seven years of her life doing penance for her past sins. Saint Zosimus gave the details of her life. It was the reading of her life that caused Saint John Colombini to become a saint.

3. Saint Richard of Chichester (1253). He was a much-loved English bishop who was persecuted by King Henry III. By his courage, simplicity and poverty, he triumphed over all his enemies. He preached one of the crusades against the Turks. There were eight great crusades against the Turks, waged by the Catholics to protect the sacred places in the Holy Land. The first crusade began in 1096 and the last one ended in 1291.

4. Saint Isidore of Seville (636). He was a bishop and a Doctor of the Universal Church. He was the brother of Saint Leander, Saint Fulgentius and Saint Florentina, whose feast days are respectively, February 27, January 16 and June 20. Saint Isidore succeeded his brother, Saint Leander, as Bishop of Seville and ruled there for forty years.

Saint Benedict the Moor (1589). He was born in Sicily, the son of African slaves. He became a Franciscan. Although he was only a lay brother and could neither read nor write, his holiness was so outstanding that he was made superior of his monastery, which he governed wisely and well.

5. Saint Vincent Ferrer (1419). He was one of the greatest saints of the Dominican Order. He was a Spaniard and was born at Valencia. He was one of the main forces that ended the Great Western Schism, a hardship of the Catholic Church, which lasted from 1378 to 1417, when two, and eventually three, cardinals, one at Rome, one at Avignon and one at Pisa, were all claiming to be Pope. Saint Vincent Ferrer had the gift of tongues. Speaking in his own language, all who listened to him could understand him in theirs. Saint Vincent Ferrer raised forty persons from the dead. He cured thousands of the blind, the lame, the deaf and the dumb. He extinguished a fire with one blow of his breath. A laborer at Valencia, who had fallen from a staging, was suspended by Saint Vincent Ferrer in mid-air until he brought him safely and slowly to the ground. A swarm of butterflies flew into Saint Vincent Ferrer's room as he was dying. A great number of angels assembled there to take his soul to God. He was in his sixty-third year when he died.

Saint Irene (304).

She was a virgin and a martyr, and a sister of Saint Agape and Saint Chionia, two heroic girls who also suffered martyrdom for the Catholic Faith

Saint Herman Joseph

under the governor Dulcitius of Macedonia. Irene's two sisters Agape and Chionia had refused to eat the food that had been offered in sacrifice to the gods. Whereupon they were burned alive. Irene was later apprehended for possessing Christian books which was against the law. Irene was ordered to be stripped and exposed in a brothel but she was unharmed there. She was given one more chance to offer incense to the gods, she refused and was sentenced to death. She and her books on sacred Scripture were publicly burnt.

6. Saint Juliana of Cornillon (1258). She was a prioress of the Order of Saint Augustine. She was responsible for the institution of the feast of Corpus Christi, which is celebrated in the Catholic Church each year on the Thursday after Trinity Sunday. This feast was set up for the Universal Church in 1264, but Saint Juliana was responsible for its being first commemorated in 1247.

7. Saint Herman Joseph (1241). He was a German, a native of Cologne. He became a Premonstratensian monk. He had a great devotion to the Blessed Virgin Mary. When the monks added the name Joseph to his original name, Herman, Our Lady gave her approval to this addition by placing a ring on his finger. Saint Herman Joseph was ardently devoted to the memory of Saint Ursula and her 11,010, companions, martyred in Cologne, all as virgins, in the year 383, and whose bodies are kept in one of the churches.

8. Saint Julie Billiart (1816).

At the age of fourteen, Saint Julie took a vow of perpetual chastity. Later, she became a cripple, but was miraculously cured when she was fifty-three years old. She founded the Sisters of Notre Dame de Namur in 1803. The French Revolutionists, in the horrible era of Napoleon, could not intimidate this courageous nun. She died when she was sixty-five years old.

Venerable Sister Mary Teresa Quevedo (1950).

Maria Teresa was born in Madrid, Spain, on April 14, 1930. She had since her childhood a tender love for the Mother of God which consisted not merely in words, but in works of generous sacrifice. She was a lively girl—a talented dancer, an expert swimmer, and an outstanding tennis player. She had everything life could offer, but it was not enough for her. One day, kneeling in the school chapel, she prayed: "Mother, give me a religious vocation..." and Our Lady gave it to her. When she was seventeen, Maria Teresa entered the novitiate of the Carmelite Sisters of Charity. Her life as a novice was simple. She did the ordinary everyday things extraordinarily well. Her greatest desire was to live for Jesus and Mary only. She died of tubercular meningitis at the age of 19. Before her death she was allowed to profess her final vows and was given Extreme Unction. Her life can be summed up in her own motto, "May all who look at me see you, O Mary."

9. Saint Mary of Cleophas (First Century).

She was one of the "three Marys" who followed Our Lord and stood at the foot of the cross, on Calvary when He died. She was the wife of Saint Cleophas, the brother of Saint Joseph. She was the mother of Saint Simon, Saint James the Less and Saint Jude, Apostles, and of Saint Mary Salome, the mother of the Apostles Saint James the Greater and Saint John. Saint Mary of Cleophas was put on a boat by the Jews in the year 47, and pushed out to sea without sails or oars. With her were Saint Mary Magdalen, Saint Martha, Saint Mary Salome, (daughter of St. Mary of Cleophas), Saint Lazarus, Saint Maximin, Saint Sidonius (the man born blind), and the body of Saint Anne, the mother of the Mother of God. Saint Mary of Cleophas died in France. The island in France where she landed, after her miraculous journey from Jerusalem, is called *les Saintes-Maries-de-la-Mer* ("the Holy Marys of the Sea") named for Saint Mary of Cleophas, Saint Mary Magdalen and Saint Mary Salome.

Pope Saint Leo the Great

10. Saint Ezechiel (Sixth Century B.C.).

Ezechiel was one of the four major prophets of the Old Testament. He was put to death by a Jewish judge and buried in the tomb of Sem, one of Noah's sons. Early Christians made many pilgrimages to the grave of this great prophet, Ezechiel, whom Catholics now call Saint Ezechiel on his feast day.

11. Saint Leo the Great (461). There have been thirteen Popes named Leo; five of them are canonized saints: Saint Leo I, Saint Leo II, Saint Leo III, Saint Leo IV and Saint Leo IX. Saint Leo I, called Saint Leo the Great, was a Pope and Doctor of the Church. He reigned for twenty-one years and fought all manner of heretics. He was "the soul of the Council of Chalcedon," in 451, which condemned the Monophysites, those heretics who held that the human nature of Jesus was absorbed into the Divine, and no longer exists. This heresy would leave Mary, the Mother of God, without a Child. Saint Leo the Great, by his personal power and fearlessness, kept Attila and the Huns from invading and sacking the city of Rome in the year 452.

Saint Gemma Galgani (1903). She was a beautiful Italian girl, of Lucca, in Italy. Because of her ardent love of God she received great visions and had conversations with her Guardian Angel. She worked many miracles and bore the stigmata, the five wounds of Our Lord, in her body. She died at the age of twenty-five. She wanted to become a Passionist nun, but her health was too poor and that Order refused her.

12. Saint Sabbas (372). He was a Goth in what is now Romania. He was captured by heathen soldiers and cruelly martyred with his companions for the Catholic Faith because he would not eat food that had been dedicated to the pagan gods. His memory is in the Catholic Church forever.

13. Saint Hermengild (585). He was a prince, the son of a Gothic king of Spain. His father commanded that he be put to death because he would not receive Holy Communion from the hands of a heretical Arian Bishop. His father had him beheaded.

Blessed Ida of Boulogne (1113). She was the daughter of a duke and a descendant of Charlemagne, the great Holy Roman Emperor. Blessed Ida was the mother of Godfrey de Bouillon who fought valiantly in the First Crusade. After her husband's death, blessed Ida dedicated herself as an Oblate in the Benedictine Order. She died a most holy death when she was seventy-three years old.

Saint Margaret of Castello (1320). Saint Margaret was born in Umbria, to a noble and powerful Italian couple. She was born blind, hunchbacked and crippled, so her parents, embarrassed by her deformity, hid her away in their castle until she was five years old. After that they locked her in a room attached to a chapel on their estate. There the local priest befriended her and helped her as much as he could.

When she was about twenty years old, her parents took her to a shrine in Citta di Castello hoping she would be cured. But when no miracle occurred, the couple slipped away leaving their helpless daughter praying in the church. The beggars and the poor of the city looked after Margaret and soon everyone discovered her extraordinary intelligence and holiness. A community of sisters then invited her to join their convent; but the sisters were lax and felt reproached by her perfection, so they asked her to leave.

After this Saint Margaret became a Dominican Tertiary and lived a life of severe penance, performing miraculous cures and bringing about remarkable conversions. She died of sheer love of God when she was only thirty-three years old. Her little body is incorrupt. Saint Margaret is the patron of the handicapped and unwanted.

14. Saint Justin, Martyr (165). He lived in Palestine. He was converted to the Catholic Faith by the reading of Holy Scripture. Seeing the heroic courage with which Catholics joyfully shed their blood for the Faith they believed, he too aspired to be a martyr. And God granted him that grace.

15. Saint Basilissa and Saint Anastasia (68). These were two noble Roman women, disciples of the Apostles Saint Peter and Saint Paul. They were the pallbearers of Saint Peter and Saint Paul, and buried the bodies of these Apostles after they were martyred, in the year 67. Saint Basilissa and Saint Anastasia were themselves martyred one year later by the Emperor Nero.

Saint Conrad

16. Saint Benedict Joseph Labre (1783). He was a saintly man who spent his life as a pilgrim and as a beggar in France and in Italy. He went about from church to church, spending most of his day in adoration of the Blessed Sacrament. His favorite shrine, to which he made a pilgrimage every year, was the Holy House of Loreto, the house where Mary was conceived and born, and where she conceived her Divine Child-and which had been miraculously transported through the air by angels, in 1291, from Nazareth to Dalmatia, and in 1294, from Dalmatia to Loreto. Saint Benedict Joseph Labre, the beggar, was canonized one hundred years after his death.

17. Saint Anicetus (175). He was the twelfth pope, a Syrian and a martyr.

18. Saint Apollonius (186). He was a Roman senator who was accused of being a Christian by one of his slaves. He stood trial before the Roman Senate, and gave a most beautiful profession of his Faith in the Catholic Church. After this, he was taken out and beheaded.

19. Saint Leo IX (1054). He was the One hundred and fifty-fourth Pope. He was the cousin of an emperor. He was imprisoned by the Normans whom he eventually changed into protectors of the Holy See. He died before the high altar of Saint Peter's in Rome. He was a friend and ally of the future great Pope, Saint Gregory VII, the famous Benedictine monk, Hildebrand.

Blessed James Duckett (1602). He was a bookseller, in London. He was imprisoned and hanged for selling Catholic books after the Protestant Reformation had taken over England. As he was dying, this is what he said to his fellow countrymen: "It is as impossible for anyone to be saved outside the Catholic Church as it was for anyone to avoid the deluge who was outside Noah's Ark."

20. Saint Agnes of Montepulciano (1317). She was a most beautiful and holy Dominican nun. She entered the Order of Saint Dominic when she was a young girl. She was later made a prioress, and died when she was only forty-nine years old. She is one of the many Dominican women religious who are canonized saints. Some others are: Saint Catherine of Siena, Saint Catherine de Ricci, Saint Margaret of Hungary and Saint Rose of Lima.

21. Saint Anselm (1109). Saint Anselm was born in Italy. He later went to France and became abbot of the famous abbey of Bec. He then went to England and became archbishop of Canterbury. His life was written by one of his monks. Every detail of it is one of edification and instruction. Saint Anselm is one of the thirty-three Doctors of the Universal Church.

Saint George

Saint Beuno (630). He was a Welsh saint, and an abbot. He founded several monasteries in Wales. The Society of Jesus in North Wales has a very noted house dedicated to his name. When Saint Beuno's niece, Saint Winifred, was beheaded by Caradog of Hawarden for resisting his impure advances, Saint Beuno took her lifeless body and her head, wrapped them in his cloak and placed them at the foot of the altar while he said Mass. During the Mass, Saint Winifred's head and body were reunited; she came to life once more. She later became a nun and is one of the greatest glories of Wales.

Saint Conrad (1894). He was a Capuchin saint of the 19th Century, who lived in Bavaria. He became a Capuchin when he was thirty-one years old, and spent more than forty years as the doorkeeper of his friary. He was canonized in 1934, only forty years after his death.

22. Saint Caius (296). He was the twenty-ninth Pope and a relative of the Emperor Diocletian. Saint Caius shed his blood for the Catholic Faith that the cruel Emperor Diocletian was persecuting. The niece of Saint Caius, Saint Susanna, whose feast day is August 11, was martyred as a Catholic Virgin because she would not marry Diocletian's son-in-law, whose wife had died.

Saint Soter (182). He was the thirteenth Pope and was martyred for the Catholic Faith. He was a great opponent of the horrible heresy of Montanism, which claimed that there are unforgivable sins that even Jesus cannot absolve us from.

23. Saint George (303). He is known as the "great Martyr." He was an officer in the army of Diocletian, the Roman Emperor. Because he refused to offer sacrifice to a pagan god, he was tortured and beheaded. Saint George is one of the fourteen Holy Helpers. He protects those who invoke him against skin diseases. Saint George is one of the great patrons of England.

24. Saint Fidelis of Sigmaringen (1622). He was a former lawyer who joined the Capuchins. He tried to convert to the Catholic Faith for the sake of their salvation the people of Switzerland who had lost the Faith during the Protestant Reformation. Saint Fidelis was so successful in bring lapsed Catholics and Protestants back to the Faith that his enemies in Switzerland grew furious. They stabbed him to death.

Saint Euphrasia Pelletier (1868). She was the foundress, in 1829, of the Good Shepherd nuns. This is one of the most charitable and apostolic orders of women in the Catholic Church. The fruits of their work among poor and wayward girls are known everywhere. Saint Euphrasia died at the age of seventy-two. This was the same age as Our Blessed Lady when she died.

25. This is the latest day on which **Easter Sunday** can fall. The earliest day Easter can occur is March 22, the feast of Saint Catherine of Sweden.

Saint Mark (68). He was an Evangelist, the disciple of Saint Peter, and the first Bishop of Alexandria, in Egypt, and the writer of the second Gospel. His full name was John Mark. He was a cousin of Saint Barnabas. His mother, Saint Mary, has her feast day on June 29. It was at the home of Saint Mark, and his mother Saint Mary, that the Last Supper was held, that the Holy Ghost descended upon the Apostles at the first Pentecost, and that Our Lady lived from the time she spent at Ephesus with Saint John. Saint Mark dropped the John from his name in favor of Saint John the Evangelist, who lived in his house. Saint Mark was martyred in Alexandria. He was tied to a rope and

Our Lady of Good Counsel

dragged through the streets until he died of bleeding and exhaustion. His body was taken in 828 to Venice, where a cathedral was built for him in 830, the famous Cathedral of Saint Mark in Venice.

26. Saint Cletus (90). He was the third Pope. He ruled the Church for eleven years before his cruel martyrdom. He was of Roman blood. He was the first Pope to set up parishes in Rome. His name is mentioned every day by every Catholic priest in the Holy Sacrifice of the Mass.

Our Lady of Good Counsel (11th century). The title, "Our Lady of Good Counsel," has been given to a miraculous fresco depicting the Blessed Mother holding the Divine Child. Believed to be a gift from Heaven since the origin of the artwork is unknown, the holy portrait is suspended in mid-air without any means of physical support! It has been situated this way ever since the fifteenth century when it made a mystical journey from Scutari, Albania to Genazzano, Italy. Albania at that time was under Islamic siege and was also undergoing moral decay. Two devout Albanians, Georgio and De Sclavis, were faced with the dilemma of leaving their country and their Virgin, or remaining under Islamic rule. Our Lady advised both of them in a dream to follow her to safety. While praying before the image, the two men saw it lift from the wall and begin to float away. They followed it all the way to its new home in Italy, even walking across the Adriatic Sea in accordance with Our Lady's instructions. The fresco was welcomed in the town of Genazzano by the miraculous ringing of the church bells. Although remaining suspended in the air, the sacred image placed itself near a wall inside the church. Innumerable miracles of every kind have been wrought through devotion to Our Lady of Good Counsel.

27. Saint Peter Canisius (1597). He was a native of Holland who was received into the Society of Jesus when he was twenty-two years old. He was the great leader of the counter-Reformation against Protestants in German countries in the sixteenth century. He worked in Germany, Austria, Switzerland, Bohemia and Poland. He has been made a Doctor of the Universal Church, one of the two members of the Society of Jesus to receive this honor. The other is Saint Robert Bellarmine. Saint Peter Canisius has been called "the second apostle of Germany." The first apostle of Germany was Saint Boniface, who died in 755, and whose feast is June 5. It is Saint Peter Canisius who assures us that Saint Maternus, the son of the widow of Naim, was the first Bishop of Cologne, in Germany.

Saint Peter Canisius

Saint Zita (1278). She became a little servant maid for a wealthy family at Lucca, in Italy, at the age of twelve. She worked for them all her life, and was sixty years old when she died. Because of her radiant sanctity in every simple and humble thing she did, she has become the patron saint of housemaids and domestic servants.

28. Saint Louis Marie de Montfort (1716).

He was born of poor parents, in France, ordained a priest in 1700, and died in 1716 when he was only forty-three years old. He founded the order of the Daughters of Wisdom and also the Company of Mary (the Montfort Fathers). He was one of the greatest apostles of devotion to the Blessed Virgin Mary in the whole of Catholic history. His masterpiece on this subject, called *True Devotion to the Blessed Virgin*, may well make him one day a Doctor of the Universal Church.

Saint Peter of Verona

He revived the practice of saying the Rosary, first begun by Saint Dominic, which was being neglected in his day. The true practice of saying the Rosary, according to Saint Dominc and Saint Louis Marie, and to another dear apostle of the Holy Rosary, Blessed Alan de la Roche, is to recite it daily and always to keep the Rosary beads on one's person and in one's house. Saint Louis Marie de Montfort was a tall, handsome, noble and heroic priest, constant in the thought of Mary, the Mother of God, in everything he did and said.

Saint Paul of the Cross (1775). He was the founder of the Passionist Order, which has done so much to revive in the hearts of all true Catholics a love for the sorrows of Jesus upon the Cross. Two other members of his Order have already been canonized as saints. They are: Saint Vincent Mary Strambi, who died in 1824, and Saint Gabriel of the Most Sorrowful Virgin, who died in 1862. Saint Vincent Mary Strambi wrote the life of Saint Paul of the Cross.

Saint Peter Louis Marie Chanel (1841). He was a French priest, a member of the Marist Order, and a missionary to Oceania. He was martyred on the island of Futuna by cannibals that he had come to convert.

29. Saint Hugh of Cluny (1109).

He is called Saint Hugh the Great, and is one of the glories of the Benedictine Order. He was the adviser to nine Popes. One of his disciples was the monk of Cluny called Hildebrand, who after his election to the papacy was named Gregory VII, and is one of the greatest of the Popes.

Saint Peter of Verona (1252). Is also known as Saint Peter Martyr. He was born in Verona, Italy to parents who were adherents of the Manichaean heresy. He was sent to study at a Catholic school and then went to the University of Bologna

Saint Catherine of Siena

where he met the great Saint Dominic, and entered the Order of Friars Preachers also known as Dominicans. Because of his great talent and zeal he was appointed by Pope Gregory IX to combat the Manichaean heresy in all of Italy. His success in converting souls resulted in many attempts on his life. He never failed to denounce the vices and errors of Catholics who confessed the Faith by words, but in deeds denied it. Finally when he was returning from preaching in the town of Como on his way to Milan he was waylaid by assassins who struck him in the head with an axe, causing him to fall down half dead. Raising himself to his knees, bleeding profusely, he recited a prayer offering his blood as a sacrifice to God. Then tracing the words "Credo in Deum" (I believe in God), on the ground with his blood he was pierced through his heart by his assailants.

30. This is the earliest day that **Ascension Thursday** can occur. The latest day on which it can fall is June 3.

Saint Catherine of Siena (1380). She was the twenty-fifth child of a wool dyer and his wife, who lived in northern Italy. She became a Third Order Dominican at the age of sixteen. Though never educated in any formal way, she was one of the most brilliant theological minds of her day. This was because of special graces and inspiration given her by God. She succeeded in persuading the Pope to go back to Rome from Avignon, in 1377, and when she died she was endeavoring to heal the Great Western Schism, which had begun in 1378. Her letters, four hundred or more of them, and a treatise that is innocently called "a dialogue," are among the most brilliant writings of the saints in the history of the Catholic Church. Saint Catherine was thirty-three years old when she died, the same age as Jesus at His death. Saint Catherine of Siena is the patron saint of Italy. By way of letting her know how much He knew she loved Him, Jesus gave her the wounds of the nail and the spear in her hands, her feet and her side.

Saint Joseph Cottolengo (1842). He has been called the "Italian Vincent de Paul." He founded several institutions for men and women, devoted to penance, the care of the poor, and the rescue of the derelict. He died at Chieri (Turin).

Blessed Marie of the Incarnation (1672). She was born in France, married at eighteen and widowed at twenty. She then became an Ursuline nun. In 1639 she came to Canada where she was the first missionary sister. She was a great contemplative but led a most active life. She is called the "Mother of the Catholic Church in Canada."

May

The Month of Our Lady

May is one of the four months especially dedicated to the Blessed Virgin. The other three months are: August, dedicated to her Immaculate Heart; September, dedicated to her Seven Sorrows; and October, dedicated to her most Holy Rosary.

1. Saint Joseph, the Patron of Workers. Saint Joseph, the virginal spouse of the Blessed Virgin Mary, who guarded and protected her in her Divine Maternity, is, as a member of the Holy Family, one of a trinity in Heaven which every Christian heart must turn to in veneration and prayer. Saint Joseph was thirty years old when he married Our Lady, and sixty years old when he died. His genealogy is the first one given in the New Testament. He is fore-typed in the Old Testament by Joseph, the son of Jacob, tall, handsome, noble, and with a coat of many colors. Saint Joseph died in the arms of Jesus and Mary. Saint Joseph has two feast days: one on March 19, to commemorate his death, and now, one on May 1, to commemorate his vocation as a carpenter and as the patron and protector of all workers. Saint Peter Chrysologus, Doctor of the Church, tells us that the Holy Family had no servants. Our Lord, as God, let Himself be innocently taught the trade of a carpenter by Saint Joseph in order to show us what sanctity can be attached to the simple and humble role of a workman, provided all one's work is done in prayerful dedication to God. Lowly and laborious trades are elevated and exalted in the sight of God because the foster father of Jesus on this earth was a carpenter. This is the child-like lesson of May 1.

Saint Athanasius

Saint Jeremias (590 B.C.).

Jeremias was one of the four major prophets of the Old Testament. His Prophecy and his Lamentations constitute a book in the Old Testament. There are forty-five books in the Old Testament and twenty-seven books in the New Testament. There are seventy-two books in the whole Bible. One of the most quoted texts from the prophet Jeremias is from his Lamentations, chapter 3, verse 27, where he says that, "It is good for a man to have borne the yoke from his youth," thereby letting us know that when one is to become a saint, or even to save one's soul, it is good to start as a child.

2. Saint Athanasius (373). He was one of the greatest Doctors of the Catholic Church. He was only a deacon at the Council of Nicea, in 325, when he courageously denounced Arius as a heretic for denying the full divinity of Jesus Christ. Saint Athanasius became Patriarch of Alexandria, in Egypt, and was its bishop for forty-six years. He suffered great hardships and persecutions. He was excommunicated by practically every influential bishop in the East and five times banished from his See, to which he always returned. Saint Athanasius is one of the four great Doctors of the Universal Church. The other three are Saint John Chrysostom, Saint Augustine and Saint Gregory the Great. A creed has been named in honor of Saint Athanasius. It is known as the Athanasian Creed, and along with the Apostles' Creed and the Nicene Creed, it is one of the three greatest dogmatic professions of Faith the Catholic Church uses in its liturgy. Saint Athanasius has been called "the Father of Orthodoxy" and "the Champion of Christ's Divinity." Saint Gregory Nazianzen calls Saint Athanasius "a pillar of the Church." So courageous was his defense of the Catholic Faith and its dogmas against the weak and sometimes heretical bishops of his day that this has given rise to the well-known saying, "Athanasius against the world!" *(Athanasius contra mundum).* This means that one courageous priest or bishop professing the true Faith can be fully suppressed or silenced by no one.

3. The Finding of the True Cross (326). Saint Helena, the mother of the Emperor Constantine, made a pilgrimage to the Holy Land in the year 326, when she was seventy-six years old. A Roman emperor, Hadrian, about two hundred years before, in order to stop Christians from venerating the mount of Calvary where Jesus was crucified, had raised a large mount of earth over it and dedicated a temple there to the goddess Venus. When Saint Helena arrived in Jerusalem, with the help of Saint Macarius, Bishop of that city, she had the Temple of Venus destroyed. She hired two hundred workmen and one hundred soldiers to dig into the ground, and they found the Holy Cross on which Our Lord was crucified. It was identified miraculously by the instantaneous cure of a little boy with a crippled arm and of a woman who was dying when it touched her. Part of the True Cross was put in a small church on Mount Calvary. Part of it was kept in Constantinople. And part of it was sent to Rome to the Basilica of the Holy Cross, where it is kept and venerated to this day.

Along with the finding of the True Cross, Saint Helena also found the four nails which were in Jesus' hands and in His feet when He was on the Cross, the spear which the centurion drove into the side of Jesus when he died and the inscription placed above the head of Jesus on the Cross, which proclaimed Him in Hebrew, in Greek and in Latin: "Jesus of Nazareth, the King of the Jews." One of the nails Saint Helena found under the hill of Calvary she later threw into the sea to stop a storm. The other three nails are kept in churches in Europe. One of them is in the Iron Crown of Lombardy. The spear that pierced Our Lord's side is kept in one of the pillars of the Vatican, in Rome. The inscription over Our Lord's sacred head is kept in the Church of the Holy Cross in Jerusalem, in Rome. There is a special feast dedicated to the nails and the spear that wounded Our Lord on the Cross, on the second Friday of every Lent.

Saint Timothy and Saint Maura (286). These were a Christian man of Egypt and his saintly wife, who, because they refused to deliver sacred books to pa-

Saint Monica

gan officials, were crucified, and died, as their Saviour, Our Lord Jesus Christ, did.

4. Saint Florian (304). He was an officer in the Roman army who courageously professed his Faith during the persecution of Diocletian. He was terribly scourged and then thrown into a river with a stone around his neck. He is the patron of firemen and also one of the great patrons of Poland.

Saint Monica (387). She was one of the most heroically beautiful Christian women in all the history of the Church. She was married by arrangement to a pagan official in North Africa who was much older than she was. She bore him three children. Her oldest child was named Augustine. She did everything possible to bring this brilliant boy into the Catholic Church. She finally was able to do so after she followed him from Africa to Milan, where Saint Ambrose baptized Augustine in the year 387, when he was thirty-three years old. This was the great Saint Augustine, the Doctor of the universal Church, without whose name and reputation and teaching there would be a great void in Catholic tradition. Shortly after the Baptism of Saint Augustine, Saint Monica died, in the town of Ostia, in central Italy, on her way back to Africa. One thousand years after the death of Saint Augustine, in the year 1430, Saint Monica's precious body was translated from Ostia to Rome, and placed in the Church of Saint Augustine. This day has a special feast for itself, on April 9. Saint Monica was twenty-two years old when Saint Augustine was born. She was only fifty-five years old when she died.

Blessed Ceferino Jimenez Malla (1936). Ceferino, known as *El Pele* (the Strong One), was a Gypsy from Fraga, Spain. He was esteemed by all who knew him for his honesty, wisdom, great charity to the poor, devotion to Our Lady and love of Our Lord in the Blessed Sacrament. During the Spanish Civil War, he was jailed for defending a priest. He was offered his liberty if he would only stop saying his rosary. He refused and was finally shot with his rosary clutched tightly in his hand. He was 75 years old.

5. Saint Pius V (1572). During the age of the so-called Reformation, in the sixteenth century, this was the greatest Pope. Saint Pius V ruled the one true Church for six years, from 1566 to 1572. He is the Pope who supported the Christians in their crusade against the Turks in the Battle of Lepanto. He set up the feast of the most Holy Rosary. He put the invocation "Help of Christians" into the Litany of Our Lady. He is the Pope who valiantly supported all the decrees of the Council of Trent. He insisted on putting these decrees into effect despite the growing Protestant opposition of his day, from Anglicans, Lutherans and Calvinists. Saint Pius V is the Pope who courageously excommunicated Queen Elizabeth of England. He was a great lover of Church music and liturgical observances. He put into the Mass such lovely prayers as the *Domine, non sum dignus*, the *Confiteor* and the *Placeat tibi Sancta Trinitas* that the priest says just before giving the last blessing. The last blessing itself and the Last Gospel were both put into the Mass by Pope Saint Pius V.

6. Saint John before the Latin Gate (95). In the year 95, Saint John the Apostle, the beloved disciple of Our Lord, and Our Lady's priest, was arrested at Ephesus and brought to Rome. He was there thrown into a caldron of boiling oil. He was eighty-three years old at the time. He miraculously came out unharmed. In fear of him, the pagan Romans exiled him to the Island of Patmos. There he wrote his great prophetical book, the Apocalypse. He then returned to Ephesus where, in the year 96, he wrote his Gospel, and later his three Epistles. Saint John died in the year 100, when he was eighty-eight years old. He was the youngest of all the Apostles, but the last to leave this world. His body as well as his soul have been assumed into Heaven, as Saint Robert Bellarmine assures us and as the tradition of the Faith clearly indicates. When his grave was opened, there was found nothing but bread, and in the eleventh century, Saint Peter Damian tells us that miraculous bread was still being renewed there whenever the tomb of Saint John was opened.

7. Saint Stanislaus of Cracow (1079). He was a saintly Polish archbishop who, because of his courage in teaching the unequivocal Catholic Faith, drew on himself the anger of King Boleslas II, who one day entered a church where Saint Stanislaus was celebrating Mass, and split his head open with a sword. Saint Stanislaus of Cracow was only forty-nine years old when this happened.

Blessed Marie Louise (1759). She was born in Poitiers, France. She was the spiritual daughter of Saint Louis Marie de Montfort and the first to adopt his consecration of slavery to Our Lady. With him she cofounded the Daughters of Wisdom to relieve the suffering of the poor and to run charitable schools and hospitals. The poor people would called her the "good Mother Jesus." She founded 36 religious houses in France before she died. She died at age 74.

8. The Apparition of Saint Michael (525). The great Archangel Michael, the special Guardian Angel of Saint Joseph, and the Guardian Angel of each one of the Popes, and one of the seven great angels who stand before the throne of God, appeared on a mountain named Gargano, in southern Italy, in 525. Saint Michael asked that a cave there be turned into a shrine, to make amends to God for the pagan worship that once occurred in that place. This was done, and the shrine was named in honor of Saint Michael. It is one of the most wonderful shrines in all Italy.

Saint Acacius (303). He was a centurion in the Roman army who was tortured and beheaded under Diocletian. He is one of the fourteen Holy Helpers and is invoked against headaches.

9. Saint Gregory Nazianzen (389). He is a Doctor of the Church and was one of the greatest saints of the fourth century. He is called Nazianzen because he was

bishop of a small town of that name in Cappadocia, in Asia Minor. His father, Saint Gregory the Elder (January 1), and his mother, Saint Nonna (August 5), are both listed in the calendar of the saints. He also had a brother and a sister who are saints-Saint Caesarius and Saint Gorgonia. Saint Gregory Nazianzen's great friend and companion was Saint Basil the Great. With Saint Basil he is remembered as one of the four great Eastern Doctors of the Church. He was the leading theologian and was in charge at the Second Ecumenical Council of the Church, held at Constantinople in 381, whose purpose it was to defend the Divinity of the Holy Ghost, and to redefine the Divinity of Jesus.

10. This is the earliest day that **Pentecost** can occur. The latest day on which it can fall is June 13.

Saint Antoninus (1459). Saint Antoninus was a little man, born in Florence. He was admitted to the Dominican Order when he was sixteen years old. He was the Pope's special theologian at the Council of Florence, and later on was made archbishop of that city. He was called "the Father of the Poor." He died holding a crucifix in his hand, and kissing it. His motto was, "To serve God is to reign."

Blessed Damien (Damien the Leper) (1889). Father Damien de Veuster was a Belgian priest who volunteered to care for the lepers on the island of Molokai in Hawaii. Because of the fear of contagion lepers were condemned to live isolated from their families and society, abandoned by all, suffering from great poverty and despair.

Father Damien completely transformed Molokai. By constant prayer before the Blessed Sacrament and devotion to his people he regenerated the spirituality of the lepers. He built houses, a hospital, a chapel, and a water-supply system for the leper colony.

FR. DAMIEN DE VEUSTER   Carey Winters '94

Blessed Damien de Veuster

Father Damien ministered to his people for eighteen years, never avoiding personal contact with them. Three years before his death he began his Sunday sermon with "We lepers" for he too had become a leper. Near the end of his life Brother Joseph Dutton from the United States and three Franciscan Sisters went to help him in his work.

11. Saint Philip (61) and Saint James (62). These are two of the twelve Apostles, whose feasts are commemorated on the same day. This is because their bodies are kept in the same church in Rome, in the Basilica of the Holy Apostles. Saint Philip was crucified for the Faith. Saint James (James the Less), brother of Saint Simon and Saint Jude, and the first Bishop of Jerusalem, was thrown from the top of the Temple of Jerusalem by the Jews, and then clubbed to death in the street.

12. Saint Pancratius (304). He is one of the best loved of all the boy saints in the Catholic Church. Saint Pancratius was martyred at the age of fourteen. By way of a gift, one of the Popes in the seventh century sent one of his relics to England. There, to this very day, English Catholics love and venerate this heroic Christian Martyr as Saint Pancras.

Blessed Imelda (1333). Blessed Imelda Lambertini was the daughter of an Italian count, at Bologna, in Italy. She was a student at a Dominican convent in that city. They accepted her as a novice at the age of nine. She had an intense love for the Blessed Sacrament, but had not received It. At the age of eleven, when she was kneeling in chapel at Mass, the Sacred host miraculously left the hand of the priest and went into her mouth. She made a long, long thanksgiving. When the nuns came to call her, they found she had died, of sheer love.

13. Our Lady of the Blessed Sacrament.
This feast was first promoted by Saint Peter Julian Eymard, in 1868, the year he died. He was fifty-seven when he died, and his feast day is August 3. He was a great friend of Saint John Marie Vianney, the Curé of Ars, and was a great admirer of Saint Philomena. The purpose of this feast is to let us know that without Mary there would be no Blessed Sacrament, because it was she who gave Jesus the body and the blood, which are sacrificed at every Catholic Mass, and then given to the faithful as their Divine Food.

Our Lady, Queen of Martyrs. This feast is to let us know how royal it is to shed our blood for the Catholic Faith, and to suffer anything so as to practice and profess it. The whole story of the Catholic Faith in the early centuries of the Church was the shedding of blood. From the year 36 to the year 306, there were eleven million martyrs, men, women and children, who shed their blood for their Faith. They were supported in their suffering by Mary, Queen of Martyrs. At their death they went immediately to heaven, to meet her in royal grandeur, and to be her children, her servants and her subjects for all eternity.

Our Lady of Fatima. The first of the great Fatima apparitions, to three children in Portugal, occurred on May 13, 1917. There were five more apparitions, one on June 13, one on July 13, one on August 19, one on September 13 and the last one on October 13. At the last of these apparitions, 70,000 people saw the sun whirl round and round in the sky for ten or more minutes. The three children to whom Our Lady appeared at Fatima were a little ten-year-old girl named Lucia dos Santos, and her two cousins, a boy and a girl, nine and seven years old respectively, whose names were Francisco and Jacinta. All three were shepherds, in a little village north of Lisbon. Before the Fatima apparitions an angel had been sent by Our Lady with a chalice containing the Precious Blood of Jesus, to give to the two younger children, and with a consecrated host for Lucia, the oldest child. In all the apparitions to the Fatima children, Our Lady held a rosary in her hand. She was seen with Jesus as a Child and with Saint Joseph. She was seen as Our Lady of Sorrows, with Jesus. She was seen as Our Lady of Mount Carmel, holding her Divine Child. Francisco and Jacinta died shortly after these apparitions. Lucia or Sister Mary of the Immaculate Heart, lived as Carmelite nun in Coimbra, in Portugal, until her death on February 13, 2005.

Saint Robert Bellarmine (1621). Saint Robert Francis Bellarmine was born at Montepulciano, in Tuscany, in Italy. He joined the Society of Jesus when he was eighteen years old. In 1599, in spite of all his protestations and entreaties, and even tears, he was made a cardinal by Pope Clement VIII, and in 1602 became Archbishop of Capua. He died on the seventeenth of September 1621, the feast of the Stigmata of Saint Francis of Assisi, a saint to whom he was very much devoted. Saint Robert Bellarmine was one of the greatest and most learned men in the history of the Church. Pope Pius XI declared him a Doctor of the Church, in 1931. He is one of the two priests of the Society of Jesus who are Doctors of the Church. The other is Saint Peter Canisius. Queen Elizabeth of England was so afraid of the writing of Saint Robert Bellarmine that she forbade any of her subjects to read them. Pope Benedict XIV called Saint Robert Bellarmine "the Hammer of Heretics," the title also given to Saint Anthony of Padua. Pope Benedict XV entitled him "the Model of the Defenders of the Faith." It is Saint Robert Bellarmine who assures us that the body of Saint John the Evangelist, Our Lady's First Eucharist child, is with her in Heaven.

14. Saint Boniface of Tarsus (307). Saint Boniface went from Rome, where Saint Paul was beheaded, to Tarsus in Cilicia, where Saint Paul was born. He went there to recover the relics of some precious Catholic martyrs. He was seized by pagans, condemned as a Catholic, and beheaded. His relics were brought back to Rome and are still kept on the Aventine Hill, together with the relics of a courageous Catholic woman whose name is Saint Aglae. There are seven great hills in Rome: the Quirinal, the Viminal, the Esquiline, the Palatine, the Capitoline, the Caelian and the Aventine. Every one of these hills has some beautiful connection with the Catholic Faith by way of Saints who were martyred on them, or churches that were built on them.

15. Saint John Baptist de la Salle (1719). He is the founder of the Christian Brothers, known technically as the "Brothers of the Christian Schools." For three hundred years they have trained young Catholic boys in their Faith in a manner so simple and clear and courageous, that almost no training of young Catholic boys can compare with theirs. Everyone knows a Christian Brother's boy almost the moment he speaks to him. Saint John Baptist de la Salle was born at Rheims, in northern France. This is where Saint Joan of Arc crowned the Dauphin after a French victory over an English army. Saint John Baptist de la Salle's special patron was, of course, Saint John the Baptist, the precursor of Our Lord. Saint John

Saint John Nepomucene

Baptist de la Salle's motto in all apostolic endeavors, for the sake of converting souls to the Catholic Faith and preserving those who have it, was to combine zeal with prudence, Faith with charity, and firmness with gentleness. Prudence without zeal for souls, and charity without the challenge of the Faith, and gentleness without the strength of a true apostle, Saint John Baptist de la Salle rejected. He was sixty-eight years old when he died.

16. Saint John Nepomucene (1393). This is the great and wonderful Catholic priest born at Nepomuk, in Bohemia, who became court chaplain at Prague and confessor to the wife of King Wenceslaus IV. Because he would not reveal to the king what the queen had told him in confession, Saint John Nepomucene was thrown into the River Moldau in Prague, and drowned. He was only fifty-three years old at the time. Lights shone on the place where the saintly priest was drowned when he had been thrown from a bridge. The morning after his martyrdom, his body was found and buried in the Cathedral of Prague. The king who killed him was later seized and dethroned by the people. In 1719, the tongue of Saint John Nepomucene was found incorrupt. This was a tribute to his fidelity in never revealing to anyone the secrets of the confessional, a fidelity, which every Catholic priest is obliged courageously to observe. In 1729 Saint John Nepomucene was canonized.

Saint Simon Stock (1265). Saint Simon was born at Kent, in England, of a distinguished family. He was called "Simon Stock" because at the age of twelve he began living a contemplative life in the hollow (the stock) of a great oak tree, which he made his little chapel and home for twenty years. He became a Carmelite monk and, in time, was made the sixth General of the Order, in England. It was to Saint Simon Stock, on July 16, 1251, that Our Lady gave the brown scapular. Our Lady promised to all who wore the brown scapular that she would obtain for them the grace of final perseverance in the Catholic Faith. Saint Simon Stock was one hundred years old when he died. During his life he visited Mount Carmel in the Holy Land, the great mountain dedicated so especially to Mary, the Mother of God, and where the first chapel ever built in her honor was erected, in the year 33.

Saint Brendan (578). There are two great Irish saints named Brendan, and both were abbots. Saint Brendan the Younger, whose feast is May 16, was educated by Saint Ita and Saint Finian. He was the first one ever to make a voyage to the shores of America, the "Land of Promise." He did this in the sixth century, nine hundred years before Columbus discovered America. He is called "Saint Brendan the Navigator." He was ninety-four years old when he died. He founded schools and monasteries. He is the patron saint of sailors.

17. This is the earliest day that **Trinity Sunday** can occur. The latest day on which it can fall is June 20.

Saint Paschal Baylon (1592). Saint Paschal Baylon was born on the feast of Pentecost, on the twenty-fourth of May 1540. That is why he was called "Paschal." He was a little peasant boy who tended sheep. In his leisure, he read holy books and became profoundly learned in all the simple mysteries of the Catholic Faith. His great love and devotion were to the Blessed Sacrament. He would spend hours kneeling before our Lord in the tabernacle. When he could not go to church, he would kneel in the fields and face the church where the Blessed Sacrament was, and adore Jesus from a distance. He became a Franciscan lay brother at the age of twenty-four. His obedience, humility and gracious manner edified everyone. His assignment as a lay brother was that of a doorkeeper. He used to spend most of his nights in prayer and adoration before the Blessed Sacrament. On a trip through France he met some Calvinists, and so defended the Most Blessed Sacrament in disputation with a Protestant minister, that he was beaten until he nearly died. When he did die, on the seventeenth of May, in 1592, while his body lay in the coffin at the foot of the altar in the church at his funeral Mass, during the elevation of the Host and the Chalice, Saint Paschal's eyes were seen to open and close by hundreds of people in the church. This angelic lay brother of the Franciscan order has been made the Patron of Eucharistic Congresses.

18. Saint Eric (1160). Saint Eric was a king of Sweden, and is one of the great Catholic patrons of that country. He was called "the Father and Lawgiver of the People." He was martyred by some pagan Danes as he was leaving a Catholic Church after Mass. He was beheaded.

Saint Felix of Cantalice (1587). He was a simple farmer at Abruzzi, in Italy. He entered the Capuchin Order as a lay brother when he was thirty years old. His constant prayer was "Deo gratias!" which means "Thanks be to God!" As a result of this simple invocation, which he continually made, everyone called him "Brother Deo Gratias." Though a simple and unlettered man, his holiness and wisdom were so great that saints, like Saint Charles Borromeo and Saint Philip Neri, consulted him, and many learned theologians went to him for advice.

19. Saint Peter Celestine V (1296). Peter of Morone was the name of Pope Celestine V before he was elected to be a successor of Saint Peter. He spent only five months as Pope. He then resigned because of his humility and his desire to return to the life of a Benedictine hermit. There has been no Pope named Peter except the first one. As Pope, Peter Celestine is called Pope Celestine V. As a saint, he is called Saint Peter Celestine.

20. Saint Bernardine of Siena (1444). Saint Bernardine of Siena was born in 1380. He became a Franciscan when he was twenty-two years old. He was one of the greatest missionary priests of the fifteenth century. His especial devotion was to the Holy Name of Jesus, which he insisted that everyone should say devoutly, reverently and with the bending of one's head. He openly rebuked anyone who dared use the Holy Name of Jesus in profanity. Everywhere Saint Bernardine went, he carried a banner with the monogram IHS on it. Saint Bernardine was canonized six years after he died. The four great apostles of the Holy Name of Jesus are: Saint Bernardine of Siena, Saint John of Capistrano (whose feast day is March 28). Saint Ignatius of Loyola (who called the Order which he founded the Society of Jesus, and whose feast day is July 31) and Saint John Colombine (whose feast is also July 31), who founded an Order whose members went about constantly and reverently and audibly invoking the Holy Name of Jesus.

21. This is the earliest day that **Corpus Christi** can occur. The latest day on which it can fall is June 24.

Saint Andrew Bobola (1657). Saint Andrew Bobola was born and died in Poland. He is called the apostle of Lithuania because of his great apostolic labors in that section. He was a priest of the Society of Jesus. He was martyred at the age of sixty-seven by the Cossacks, who beat and scourged him so severely, dragged him through the streets, half burned and choked him, that when he was beatified, the sacred congregation of Rites in Rome declared that his was the most cruel martyrdom ever submitted to that court. Saint Andrew Bobola was beatified in 1853 by Blessed Pope Pius IX. He was canonized in 1938 by Pope Pius XI.

Saint Eugene de Mazenod (1861). Charles Joseph Eugene Mazenod was born in France in 1782. As a young man he resolved to become a priest to help remedy the moral and religious decay left in the wake of the French Revolution. In 1816 he founded the Missionaries of Provence, which developed later into the Oblates of Mary Immaculate, to work with the poorest of the poor. Saint Eugene's missionaries today range from Alaska to Sri Lanka. Saint Eugene was made Bishop of Marseilles in 1837.

22. Saint Rita of Cascia (1456).
Saint Rita's full name was Margherita, which means *pearl*. She was born of a peasant family in the mountain country of Umbria, in Italy. Her birth was an answer to the prayer of her parents, who had for years waited for a child. She wished to become a nun at eighteen, but was forced to marry. After her husband's death she fulfilled her first vocation, and at the age of thirty became an Augustinian nun. The convent of that Order first refused her, but her patron saints, Saint Augustine, Saint John the Baptist and Saint Nicholas of Tolentino, miraculously carried and placed her at the foot of the altar, before the Blessed Sacrament, in the chapel of the convent where she desired to enter. There the nuns found her, and knew they must keep her. Saint Rita begged Our Lord to share His Passion with her in the matter of wounds. One night, when she was kneeling before a fresco on the wall of her convent, a bright light came from a figure of Jesus with His crown of thorns to her own forehead, and pierced it, and left the mark of a thorn there for the rest of her life. Saint Catherine of Bologna, Saint John of Capistrano and Saint James of the Marches were her contemporaries. She died when she was seventy years old. Because of her power in Heaven to grant favors of any kind that are asked of her, Saint Rita is called, in childlike affection, "the saint of the impossible."

23. Saint John Baptist de Rossi (1764).
This heroic Roman priest was the great apostle to the farm laborers and city workers of Rome and its suburbs. He loved to do work among prisoners, the poor and the illiterate. He preached to simple folk at all hours of the day. He visited them in their hospitals and in their homes. He was given permission to hear confessions at any time in any one of the churches in Rome, and penitents constantly came to him. The sick poor were those he especially loved and protected; also the abandoned in the streets, and those who walked the streets by night. Saint John Baptist de Rossi is known as "the apostle of the abandoned." He was sixty-six years old when he died.

24. Our Lady, Help of Christians.
There are fifty-one invocations to Our Lady in the Beautiful Litany of Loreto. The invocation. "Our Lady, Help of Christians" was first put into the Litany of Loreto by the Pope, Saint Pius V, in 1571, after the Battle of Lepanto. This was a great battle in which an army of valiant Catholic soldiers, fighting against the Mohammedans, completely defeated these Turkish enemies of Our Lord and Our Lady. In 1814, when Pope Pius VII was freed from a five years' stay in prison, where he had been put by the brutal Napoleon, this Holy Father set up May 24 as the feast of Our Lady, Help of Christians. Catholic priests may say Mass in honor of the Mother of God under this title on this day.

Our Lady of the Way. The title "Our Lady of the Way" (*Madonna della Strada*) comes from a beautiful shrine kept in one of the streets of Rome, where a picture painted in the fifth century was venerated. This lovely picture, to which Saint Ignatius of Loyola, the founder of the Society of Jesus, was so devoted—and before which he and his early companions used to assemble when first they came to the Eternal City—is now kept in the Church of the Gesú, in Rome, a church of the Society of Jesus. Pilgrims visit it there every day and keep constantly telling of the favors they receive from the Mother of God after kneeling and praying before it.

Saint Joanna (First Century). She was the wife of Chuza, the steward of King Herod Antipas. She was one of the holy women who brought spices and ointments to the Holy Sepulcher on Easter morning to anoint the body of Our Lord, which they found had risen from the grave. Her name is mentioned twice in the Holy Gospel of Saint Luke.

25. Saint Gregory VII (1085). Saint Gregory VII's baptismal name was Hildebrand. He was a counsellor to many Popes before he was elected Sovereign Pontiff himself. He reigned

Saint Philip Neri

for twelve years, from 1073 to 1085. So heroically did he fight for the truths and regulations of the Catholic Faith, and so bitterly was he opposed and hated by the powerful enemies of the Church, that he had to flee from Rome to Salerno, where he died. His famous last words were, "I have loved justice, and hated iniquity; therefore I die in exile." He was sixty-five years old when he died.

Saint Madeleine Sophie Barat (1865). Born before the Reign of Terror brought on by the French Revolution, Madeleine Sophie Barat was one of the most brilliant and courageous French Catholic girls in the history of the Church. With heroism and charm combined, with devotion and genius mingled together, she rallied hundreds and hundreds of young women to the cause of the Church Militant in those dreadful days. In 1801, she founded the Religious of the Sacred Heart, familiarly known as the Madams of the Sacred Heart. The fruit of her work was one hundred and five religious houses, and four thousand nuns, right in her own day. Her spiritual daughters are found now in all parts of the world. The United States owes them a great debt for what they have done for young Catholic girls who want to be educated in the goodness and the grace that go together in the true Catholic Faith. One of the spiritual daughters of Saint Madeleine Sophie Barat is Blessed Rose Philippine Duchesne, who is buried in Saint Charles, Missouri, outside Saint Louis. Saint Madeleine Sophie was eighty-six years old when she died.

26. Saint Philip Neri (1595). Saint Philip Neri lived in the century when Protestantism was first raging. He founded the noted Congregation of the Oratory. He was such a clear and authoritative teacher of the Catholic Faith to simple and poor people in the streets, as well as to the highborn and noble of his day, that he is called "the second apostle of Rome." He kept thousands of Catholics from being infected with the heresies of such groups as the Episcopalians, the Lutherans and the Calvinists. He used to spend from twelve to fifteen hours a day in the confessional. Saint Philip Neri was noted for his radiant cheerfulness and friendliness and grace and good humor. He frequently went into an ecstasy while saying Mass. The beating of his heart for the love of God was so strong it broke two ribs in his side. He was eighty years old when he died.

27. Saint Bede the Venerable (735). Saint Bede was called the Venerable while he was still alive. He is the one English Doctor of the Catholic Church. Saint

Saint Mary Magdalen de Pazzi

Bede was educated by a saint, Saint Benedict Biscop, and was ordained by a saint, Saint John of Beverley. He was crystal clear, simple and childlike in all his positive affirmations about the beauty, the clarity and the necessity of the Catholic Faith for the salvation of souls. He died on the eve of the Ascension, in the year 735, at the age of sixty-two. His last words were, "Glory be to the Father, and to the Son and to the Holy Ghost!" Saint Bede was called Venerable during his life because his writings were so challenging and holy that they were read from pulpits at Mass by other Catholic priests.

28. Saint Augustine of Canterbury (604). He was the great apostle of England, sent there by Saint Gregory the Great in 597.

He brought forty Benedictine monks with him. On the Christmas Day after he arrived he baptized ten thousand Englishmen. Even King Ethelbert was converted. This was the beginning of the great age of the Catholic Faith in England, once a country so devout and loyal to the true Faith, and so lovingly prayerful toward the Blessed Virgin Mary that it was called as a land, "Our Lady's Dowry." The best traditions of England are all Catholic. No heretic has been able completely to destroy them.

Saint Bernard of Menthon (1008). He was an Augustinian monk who visited every mountain and valley in the Alps. He took care of all travelers there for over forty years. He is the patron saint of mountain climbers. The celebrated Saint Bernard dogs are named in his honor.

Saint Joan of Arc

29. This is the earliest day the feast of the **Sacred Heart** can occur. The latest day on which it can fall is July 2.

Saint Mary Magdalen de Pazzi (1607). She was an Italian girl, born in Florence in 1566. Her baptismal name was Catherine. As a little child, she would place a crown of thorns on her head when she went to bed at night. She received her first Holy Communion when she was ten years old. She immediately bound herself by a vow of virginity to be the spouse of Jesus. At the age of sixteen she joined the Carmelite Order, and took the name of Mary. She joined that Order because the sisters there, by special permission, were allowed to receive Holy Communion every day. Because she was so sick and not expected to live, she was allowed to make her religious vows two years after her entrance. Saint Mary Magdalen de Pazzi enjoyed great ecstasies of love and union with God. She also suffered great darknesses of soul, sicknesses and attacks by the devil. She offered all her suffering to God for the conversion of sinners, heretics, pagans and unbelievers. She spent the last three years of her life in bed. Her motto was, "To suffer and not to die." She did die, at the age of forty-one. Her body is preserved incorrupt in the Carmelite convent, in Florence, adjacent to the church there.

30. Saint Joan of Arc (1431). She is known as the Maid of Orleans. Her fame has spread to every corner of the world. She was a young shepherd girl in France, who, at the command of three saints, took up arms and led a French army against English invaders of France who were threatening to destroy its culture and its freedom.

Saint Joan of Arc was only seventeen years old at this time. She was later captured and martyred by the English. Because her martyrdom occurred, according to detail, for secular reasons, she is given the title of *virgin*, and not martyr. She died in 1431, when she was nineteen years old. She is the patroness of France. Saint Denis is its patron. Saint Genevieve is the patroness of Paris. The voices of three saints led Saint Joan of Arc to go to battle as a young girl to save her country from dishonor. These were the voices of Saint Michael the Archangel, Saint Catherine of Alexandria and Saint Margaret of Antioch. The last word Saint Joan of Arc spoke was the Holy Name of Jesus, as she was being burned to death. Saint Pius X espoused her cause for canonization. Pope Benedict XV canonized her in the year 1920.

Saint Ferdinand (1252). He was a King of Castile and Leon in Spain. He fought against the Moors. He made the soldiers in his army always carry an image of Mary when they marched. He wore an image of Mary over his heart. He said he "feared more the curse of one old woman than the whole army of the Moors."

31. The Queenship of Mary. The last day of May, the glorious month of Our Blessed Mother, honors her with three outstanding titles: Our Lady, the Queen, Our Lady, Mediatrix of All Graces and Our Lady, the Mother of Fair Love. The Queenship of Mary refers to her absolute dominion over all creation by virtue of being the mother of the King by whom the world was created. Mary is the virgin Mother who brought forth the King of heaven and earth. She is, and should be called, Queen of All Creation. Everything we look at in the order of grace and of nature should be immediately related to her. Nothing is ever done by God, or ever was done, without Mary in His mind. Hers is the Sovereign Majesty of everything God made and of everything He bestows by grace. In the Litany of Loreto, Mary is called Queen twelve times. The authors and dispensers of this book love to call Our Lady, Queen of the Slaves of the Immaculate Heart of Mary

Our Lady, Mediatrix of All Graces. This title of Our Lady means that anything we get from God we get *when* Mary asks it, *as* she asks it, and *to the degree* with which she makes her request. She is the Mother of all favors for everyone. God will not listen to any prayer that is not offered to Him through the intercession of Mary, the Mother of God.

Our Lady, the Mother of Fair Love. The children of Mary should not be merely loving; they should be beautifully and divinely so in all they do. Everyone who sees a Catholic, meets a Catholic, talks with a Catholic, should behold in his or her manner the ways, the looks, the voice, the gestures, the manner of dress, the simplicity and the purity of Mary, the Mother of Fair Love. Mary is the Mother of beautiful Love, of the love, which entrances all who see it. She wants to abide royally in all her children who call her their Mother and their Queen.

Saint Petronilla (First Century). She was a Roman virgin, converted to the Catholic Faith by the Apostle Saint Peter. She stayed with him and ministered to him until her death, at an early age. She ended her life as a martyr. She is the spiritual daughter of Saint Peter. It was his delight to have their names substantially the same: Peter, which means *rock*, and Petronilla, which means *little stone*.

June

1. Saint Angela Merici (1540). A little Italian girl of northern Italy, she lost her parents and was completely orphaned at the age of ten. When she was thirteen, the priest, by special favor in those days, used to give her Holy Communion several times during the week. When she was twenty-one years old, she was told in a vision to found a Religious Order for the instruction of young girls. She thought no group of young girls in all the history of the Church was more beautiful than Saint Ursula and her 11,010 companions, all martyred for their Faith and their virginity in Cologne, in Germany, in the year 383. And so Saint Angela Merici, with twelve girl companions, in 1535, founded the famous and beloved order of nuns known as the Ursulines. They now have convent schools for girls all over the world. The last word Saint Angela Merici

Saint Angela Merici

spoke was the Holy Name of Jesus, just before she died, at the age of sixty-six.

2. Saint Erasmus (303). He was a bishop in Campania in Italy who was martyred after undergoing terrible torments. He is one of the fourteen Holy Helpers and is invoked against stomach ailments. He is also the patron of sailors, who call him Saint Elmo.

Saint Marcellinus and Saint Peter (304). Saint Marcellinus was a priest and Saint Peter an exorcist (one of the minor orders), who both lived in Rome and labored there under the cruel Emperor Diocletian. They were martyred together.

So great was the veneration of the Catholics for them that a basilica was built over their tomb in Rome. Their names are mentioned every day by every Catholic priest in the Canon of the Mass. If "the law of praying is the law of believing," we may know from this simple recognition how great and heroic these two martyrs were, and how much they should be remembered and invoked.

3. This is the latest day on which **Ascension Thursday** can occur.

Saint Clotilde (545). She was queen, the wife of King Clovis of the Franks, who brought the French people as a nation into the Catholic Church in 496, when he was baptized at Rheims by Saint Remigius. Her husband, King Clovis, died in 511. Saint Clotilde was left a widow for thirty-four years.

Saint Boniface

She lived the rest of her life as much a nun as she was a queen. She endured great sufferings for the Catholic Faith. Her favorite patron saint in Heaven was Saint Martin of Tours. She died not far from his tomb, at the age of seventy-one.

Saint Kevin (618). He is one of the great Irish saints. He was the founder of the famous monastery of Glendalough. Along with Saint Laurence O'Toole, he is one of the patron saints of Dublin.

Saint Charles Lwanga and Companions (1886-1887). Commonly referred to as the 22 Ugandan Martyrs. These twenty-two young men and boys, ranging in age from thirteen to thirty years, were the first martyrs among the African Blacks. They were pages of the Ugandan court who enraged the King because they refused to commit the sin of sodomy. When they were arrested four had not yet been baptized, but these were baptized by Charles Lwanga in prison. They were put to death after undergoing cruel torments and were canonized in 1964. Saint Charles Lwanga is the patron saint of African young people.

4. Saint Francis Caracciolo (1608). He was born of a royal family in the

Kingdom of Naples. As a little boy he started reciting daily the rosary. Very early in his life he contracted leprosy, and was miraculously cured of it. He spent every possible moment of his life in the presence of the Blessed Sacrament. His thought was that it was for men that Our Lord came to us in the Eucharist, and while the angels throng Catholic churches to worship God there, men desert Him. While kneeling before the Blessed Sacrament, his face blazed with light, which everyone could see. His favorite devotion was visiting the Blessed Sacrament in unfrequented churches, where few people came. Saint Francis Caracciolo, in 1588, founded the Clerics Regular, whose main work was the perpetual adoration of the Blessed Sacrament. He died when only forty-four years old, on the eve of Corpus Christi, at the same age as Saint Francis of Assisi when he died. Saint Francis Caracciolo's last words were, "Let us go, let us go to Heaven!" When his body was opened after death, these words were found imprinted on his heart: "The zeal of Thy house hath eaten me up."

5. Saint Boniface

(755). Saint Boniface was born in England, in 680. His name in English was Winfrid, which in Latin is translated to *Boniface*, and means "he who does good." He entered a Benedictine monastery at the age of five. In 719, he was sent by Pope Saint Gregory II to be the apostle of Germany. He reconverted that whole country to the Faith, and many of its neighboring countries as well. At seventy-five, he set out with fifty-two companions to finish his work in the conversion of Friesland. Saint Boniface and all his companions were martyred there by the pagans. Saint Boniface was killed while he was putting on his vestments to say Mass.

6. Saint Norbert

(1134). He was born near Cologne, in Germany, and was educated at the court of the emperor. After a somewhat

Saint Norbert

worldly life, he was struck down one day by lightning while riding on a horse. He cried out to God, like Saint Paul, "Lord, what wilt Thou have me do?" He heard a voice from Heaven saying to him, "Turn from evil unto good." He was ordained a priest when he was thirty-five. He later became a bishop. In a hidden and lonely valley named Prémontré, with thirteen disciples, he founded the Religious Order known as the Premonstratensians. It is a branch of the Augustinian Order. His great devotion, and that of his monks, was to the Blessed Sacrament. He is usually pictured with a monstrance in his hand, holding Our Lord in the Blessed Sacrament. He converted great numbers to the Catholic Faith.

Saint Philip the Deacon (First Century). He was one of the Seven Deacons ordained by the Apostles, as we are told in the Acts of the Apostles, Chapter 6. It was he who baptized the eunuch of Queen Candace, of Ethiopia, to let us know how much God values every soul of good will, no matter how socially low or useless he may be according to the standards of the world. Saint Philip the Deacon was a great friend of Saint Paul. Saint Philip was the father of four daughters, virgins, all of whom are honored as saints, and all of whom were given by God the gift of prophecy.

There are five great Philips among the saints: Saint Philip the Apostle, Saint Philip the Deacon, Saint Philip Neri, Saint Philip Benizi and Saint Philip of Jesus, the last of whom was a Mexican, martyred in Japan in 1597.

7. Saint Robert of Newminster (1159).
He was an English priest from Yorkshire, in England, who became a Cistercian monk, and was made the first abbot of the famous Abbey of Newminster, founded in 1137. He was a great friend of Saint Bernard of Clairvaux and of Saint Norbert. He made many prophecies and worked many miracles.

8. Saint Medard and Saint Gildard (558).
These two saints of France were, as we are told in the Roman Martyrology, twin brothers. They were born on the same day, consecrated bishops on the same day, and on the same day they died. Saint Medard was Bishop of Noyon. Saint Gildard was Bishop of Rouen. Their memories are most loving ones in northern France. Saint Medard began the custom of crowning each year as the Rose Queen the most virtuous and holy young Catholic girl of his diocese. If it rains on the feast of Saint Medard, the loving Catholic peasants of northern France take it as a sign that it will rain for forty days more. This same custom prevails in England with regard to Saint Swithin, whose feast day is July 2 and the feast of the translation of whose body is July 15, which day, for weather reasons, is called Saint Swithin's Day.

9. Saint Columbkille (597).
Saint Columbkille, also called Saint Columba, was born in Donegal, in Ireland, on the feast of Saint Ambrose, December 7, 521. He founded many monasteries there. He was also the great apostle to Scotland, where he built many monasteries and churches. He landed in Scotland, on the Island of Iona, on the eve of Pentecost, 563, with twelve companions. He erected on this island the greatest and most famous of his monasteries. Many of the people of northern England were converted to the Catholic Faith by Saint Columbkille. He was called "loving to all," and was said to have himself the face of an angel. He died an abbot, kneeling before the altar. He is buried in the same tomb as Saint Patrick and Saint Bridget.

10. Saint Margaret of Scotland (1093).
This great and saintly princess and queen was the granddaughter of King Edmund Ironside of England. She was the wife

of King Malcolm III of Scotland, whose father, Duncan, was murdered by the noted Macbeth. There never was a more royally holy woman, wife and widow than Saint Margaret. Of her eight children, two of her sons became monks. One of her daughters became a queen, married King Henry I of England, and because of her heroically holy life was, like her mother, a saint. Her name is Saint Matilda, and she is known in history as Good Queen Maud.

Saint Margaret of Scotland was a relative of Saint Stephen of Hungary. She was only forty-three years old when she died. She thanked God for the afflictions He sent her in her illnesses. She spent hours and hours in prayer, and was always grateful to God for every gift she had received. Her beautiful grace after meals is known as "Saint Margaret's blessing." Saint Margaret is the patroness of Scotland.

11. Saint Barnabas (60). Saint Barnabas was the cousin of Saint Mark the Evangelist. He is given the honorary title of apostle, even though he was not one of the Twelve. He was the disciple and companion of Saint Paul. He labored with Saint Paul in various cities and places. He was stoned to death on the Island of Cyprus, where he was born. The Jews stoned him to death because they were infuriated by the power with which he preached the Gospel of Jesus Christ. When his tomb was opened, several

Saint Barnabas

hundred years after his death, he was found holding the Gospel of Saint Matthew in his hand. He is beautifully associated with Saint Matthew, whose Gospel he loved; with Saint Mark, whose cousin he was; and with Saint Paul, of whom he was a disciple. Saint Barnabas' name was originally Joseph. He was called Barnabas, which means *son of consolation*. Saint Charles Borromeo calls him the apostle of Milan. He was one of the seventy-two disciples of Our Lord. The name of Saint Barnabas is mentioned every day in the Canon of the Mass, and always in the Litany of the Saints.

12. Saint John of Saint Facundo (1479). He was born in northern Spain, in the town of Saint Facundo. He was a brilliant and attractive young boy, educated in the household of a bishop. He became one of the Hermits of Saint Augustine. His devotion to the Blessed Sacrament was so great that he spent every night, from the hour of Matins at midnight, to the hour of Mass in the morning, in adoration of Our Lord in the Blessed Eucharist. He was often privileged in the saying of Mass to see Our Lord visibly in the Blessed Eucharist. Saint John of Saint Facundo is the patron saint of Salamanca in Spain. He died when he was sixty years old.

13. This is the latest day on which **Pentecost** can occur.

Saint Anthony of Padua (1231).

There is no more loved and admired saint of the Catholic Church than Saint Anthony of Padua. Though his work was in Italy, he was born in Portugal. He first joined the Augustinian Order, and then left it and joined the Franciscan Order, in 1221, when he was twenty-six years old. The reason he became a Franciscan was because of the death of the five Franciscan protomartyrs— Saint Berard, Saint Peter, Saint Otho, Saint Accursius and Saint Adjutus—who shed their blood for the Catholic Faith in the year 1220, in

Saint Anthony

Morocco in North Africa, and whose headless and mutilated bodies had been brought to Saint Anthony's monastery on their way back for burial. Saint Anthony became a Franciscan in the hope of shedding his own blood and becoming a martyr. He lived only ten years after joining the Franciscan Order.

So simple and resounding was his teaching of the Catholic Faith, so that the most unlettered and innocent might understand it, that he was made a Doctor of the Church by Pope Pius XII in 1946. Saint Anthony was only thirty-six years old when he died. Saint Anthony is called "the Hammer of Heretics." His great protection against their lies and deceits in the matter of Christian doctrine was to utter, simply and innocently, the Holy Name of Mary. When Saint Anthony of Padua found he was preaching the true gospel of the Catholic Church to heretics who would not listen to him, he then went out and preached it to the fishes. This was not, as the liberal and naturalists are trying to say, for the instruction of the fishes, but rather for the glory of God, the delight of the angels and the easing of his own heart. Saint Anthony wanted to profess the Catholic Faith with his mind and his mouth and his heart, at every moment of his life.

14. Saint Basil the Great (379). Saint Basil is one of the thirty-three Doctors of the Catholic Church. He came from a family of saints. Saint Macrina the Elder was his grandmother. Saint Basil the Elder and Saint Emmelia were his father and his mother. Saint Gregory of Nyssa, Saint Peter of Sebaste and Saint Macrina the Younger were his two brothers and his sister. He is called the father of Eastern monasticism. He declared that he would not allow his soul to be turned aside from God by his love of any single earthly thing. Saint Basil is one of the four great Eastern Doctors of the Church. The other three are Saint Athanasius, Saint Gregory Nazianzen and Saint John Chrysostom. Saint Basil was only forty-nine years old when he died. Five saints of the Catholic Church are commonly give the title "the Great" when they are referred to. These are: Saint Gregory the Great, Saint Leo the Great, Saint Basil the Great, Saint Albert the Great and Saint Gertrude the Great.

Saint Eliseus (Ninth Century B.C.). He was an Old Testament prophet, the disciple and companion of Saint Elias. When Saint Elias, whose feast is July 20, was taken up in a fiery chariot, he let his cloak fall upon Saint Eliseus, who thereupon became his successor.

15. Saint Vitus (303). Saint Vitus, whose name can also be *Guy*, was a child saint. He was entrusted by his pagan parents to the care of a Catholic nurse, Crescentia, and her husband, Modestus. They secretly baptized him and brought him up as a Catholic. When his father discovered that he had become a Catholic, he handed him over to the pagan governor of Sicily, where he lived, for punishment. Vitus, Crescentia and Modestus all escaped to southern Italy. All three were captured by pagan soldiers there, most cruelly tortured, and then put to death. All three are lovingly remembered by the Catholic Church as Saints. Saint Vitus is one of the fourteen Holy Helpers. He is the protector against nervous diseases, epilepsy and paralysis. He is also the protector against the nervous affliction known as "Saint Vitus' Dance."

Saint Germaine Cousin (1601). She was the daughter of the poor farmer who lived

Saint Adolph

near Toulouse in France. She was born with a deformed hand and was afflicted with the disease of scrofula. Her mother died when she was an infant. Her father then married a most cruel woman who treated Saint Germaine very harshly. The great loves of Saint Germaine were the Blessed Eucharist and the Blessed Virgin. She delighted to roam among the children of her town, and tell them about Jesus and Mary. She died when she was only twenty-two years old. She is beloved in southern France, even to this day, especially in the town of Toulouse. This is the town where Saint Dominic was given the rosary, in the year 1214, by the virginal Mother of God.

16. Saint John Francis Regis (1640). He was one of the greatest priests of the Society of Jesus. He entered the Society of Saint Ignatius when he was nineteen years old, on the feast of the Immaculate Conception. His great crusade was to bring all Protestants back from the heresies into which they had fallen in the sixteenth century. He wanted to make them members again of the one true Church, outside of which they could not be saved. He wanted very much to go to foreign missions, but was not allowed to go. He loved to climb mountains and find lonely people to whom he could teach the simple and innocent truths of the Catholic Faith. He died in the middle of a cold winter in La Louvesc in southern France. Blessed Rose Philippine Duchesne chose him as one of her patrons. His most devoted client was the Curé of Ars, Saint John Marie Vianney, who got encouragement to pursue his vocation to the priesthood while praying at the tomb of Saint John Francis Regis. When the Curé of Ars was dying, he declared concerning Saint John Francis Regis, "Everything good that I have done, I owe to him." Saint John Francis Regis established confraternities in honor of the Blessed Sacrament. He spent hours every day in the confessional. He was hated by the Huguenots. He died saying, "I

Saint Aloysius Gonzaga

see Our Lord and His Mother opening Heaven for Me." Saint John Francis Regis is the patron saint of the nuns called the Religious of the Cenacle. He is also the patron saint of Kansas City, Missouri.

17. Saint Adolph (680). He was the brother of Saint Botolph and a Benedictine. Saint Adolph was made a bishop in Germany

Saint Botolph (680). Saint Botolph was a Benedictine, and an Englishman. Over seventy churches have been dedicated to him in England. An English town, originally called Saint Botolphstown, was later contracted by the style of utterance for which the English are famous, to Botolphstown, then Botolphston, then Botoston, and then *Boston*. And so, by reason, at least of its name, Boston, Massachusetts, is dedicated to this saintly seventh-century saint. Anyone walking along the side streets of Boston, Massachusetts, will see a street called "Saint Botolph's Street." This keeps many Bostonians from forgetting the saint for whom the original Boston was named.

Saint Ranier (1160). He was a young nobleman of Italy, born at Pisa. He dedicated his life to prayer, penance and good works. He even made a pilgrimage to the Holy Land so that he could see the holy places with his own eyes and kiss the spots where Our Lord and Our Lady had been. He gave up all his noble titles, and retired to a monastery in the suburbs of Pisa. He died there when he was only thirty-two years old, the same age as Saint John the Baptist when he died.

Saint Gregory Barbarigo (1697). He was born at Venice in Italy, became a bishop, first at Bergamo and then at Padua. He was made a cardinal, and because of his holiness he was canonized in 1960.

18. Saint Ephrem (373). Saint Ephrem the Syrian is both a Father and a Doctor of the Church. He was born in Mesopotamia, not far from the place where Adam and Eve lived in the Garden of Eden. He became a monk when a young boy. Through humility, he refused to become a priest, and stayed a deacon all his life. He was one of the great defenders of the Divinity of Jesus Christ at the Council of Nicea, in 325. He lived in solitude in his later years. He died when he was sixty-seven. His death occurred in the same year as that of Saint Athanasius, another glorious Doctor of the Church. Saint Ephrem wrote the life of Saint Abraham the Hermit. His own life was written by Saint Gregory of Nyssa. Saint Ephrem was a great hymn maker, and is called, "the harp of the Holy Ghost." He wrote countless hymns and prayers in love and praise of the Blessed Virgin Mary, the Immaculate Mother of God. Saint Ephrem greeted her: "Hail, Reconciler of the whole world!"

19. Saint Juliana Falconieri (1340). She is the niece of Saint Alexis Falconieri, one of the seven founders of the Servites of the Blessed Virgin Mary. Her spiritual father was Saint Philip Benizi, a member of the Servite Order. She became the foundress of the Third Order of the Servites. She took a vow of virginity, and began to dress and live like a nun, when she was only fifteen. Her great devotion was to the sorrows of the Blessed Virgin Mary. Our Lady led her, because of this devotion, to a most ecstatic love of the Blessed Sacrament. Saint Juliana Falconieri is called "the saint of the Holy Eucharist." She was seventy years old when she died. This was after years of great sickness. She was so ill in her stomach that she could not receive Our Lord in the Eucharist by way of Viaticum. She asked the priest as a favor that the Sacred Host be placed on a corporal, and laid on her heart. At the moment she died, the Sacred Host disappeared. After the death of Saint Juliana

Falconieri, the form of the Host was found stamped on her heart in the exact place where the Blessed Sacrament had been laid when she was dying.

Saint Gervase and Saint Protase (165). These are two heroic brothers who shed their blood for the Catholic Faith in the city of Milan, in Italy, in the second century. They are called the protomartyrs of Milan. The relics of Saint Gervase and Saint Protase were discovered by Saint Ambrose in the fourth century. Their bodies now repose in the Church of Saint Ambrose in Milan. Saint Gervase and Saint Protase are mentioned always in the Litany of the Saints. They are two of the eleven holy martyrs especially remembered in this sacred litany. The other nine are: Saint Stephen, Saint Laurence, Saint Vincent, Saint Fabian and Saint Sebastian, Saint John and Saint Paul, and Saint Cosmas and Saint Damian.

20. This is the latest day on which **Trinity Sunday** can occur.

Saint Silverius (538). He was the sixtieth Pope of the Catholic Church. He suffered great persecution for defending the dogmatic truths of the one true Church founded by Jesus Christ. He was exiled by the Empress Theodora to an island off Naples after only two years on the papal throne. He died on this island, a martyr.

21. Saint Aloysius Gonzaga (1591). Saint Aloysius Gonzaga was born on March 9, 1568. He is the model of the virtue of holy purity to all young Catholic boys. Any Catholic boy named Aloysius is committed to a crusade for the preservation of holy purity in thought, word and deed. In honor of the Blessed Virgin Mary, the most pure and immaculate Mother of God, he must be a crusader against all impurity and immodesty. The first words Saint Aloysius spoke as a little child were the Holy Names of Jesus and Mary. So rich was his wisdom as a young boy that at the age of nine he made a vow of perpetual virginity. God arranged it that a saint should give Saint Aloysius his first Holy Communion. This saint was Saint Charles Borromeo, whose feast day is November 4, and who died in 1584. In 1585, when Aloysius Gonzaga was seventeen years old, he joined the newly-founded order of the Society of Jesus. Saint Aloysius died speaking the holy Name of Jesus, on the octave of Corpus Christi, June 21, 1591, when he was only twenty-three years old. There is not a land in the whole world, or a region, or a place, or a town, which has not somehow heard of this angelic and saintly young member of the great Order of Saint Ignatius of Loyola. The name of Saint Aloysius in Italian is *Luigi*, and countless Italian boys have been called by that name, after him. His name in French is *Louis*. He himself was named for Saint Louis of Toulouse, who in turn was named for the great King, Saint Louis of France. Saint Robert Bellarmine wrote, by way of eulogy, the life of Saint Aloysius.

Saint Terence (First Century). He was the first Bishop of Iconium, in Lycaonia, in Asia Minor. He was one of the seventy-two disciples of Our Lord. At Saint Paul's dictation, it was he who wrote down the Epistle to the Romans. His name is mentioned in this Epistle as Tertius, in Chapter 16, verse 22. He is, at least by way of name, one of the favorite saints of the Irish people. Many thousand of Irish boys have been called after Saint Terence.

22. Saint Paulinus of Nola (431). Saint Paulinus was born at Bordeaux, in France, of one of its noblest and wealthiest families. He was appointed, by the Roman Emperor, Prefect of all France. He was an orator and a poet. In rank, he finally became a Roman senator, and then Prefect of Rome. He married a Catholic Spanish

Saint William the Abbot

girl named Therasia. She brought him into the Catholic Church. Paulinus was baptized when he was thirty-one years old. The only child of Paulinus and Therasia died in infancy. After this, they both consecrated themselves to God. Therasia sold all her possessions, gave them to the poor, and became a nun. And Paulinus, under the direction of Saint Ambrose of Milan, and under the inspiration of Saint Felix, the martyred Bishop of Nola, was raised to Holy Orders and elected the Bishop of Nola. He was renowned through all Italy and France and Spain for his sanctity. He said he was "glad to sell earth so as to buy Heaven." Saint Ambrose, Saint Augustine, Saint Jerome and Saint Gregory, the four Great Western Doctors of the Church, were all ardent admirers of Saint Paulinus, and all wrote much in his praise.

23. Saint Audrey (Etheldreda) (679). Saint Audrey was an East Anglian princess, and later a queen. Driven to do so by her parents, she first married a prince named Tonbert. Three years after their marriage, he died. He had permitted her to keep perfectly preserved her virginity. Later, she was forced to marry a powerful king from Northumberland, named Egfrid. After twelve years of married life, still preserving her virginal purity, she was permitted, with her husband's consent, to become a nun. She founded a monastery on the Island of Ely. Three of her sisters are saints: Saint Sexburga, Saint Withburga and Saint Ethelburga. The great Saint Wilfried was one of her spiritual advisers and protectors. Saint Audrey for centuries was one of the most loved and venerated saints England ever had. She was not quite fifty years old when she died. Her precious body is still incorrupt.

Saint Joseph Cafasso (1860). Saint Joseph Cafasso was a secular priest of Turin. He was small in stature and had a deformed spine, which caused him much suffering. As a rector of the seminary he quickly became renowned for his teaching ability and wonderful influence on young priests, telling them that worldliness was their greatest enemy. He founded the Society of Mary later called Marianists. He spent many hours in the confessional. "When we hear confessions," he would say, "Our Lord wants us to be loving and pitiful, to be fatherly towards all who come to us, without reference to the matter, who they are, or what they have done. But he is best known for his work with convicts. He was a compassionate confessor with a gift for reaching the most hardened criminals. He accompanied over sixty men to the scaffold, and not one died impenitent. He called them his "hanged holy ones." When young John Bosco first met Father Cafasso, he told his mother that he had met a saint. For over twenty years Saint Joseph Cafasso was Saint John Bosco's teacher and spiritual director. It was Joseph Cafasso who directed Don Bosco toward his apostolate of forming the youth in Turin.

The Child Jesus and the Child John the Baptist

24. This is the latest day on which **Corpus Christi** can occur.

The Nativity of Saint John the Baptist (1 B.C.).

Saint John the Baptist was the miraculous son of Saint Zachary and Saint Elizabeth, given to them when Saint Elizabeth was well beyond the years of childbearing. He was sanctified in his mother's womb three months before his birth. This was when Our Lady came to Saint Elizabeth's house at the time of the Visitation, with the Child Jesus in her womb.

Saint John the Baptist is the last of the prophets. The other prophets had foretold what would come, but Saint John the Baptist pointed to Jesus directly, and showed what had come when he declared, "Behold the Lamb of God Who takest away the sins of the world!" Saint John the Baptist was six months older than Jesus. But he died six months younger than Jesus was when he died. Saint John the Baptist died just one year before Our Lord.

Saint John the Baptist was confined for a year in prison, and then his head was cut off by the wicked Jewish tetrarch, Herod Antipas, at the order of an indecent woman named Herodias. The head of Saint John the Baptist was served on a dish to her and her guests at table by her daughter Salome. When Saint John the Baptist's head was placed on the table where Herodias was eating, she took a knife and stabbed again and again the tongue which had rebuked her for her viciousness and impurity. Saint John the Baptist was the one who baptized Jesus in the River Jordan. The sacrament of Baptism was instituted by Jesus. This is the sacrament of water and the Holy Ghost that is necessary for all for admission to the Catholic Church and for salvation. Saint John the Baptist's body was destroyed and dispersed under Julian the Apostate, but part of his head has been preserved and is kept in the Church of Saint Sylvester in Capite, in Rome. Saint John the Baptist has two feast days, one for his birth, on June 24, and one to honor his beheading, on August 29. The feast of the father and mother of Saint John the Baptist, Saint Zachary and Saint Elizabeth, is on November 5.

25. Saint William the Abbot (1142). Of the many saints and blesseds named William, none is better remembered that Saint William of Monte Vergine, in Italy. After a pilgrimage to the tomb of Saint James at Compostella, in Spain, he retired to a mountain named Monte Vergine (Mount of the Blessed Virgin), and lived there until his death. This is where a beautiful picture of Our Lady is preserved, and works miracles. Saint William lived, and gave his monks to live, the Rule of Saint Benedict, the father of Western monasticism.

26. Saint John and Saint Paul (362). Saints John and Paul are two notable Roman martyrs. Both were soldiers and were killed under the cruel Julian the Apostate for the courage with which they refused to support him in his defection from the dogmatic truths of the Catholic Church. Saint John and Saint Paul were asked to worship idols. With the beautiful clarity and courage of soldiers, they refused, and were put to death. They are two of the most beloved saints in the Catholic Church. Their names are mentioned every day by every Catholic priest in the Canon of the Mass, and always in the Litany of the Saints.

27. Our Lady of Perpetual Help (Thirteenth Century). In the thirteenth century, a beautiful picture of Our Lady holding the Child Jesus, with the Angels Michael and Gabriel on either side of her, was painted in the East. In the fifteenth century, this picture was brought from the Island of Crete and was taken to Rome. It was placed in the Church of Saint Matthew, in Rome. There, for three hundred years, pilgrims came to reverence and pray before this holy picture, because everyone loved its simplicity, its beauty and its truth. After the French Revolution, when the vicious Napoleon desecrated thirty Catholic Churches in Rome, this precious picture of Our Lady of Perpetual Help was hidden away, but it was rediscovered in 1862. It was then placed in the Church of Saint Alphonsus Maria de Liguori, founder of the Redemptorist Order, in Rome, where it is now kept. The purpose of this lovely picture is by way of simple and innocent symbol to teach us that Our Lady is our help in all things, and our help at all times. Many Catholic Churches in all countries are called by the name, Our Lady of Perpetual Help.

28. Saint Irenaeus (202). This great saint was born to Christian parents in Asia Minor. He died when he was seventy-two years old, the same age as Our Lady when she died. He is one of the Fathers of the Church and is sometimes called "the father of Catholic theology." He was a disciple of Saint Polycarp who was in turn a disciple of Saint John the Evangelist. Saint Irenaeus was sent to Lyons, in France, and was ordained a priest. There he opposed the heresy of Montanism, started by a blasphemer named Montanus, who pretended to be, for all practical purposes, the Holy Ghost. Saint Irenaeus was Bishop of Lyons for twenty-four years. He laid the foundation of the Faith the French had in those days, and were to have completely as a nation when Clovis, their King, became a Catholic in 496. During a fierce persecution of the Catholics in Lyons, when the streets were full of blood, Saint Irenaeus himself was killed, and became a martyr. His body and his relics were placed in the Church of

Saint John in Lyons. They were desecrated there by the Calvinists in the year 1562, in the century of the so-called "Reformation." The most noted of the books he wrote is one called *Against Heresies*.

29. Saint Peter and Saint Paul (67).

Whenever Saint Peter, the first Pope of the Catholic Church, has a feast day, Saint Paul is always commemorated, and on all of Saint Paul's feast days, Saint Peter is commemorated. Saint Peter's special feasts are now four: the Chair of Saint Peter on February 22; the crucifixion of Saint Peter and the beheading of Saint Paul on June 29; the commemoration of Saint Paul and the commemoration of Saint Peter on June 30; and the Basilicas of Saint Peter and Saint Paul on November 18.

"Thou art Peter and upon this Rock I will build My Church..."

Saint Peter the Apostle, the first Pope of the Catholic Church, was the son of a fisherman in Galilee, named Jona. He was born and lived in the town of Bethsaida. Saint Peter's name was originally Simon, but Jesus changed it to Peter because of its meaning, which is *rock*. Saint Peter was the Rock upon which the Catholic Church was built. Saint Peter and his brother, Saint Andrew, were disciples of Saint John the Baptist. Both were fishermen. They saw Our Lord, heard His teachings, and gave up all to follow Him. The whole Gospel story is concerned, in one place or another, with Saint Peter, and with what he said and did and preached. One third of the book called the *Acts of the Apostles* is concerned with Saint Peter. Two thirds of it relates to Saint Paul. Saint Peter wrote two Epistles in the New Testament. After staying in Jerusalem for three years, in the year 36 he went to Antioch, and was Bishop there. His presence at Antioch made it the primatial see of the Catholic Church for over six years.

Saint Peter went to Rome in the year 42, the year Saint James, the brother of Saint John, was beheaded by the Jews. Saint Peter ruled the Church at Rome for twenty-five years. His hostess in Rome was a beautiful noblewoman named Priscilla who, with her son who was a senator, Pudens, and his wife, Claudia—an English girl—and their four children, Praxedes, Prudentiana, Novatus and Timothy, made it possible for the Holy See to have a place in Rome where the truths of salvation could be dispensed, taught and regulated. Every mentioned member of this charitable family—so holy did their lives become under Saint Peter's influence—is honored in the

Catholic Church as a saint.

Saint Peter was the first Pope. There has been no Pope named Peter since his time. There was a Pope in the thirteenth century who is now called Saint Peter Celestine, but this was only because after he resigned from the papacy he was given back his baptismal name, which was Peter. His name as Pope was Celestine.

Saint Peter, the first pope, was crucified in the year 67, in the same year and on the same day on which Saint Paul was beheaded. It is in order to give Catholics sufficient time to commemorate both these glorious Apostles that two days, June 29 and June 30, are dedicated to them by way of feast.

At his own request, Saint Peter was crucified upside down. It was, as we have said, on the twenty-ninth day of June. Saint Peter's name occurs everywhere in the prayers of the Church, at Mass, in the Holy Office, in the litanies and invocations.

The feast of the Finding of the Chains of Saint Peter, which has been celebrated for hundreds of years on August 1, makes us remember the chains that bound him when he was imprisoned in Jerusalem. He escaped from these chains by a miracle. And these chains, when joined to the chains that bound him when he was imprisoned in Rome, were found to make a perfect link of chains. This was a miracle.

The Basilica of Saint Peter is the great church of the Roman Pontiff in Rome, called simply *Saint Peter's*, and, because of the hill on which it is placed, it is also called the *Vatican*.

Saint Mary, the Mother of Mark (First Century).

Saint Mary was the mother of Saint Mark the Evangelist, whose full name was John Mark. She was a wealthy woman who lived in Jerusalem. It was at her house that the Last Supper was held, and the Blessed Sacrament instituted. It was at her house that the Holy Ghost descended upon the Apostles at the first Pentecost. It was at her house that Our Lady lived, in Jerusalem, until she died in the year 58. It was at her house that Saint Peter, the first Pope, often visited, and to her house he immediately went on his deliverance from prison in Jerusalem, as we are told in the Bible. It is simple to say and to prove that Saint Mary, the mother of Mark, was the greatest hostess in the history of the Catholic Church. Her house after the Last Supper was called "the Cenacle."

Mary, the mother of Saint Mark, was the hostess to Jesus at Jerusalem. Priscilla, the mother of Saint Pudens, was the hostess to Saint Peter in Rome.

30. Saint Paul (67).

Saint Paul, the great Apostle of the Gentiles, though a Jew, and of the tribe of Benjamin, was born in the Gentile country of Cilicia, in a city called Tarsus. He was born a Roman citizen. Saint Paul was a disciple of Gamaliel, the renowned teacher who became a Christian and a saint. Saint Paul first opposed the Christians. And he was present at the stoning of Saint Stephen, the first martyr, in Jerusalem. Saint Paul's name was Saul, when he lived as a Jew. On the road to Damascus, after the martyrdom of Saint Stephen, Saint Paul heard the voice of Our Lord speaking to him from Heaven and saying, "Saul, Saul, why presecutest thou Me?" Saul was his Jewish name, but so anxious was he after his conversion to become the true apostle to the non-Jews that he changed his name to Paul, after meeting and converting a notable Gentile named Sergius Paulus. Saint Paul was baptized a Christian at Damascus by Saint Ananias.

Saint Paul, after his conversion, became very devoted to the Blessed Virgin Mary, the Mother of God. He would not let his name be connected with hers overtly because of the way he had persecuted Christians before his conversion. But in the midst of all his journeys, he was constantly returning to Jerusalem to see her. It was

Our Lady who caused Saint Paul's name to be put immediately after Saint Peter's in all the litanies where the Apostles are mentioned. It was Saint Paul's disciple, Saint Luke—a Gentile—who wrote the third Gospel, which is properly called "the Gospel of Our Lady." Saint Paul wrote fourteen Epistles in the New Testament.

One can see from these simple leads how devoted Saint Paul was to the Mother of God. As soon as Saint Paul had converted Denis the Areopagite in Athens, he brought him to Jerusalem to see Mary, the Mother of God. Saint Denis said that if he had not been stopped from doing so, he would have fallen on his face before Mary and adored her as God, so radiant was her holiness and so transcendent was her beauty.

The head of Saint Paul is kept with that of Saint Peter in the Church of Saint John Lateran in Rome. Part of his body, along with a part of Saint Peter's, is lovingly guarded at the Vatican. The rest of his body, along with the rest of Saint Peter's, is kept in the Church of Saint Paul's-outside-the-Walls. Saint Paul was beheaded, just outside the city of Rome, at a place now called Tre Fontaine, in the year 67. As his head bounced three times on the ground, his mouth was heard to utter, "Jesus! Jesus! Jesus!" Three fountains of water miraculously sprang up from the three places where the head of Saint Paul struck the ground. Three of the Roman soldiers who assisted at the execution of Saint Paul were at once converted to the Catholic Faith.

Seventeen Irish Martyrs (1579-1654). These seventeen martyrs are representative of the thousands of Irish Catholics who died for their Faith during the sixteenth and seventeenth centuries in Ireland. They died under Henry VIII, Elizabeth I and Oliver Cromwell. The sixteen men and one woman who were beatified widely differed in occupation and education, but were alike in their decision to accept death and at times great torture rather than compromise their Faith.

Blessed Dominic Collins was a courageous and brilliant soldier who left his distinguished military career to become a humble serving brother in the Society of Jesus. He was cruelly tortured and executed for refusing to abandon his Holy Faith. Blessed Margaret Ball, betrayed by her own son for giving refuge to priests, and Blessed Francis Taylor suffered to their deaths in the filth and stench of the Dublin prisons rather than take the Oath of Supremacy, which declared the British monarch head of the church. Blesseds Father William Tirry and Father John Kearney were hanged for remaining in Ireland after all priests were ordered to leave the country on pain of death. In his last words, Father Kearney proclaimed "…I not only confess but do affirm that no one can be saved outside the Catholic and Roman Faith, for which Faith I gladly die." Blesseds Bishop Terence Albert O'Brien, Bishop Conor O'Devany, Father Patrick O'Loughran and Father Peter Higgins were condemned to the gallows for their Catholic Faith and their priesthood. Blessed Father Maurice MacKenraghty, Bishop Patrick O'Healy, Father Conn O'Rourke, a baker named Matthew Lambert, and five sailors were executed for refusing to take the Oath of Supremacy.

Blessed Archbishop Dermot O'Hurley was a lawyer who at age fifty was asked by Pope Gregory XII to abandon a prosperous career and become a priest and archbishop in Ireland. Despite the danger of the offered position, Blessed Dermot, being a generous man of great faith, accepted. Shortly after arriving in Ireland, and before he arrived at his diocese, he was imprisoned. Because he refused to abandon his office or his Faith, he was savagely tortured and later secretly hanged. Many miracles and special favors have been granted at the grave and the execution site of this holy martyr.

July

The Month of the Most Precious Blood

1. The Most Precious Blood of Jesus. Both halves of the year, in January and July, begin with the commemoration of the Precious Blood of Jesus. January 1 is the feast of the Circumcision, when the Precious Blood of Jesus was first shed. July 1 is the commemoration of the Most Precious Blood of Jesus as it is preserved in all Catholic Churches at the hour of Mass. The Precious Blood of Jesus was given to Him to divinize by Mary, the Mother of God. Between Jesus and Mary there was a perpetual interflow of blood for nine months when He was a Child in her womb. Anyone can see how divinized Mary became by this interchange of blood for nearly a year. Everyone who wishes to become a son of God the Father, as he becomes by Sanctifying Grace, must also become a child of Mary the Virgin, by receiving in his mouth the Blessed Eucharist which is the Body, Blood, Soul and Divinity of Our Lord and Saviour, Jesus Christ. All the Saints of the Old Testament, when their bodies rise from the grave on the Last Day, will receive the Precious Blood of Jesus. Our Lord said of the chalice which contained His Precious Blood at the Last Supper, "I will not drink of this fruit of the vine, until that day when I shall drink it with you new in the Kingdom of My Father." The Kingdom of God the Father, Whose sons we are divinely by adoption, is also the Queendom of Mary the Virgin, whose children we must incarnately become in order to enjoy the happiness of Heaven forever.

Saint Aaron (Fifteenth Century B.C.).

Aaron was chosen by God to be the first High Priest of the Old Law. It is fitting in the New Law that his feast should be observed on the feast of the Most Precious Blood of Jesus. Aaron was the brother of Moses and Miriam. He belonged to the tribe of Levi, the clerical (Levitical) tribe of the Jews. Aaron lived fourteen hundred years before the coming of Christ. Aaron was the ancestor in blood and in priestly lineage of Saint Zachary, the father of Saint John the Baptist. Saint Elizabeth, the mother of Saint John the Baptist—who gave us the second invocation in the *Hail Mary*, "Blessed art thou among women and blessed is the fruit of thy womb"—was, as we are told in the Gospel of Saint Luke, "one of the daughters of Aaron."

Aaron died, and was buried on a mountain (Mount Hor) just outside the Promised Land. Aaron as a priest was a type of what Jesus was to be. That is why he is honored among the saints. Jesus is the sole High Priest of the New Law. He gave us His Precious Blood in sacrifice at the Last Supper. And in the Sacrament of Holy Orders, administered by Catholic bishops—the successors of the Apostles—Jesus has given us the true priesthood of our day. Aaron's priesthood perished on the first Good Friday with the rending of the veil of the Temple of Jerusalem. In the year 70 A. D., with the total destruction of the Temple, Aaron's credentials were no more.

Blessed Junipero Serra (1784).

Blessed Junipero was the Franciscan priest who founded the missions of California. Junipero was born in Spain in 1713, the son of a farmer. He joined the Franciscan Order in 1730, and shortly thereafter received a Doctorate in Theology. Nineteen years later, he asked to join the missionary college of San Fernando in Mexico. A renowned professor of philosophy, suffering from chronic bronchitis and an ulcerated leg that made walking an agony, he seemed an unlikely person for missionary work. Yet in his work he covered 6000 miles on foot and mule-back.

Father Serra preached in Mexico until he was appointed superior of a band of 15 Franciscans for the California missions. Through his zeal, twenty-one prosperous missions were founded, which were held in trust for the more than 5000 Indian converts who studied and labored with the Franciscans. The missions produced an abundance of crops and livestock. Reservoirs and aqueducts were built, making the desert bloom.

Mexico revolted from Spain in 1821 establishing an anti-Catholic government. Government authorities expelled the Franciscans and forced the missions to disband. The mission property was not given to the Indians, the rightful owners. Instead, the great mission tracts were divided into smaller ranchos which were granted to soldiers and provincial officials, and the buildings turned into government centers. When California became part of the United States the mission buildings were restored and returned to the Franciscans. Today they are national monuments and bear witness to Blessed Junipero's missionary spirit.

2. This is the latest day on which the feast of the **Sacred Heart** can occur.

The Visitation of Our Lady (1 B.C.). to the house of Elizabeth and

Zachary, the mother and father of Saint John the Baptist. As soon as Mary, the spouse

The Blessed Virgin Mary and Saint Elizabeth

of Saint Joseph, had learned from an angel that, as she had conceived a Child virginally, so Elizabeth, her cousin, had conceived one miraculously, she made haste to go and visit Elizabeth. Mary arrived at the house of Elizabeth at Ain Karim, a little town southwest of Jerusalem, on April 2. She stayed there for three months. Elizabeth greeted Mary with the phrase, "Blessed art thou among women, and blessed is the fruit of thy womb." It was standing in the door of Elizabeth's house that Our Lady sang her canticle, the *Magnificat*. Mary waited for the birth of John the Baptist on June 24, and left for Nazareth on July 2, the day after Saint John the Baptist was circumcised and given his name. This day, the day of Mary's leaving Elizabeth, is celebrated as the feast of the Visitation.

Mary's visit to Elizabeth was the greatest visit paid by anyone to anyone in the history of the world. All Catholics call it, in simple reference, the Visitation. The moment Mary, with Jesus in her womb, entered the house of Elizabeth, on April 2, John the Baptist was sanctified in his mother's womb. He received at that moment the use of reason, and for three months antecedent to his birth, he knew, in humility and love, Who was dwelling in his house. He also knew his own purpose as the Precursor of Christ.

John the Baptist was born six months before Jesus. John the Baptist was martyred one year before Jesus. The day Jesus was born, the days begin to increase. The day John the Baptist was born, they begin to decrease. "He must increase and I must decrease," is the beautiful way this seasonal fact is referred to in liturgical love in Holy Scripture by Saint John the Baptist.

3. Saint Leo II (683). Born in Sicily, he was elected Pope on January 10, 681. He approved of the acts of the Sixth General Council, the Third Council of Constantinople (680-681), which condemned those who taught that Christ has only one will (Monothelites). He also censured Pope Honorius I for not formally condeming that heresy. Pope Leo II was well versed in sacred music and he perfected the melodies of the Psalms and the Hymns of the Church. He was truly the father of the poor and by his example and preaching led every one to virtue.

4. Saint Theodore (310). He was a bishop of Cyrene in Lybia, and had great skill in copying holy manuscripts, especially those of the Holy Scripture. For refusing to give these sacred manuscripts to pagans to desecrate, he was seized, fiercely tortured and finally beheaded.

5. Saint Anthony Mary Zaccaria (1539). He was born at Cremona in Lombardy, in northern Italy. He was first a doctor of medicine, and later became a priest. He founded the Clerics Regular of Saint Paul, who, because they ministered to the people in the Church of Saint Barnabas in Milan, are called "the Barnabites." Saint Anthony Mary Zaccaria was only thirty-seven years old when he died, one year older than his patron saint, Saint Anthony of Padua.

6. Saint Thomas More (1535). He was the wonderful English martyr, Chancellor of the Realm, who was beheaded on Tower Hill, just outside London, for not giving in to the heretical diabolicism of Henry VIII, who denied the supremacy of our Holy Father the Pope over the whole Catholic and Christian world. Henry VIII, the founder of the Episcopal Church, was an English king who married six wives, and murdered two of them. Saint Thomas More would not submit to him as head of the Church that Christ founded. Because Henry VIII set up bishops in place of the Pope (which accounts for the name Episcopalian, taken from *episcopi*, the Latin word for bishops), other groups were induced by various influences, to set up: ministers for the Presbyterians, congregations for the Congregationalists, liturgies for the Baptists, ideas for the Methodists, or ideas with some sort of hierarchical setup for the Methodist Episcopals. Saint Thomas More was only fifty-seven years old when the Anglicans (the Episcopalians) martyred him.

Saint John Fisher (1535). Saint John Fisher, Bishop of Rochester in England, and Chancellor of the University of Cambridge at the time when the adulterous and murderous Henry VIII was seceding from the Catholic Church and founding a religion of his own, was the most notable Catholic bishop who opposed this heretical king. Saint John Fisher was a brave supporter of the Catholic queen, Catherine of

Aragon. He refused to take an oath of supremacy to the heretical Henry VIII. He was seized and thrown into the Tower of London. While there, the Holy Father, Pope Paul III, made him a cardinal. Henry VIII, when he heard this, in furious anger swore that Cardinal Fisher would not have a head on which to put the red hat that the Pope would give him. Saint John Fisher was beheaded. Anne Boleyn, the illegitimate wife of Henry VIII, whom he later murdered, asked for the head of Saint John Fisher, and, like Herodias with the head of Saint John the Baptist, struck it with her hand. Some of his teeth made a wound in her hand, which never healed.

There were, from 1535 to 1681, only six hundred candidates for heroic sanctity among all the English Catholic people. Fifty-four of these were beatified by Pope Leo XIII, on December 29, 1886, and nine others on May 13, 1895. One hundred and thirty-four more were beatified by Pope Pius XI in 1929. Saint Thomas More and Saint John Fisher were both canonized by Pope Pius XI on May 19, 1935. Forty martyrs of England and Wales were canonized by Pope Paul VI in 1970. In 1987 Pope John Paul II beatified eighty-five martyrs of England, Scotland and Wales. The scarcity of the English martyrs shows us that Henry VIII did not completely lose the Faith for England. The English people lost it for themselves.

Saint Isaias (Seventh Century B.C.). The great prophet Isaias, who deserves to be remembered as a saint on his feast day, was the one who foretold of the Blessed Virgin Mary—in Chapter 7, verse 14 of his great prophetical book—"Behold a virgin shall conceive and bear a son, and His name shall be called Emmanuel." No reader of the Old Testament can ignore this prophecy. One who does not sincerely look in the Old Testament for the beautiful, virginal maiden who was to be its fulfillment, and one who does not immediately find her in Mary, the virginal spouse of Joseph, is an unbeliever and a desecrator of the inspired word of God. He pretends to love the Bible, while he ignores its greatest prophet and its greatest prophecy.

7. Saint Cyril and Saint Methodius (869 and 885).

Saints Cyril and Methodius were brothers. They were born in Greece and educated in Constantinople. They were the great apostles of the Faith to the Slavs in southern Russia, in Bohemia and Poland during the ninth century. Though Saint Cyril and Saint Methodius died sixteen years apart, their feasts are celebrated together on July 7. They are responsible for the Slav alphabet, and indeed, for the Slav language.

Blessed Roger Dickenson and Blessed Ralph Milner (1591).

These English martyrs were killed during the reign of Queen Elizabeth I because they would not forsake their Catholic Faith. Blessed Roger was a secular priest and Blessed Ralph was a layman with a family. Blessed Roger's crime was his priesthood. Blessed Ralph was accused of helping Father Dickenson. They were hanged on July 7, 1591.

8. Saint Elizabeth of Portugal (1336).

She was Queen of Portugal. She was the daughter of Peter II, King of Aragon. She was espoused when a young girl to Denis of Portugal. Her husband was a weak and unsaintly man. Elizabeth's whole life as his queen was a trial. She considered the first of her queenly duties to be that of hearing Mass and reciting the Divine Office every day. Frequent reception of Holy Communion was her greatest joy. When her husband died, she took off her queenly robes and put on the habit of the Third Order of Saint Francis. She was the great grandniece of Saint Elizabeth of Hungary, whose feast is November 19. She died when she was sixty-five years old.

Saint Veronica Giuliani

9. Saint Veronica Giuliani (1727).

Saint Veronica Giuliani was a Franciscan nun who lived in Italy. Because of her transcendent holiness, Jesus gave her visions, revelations and the imprint of His Five Wounds on her body. She died at Città di Castello in Italy, when she was sixty-seven years old.

Saint Maria Goretti (1902).

Maria Goretti was a little Italian girl, almost twelve years old, martyred for the preservation of her purity. The young man who killed her was nineteen. He stabbed her with a dagger while she cried out in protestation of what he would do to her: "No! No! It is a sin! God does not want it!" Saint Maria Goretti is one of the glories of the 20th century. She was canonized by Pope Pius XII in 1950.

120 Chinese Martyrs (1281-1930).

Of these 120 martyrs, 87 are Chinese and 33 are foreign missionaries. Among them were six bishops, 23 are priests, one brother, seven sisters, seven seminarians, and 76 lay people. The oldest was 79 years old, and the youngest only seven years old. Thirty-two gave their lives between 1814 and 1862; 86 died in 1900; and two were martyred in 1930. There were three periods of persecution of the Church in China. The first period was in the Yuan dynasty (1281-1367); second, the Ming dynasty (1606-1637); and third, the most violent, the Ching dynasty (1648-1907). The Boxer Rebellion was part of this period.

In Shanxi, on July 5, 1900, seven sisters, Franciscan Missionaries of Mary with 19 others—including bishops, priests, seminarians, and lay people were arrested and imprisoned. On July 9, a mock trial was held: "Why did you come to China?" "To save souls," answered Bishop Fogolla, speaking for all 25 prisoners. Without further questions the order was given, "Kill them!" To frighten the sisters more, they were the last to be beheaded. On July 20, 1900, anti-Christian Boxers surrounded the church in the province of Hebei, where the people had fled for protection. A courageous lay woman, Mary Zhu-Wu, outstretched her arms in the form of a cross to defend the priest while he administered absolution and the plenary indulgence to all present. The Boxers shot her and the priest, Father Ren (Ignace Mangin, S.J.). Then they set fire to the church with all the people in it. All who tried to escape through the openings were stabbed by the Boxers.

10. Saint Felicitas and Her Seven Sons (165).

There are three glorious mothers among the saints who were martyred along with their seven sons. They are: Saint Felicitas, Saint Symphorosa and, from the Old Testament, Saint Samona. This last is known as the Mother of the Machabees.

Saint Felicitas was a widow. She was tried with her seven boys before the Emperor Marcus Aurelius in Rome. She encouraged every one of her sons to shed his blood for the Catholic Faith. She stood by and watched each one of them as he suffered and died. Four months later, on November 23, she was herself beheaded. But it is beautiful to put her in commemoration along with her seven sons on July 10, in the month of the Precious Blood of Jesus.

11. Saint Pius I (167).

There have been twelve Popes named Pius. Four of them have been de-

Saint Veronica

clared saints by the Church: Saint Pius I, who died in 167; Saint Pius V, who died in 1572 and who established the feast of the Most Holy Rosary; Blessed Pope Pius IX who died in 1878, and defined the dogma of the Immaculate Conception on December 8, 1854 and the glorious Pope Saint Pius X, who died in 1914 at the beginning of the First World War, and who was the great Pope of daily Communion for all, and of early Communion for children. Saint Pius I was a martyr. He was the great opponent of the Gnostic heretics who contended that man could reason out things better than they have been revealed by God. This is still one of the great heresies of our day, and infects most colleges and universities of the United States.

Saint Oliver Plunket (1681).

Saint Oliver Plunket was born in 1629. He was an Irish saint. He was one of the successors of Saint Patrick as Archbishop of Armagh. He did everything possible to keep his people free from the horrors of heresy. He was taken to London and after a mock trial was hanged, drawn and quartered by Protestant heretics. With the words "I desire to be dissolved and to be with Christ" on his lips, he shed his blood for the one true Faith.

12. Saint Veronica of the Veil (First Century). The greatest and most loved Veronica of the Church is a heroic Gentile woman who met Our Lord on His way to Calvary, and wiped His sacred and bleeding face with her veil. This is commemorated in the Sixth Station of the Cross. Jesus left the imprint of His sacred face on Veronica's veil. This veil is now kept in one of the pillars of Saint Peter's in Rome, facing the altar where the Pope says Mass. Saint Veronica left Jerusalem after Our Lord's death and came to Rome. She gave her precious veil to the Holy Father. Saint Veronica was martyred for the Faith.

13. Saint Mildred (700). She was a daughter of Saint Ermenburga. She was born in England and was educated in France. She gave up her title as a princess to become a Catholic nun. She was made an abbess. The Order to which she belonged was the Benedictines. She is one of the most loved saints in England. Thousands and thousands of English girls have been named for her.

Saint Bonaventure

Saint Teresa of the Andes
(1920). Saint Teresa of the Andes was born Juana Enriquita Jarequemada in Santiago, Chile in 1900. She was impetuous by nature and extremely bright. Her mother instilled in her a great devotion to the poor, and Juanita spent much of her time relieving their suffering. From the time of her First Holy Communion she was often favored with spiritual gifts. At the age of fifteen she consecrated herself to God by making a vow of virginity. Juanita had a tremendous devotion to Our Lord's Passion and often wrote in her diary of how great a privilege it is to suffer for Christ. Her father was reluctant to give permission for his favorite daughter to enter the Carmelite Order. Finally he yielded, and she entered in May, 1919 when she was still eighteen. Juanita was made a novice in October and given the name Sister Teresa of Jesus. Six months later she was diagnosed with typhus that she had unknowingly contracted while ministering to the poor. Saint Teresa made her profession as a Carmelite Nun on her deathbed and died having been in Carmel only eleven months.

14. Saint Bonaventure (1274). He was a Franciscan who died when he was fifty-three years old. His name in Baptism was John (Giovanni), and his last name was Fidanza. The name Bonaventure, which means *good fortune*, was given to him by Saint Francis of Assisi, who cured him of a serious illness when he was a small child. Many believe that Saint Bonaventure was the little boy taking the place of Jesus, put in the first Christmas crib built by Saint Francis of Assisi in 1223, and that he was two years old when he portrayed Baby Jesus. When Saint Bonaventure was twenty years old he became a Franciscan. Later, he was created cardinal-bishop of Albano. He was a great friend of the Dominican, Saint Thomas Aquinas. Saint Thomas Aquinas is known as the Angelic Doctor. Saint Bonaventure is called the Seraphic Doctor. Saint Bonaventure says of the Blessed Virgin that when she saw the love of the Eternal Father toward men to be so great that He willed the death of His Son to redeem and save us, she united her will to His, and made an entire offering and consent to the death of her Divine Son on the Cross, that we might be saved. Thus did the *Our Father* and the *Hail Mary* blend together in the mind of this noble Doctor of the Church, Saint Bonaventure.

Saint Francis Solano (1610). He was a Spaniard who professed the Franciscan rule in one of the branches of that Order, known as the Observantines. He left Spain, and went to Peru, in South America. There he preached the one true Faith for twenty years. He converted thousands of Indians to the way of salvation in South America. He died at Lima, the town of Saint Rose, who was to be the first canonized saint of the New World. Through his intercession, the dead have been raised to life.

Blessed Kateri Tekakwitha (1680). Blessed Kateri was an American Indian born at Ossernenon (Auriesville), New York in 1656. She was baptized at the age of twenty by a Jesuit missionary and lived a life of prayer, penance and care of the sick. She took a vow of perpetual virginity. On April 17, 1680, she died, at the age of twenty-four. The "Lily of the Mohawks," as she is called, was beatified by Pope John Paul II in 1980.

15. Saint Henry the Emperor (1024). The greatest of all the many saints named Henry is Saint Henry II, the Roman Emperor. He was a disciple of Saint Wolfgang, whose feast is October 31. He was the husband of the illustrious Saint Cunegunda, whose feast is March 3. Saint Henry the Emperor lived from 972 to 1024. He was fifty-two years old when he died. He was one of the great supporters for the Benedictine Order. Countless Benedictine monasteries were built or restored by him. He himself wanted to become a Benedictine, but it was his destiny to become a king. Saint Pius X declared him the patron saint of all the Oblates of the Benedictine Order. Saint Henry and his wife, Saint

Saint Henry the Emperor

Cunegunda, lived in perpetual chastity during the whole of their married life. Though a king and a queen, he lived like a monk and she like a nun.

Saint Swithin's Day (862). Saint Swithin, a most saintly monk and bishop in England, died in 862. His feast day is July 2. On July 15, 964, his relics were being carried to a church built in his honor. Torrents of rain fell on that day and delayed the translation of his body. This is the origin of the tradition that if it rains on Saint Swithin's Day, July 15, it will continue to rain for forty days. This is not necessarily so. But it is nice to remember Saint Swithin in any connection.

16. Our Lady of Mount Carmel.

Mount Carmel is the beautiful mountain, facing west, just north of the Holy Land. It is midway between the country of the Jews and the cities of the Gentiles. It is the mountain where the Prophet Elias dwelt and started the long tradition of contemplative life and prayer that still prevails in the Catholic Church. It was from the mountain of Carmel that the first group wanting to be baptized by water came down to Jerusalem on the feast of Pentecost. They were many Gentiles, with a few believing Jews. They were the first large group of official and sacramental Christians given to the Church. One of the fruits of the tradition of Mount Carmel has been the Carmelite Order. This is a religious group of both men and women which has given the Catholic Church such illustrious saints as Saint John of the Cross and Saint Simon Stock, among men, and Saint Teresa of Avila and Saint Thérèse of the Child Jesus, among women. It was on the feast of Our Lady of Mount Carmel, in 1251, that the Blessed Virgin Mary appeared to a Carmelite priest in England, Saint Simon Stock, and gave him the brown scapular. She promised that anyone who would wear this little emblem of love and loyalty to her would receive the grace of final perseverance. Such is the generosity of the Virgin Most Powerful, the Mediatrix of All Graces, in return for a simple favor of devotion shown her by those who truly want her to be their Queen.

These were the words spoken by the Mother of God to Saint Simon Stock with regard to the brown scapular: "This shall be the privilege for you and for all Carmelites that anyone dying in this habit shall be saved." This privilege is extended to all the laity who are willing to be invested in this scapular, and who perpetually wear it.

17. Saint Alexis the Beggar (417).

He was born in Rome, and wishing to give up, for the sake of Our Lord, all honor and prestige, left home on his wedding day, and set sail for Syria. He lived at Edessa, in Syria, for seventeen years. He prayed for hours and hours in church, and worked as a lowly servant in hospitals. He returned to Rome as a beggar, and died unrecognized in his noble father's rich palace where he worked as a slave, and where he slept in a small room under the stairs. His parents came to know who it was they had been sheltering from a manuscript found after his death on his body, and written in his own hand. All the bells in Rome miraculously started ringing at the moment of the death of Saint Alexis, as a tribute to this selfless beggar, known as "the man of God." There is a Religious Order in the Catholic Church, founded in the fifteenth century, named for him and called "the Alexian Brothers." They devote themselves to taking care of the old, the insane and those suffering from nervous collapse.

Saint Chester (Ceslas) (1242). He was the brother of Saint Hyacinth. These two brothers were educated by their uncle who was a priest. They were both ordained and made canons in the cathedral of Cracow. Later they traveled to Rome with their uncle and met with the great preacher, Saint Dominic, the founder of the Order of Friars Preachers, and became his disciples. After their novitiate training Ceslas and Hyacinth, were sent back to their native country as missionaries. Ceslas preached in Prague, Silesia and Bohemia, and was the spiritual adviser to the duchess, Saint Hedwig of Poland. His life is filled with countless miracles of cures and miracles of grace. He raised four persons from the dead one of whom had been dead for eight days. In an invasion of Tartars in the year 1241 his community fasted and prayed incessantly that their city would be spared. When the situation seemed hopeless, Ceslas mounted the city wall

Saint Ceslas

with a crucifix in his hand. A huge ball of fire desceded from Heaven and rested above the saint. The fear-stricken Tartars fled as arrows of fire shot out at them from the heavenly weapon, the city was saved! One year later Our Lady herself came to receive the soul of Saint Ceslas into Heaven. Ceslas is Polish for Chester.

Blessed Teresa of St. Augustine and Companions (1794). Blessed Teresa and fifteen other Carmelite nuns were guillotined during the "Reign of Terror" of the French Revolution. They are also called the Martyrs of Compiegne. Two years earlier they had made an Act of Consecration by which they offered themselves as a holocaust to bring peace to the Church and the country. When they were arrested Sister Henriette exclaimed, "Let us rejoice in the joy of the Lord, that we shall die for our Holy Religion." As each Sister ascended the guillotine, her companions sang the *Veni Creator Spiritus.* The normally noisy crowd was strangely silent, and a witness remarked, "They looked as if they were going to their wedding." Within ten days of their death, the Reign of Terror ended.

18. Saint Camillus de Lellis (1614). He is one of the great patrons of the sick. He founded a Religious Order to take care of them. He himself suffered great sickness all his life, until he died, at the age of sixty-four. Doctors and nurses pray to him for help in caring for the sick. None who do so lovingly ever find him wanting. He lived in Rome, and the Order he founded is called "the Fathers of the Good Death," or "the Camillians." The last two words Saint Camillus spoke as he died were the Holy Names of Jesus and Mary.

19. Saint Vincent de Paul (1660). He was a Frenchman who founded the great Order known as the Congregation of the Priests of the Missions, popularly known as the Vincentians. Along with Saint Louise de Marillac, he founded the Sisters of Charity, in the year 1634. He was one of the greatest apostles of his day. He is the patron saint of all organizations in the Catholic Church devoted to charity. Saint Vincent de Paul was eighty-four years old when he died.

20. Saint Margaret of Antioch (304). She was a young girl from Antioch in Pisidia. Her father was a pagan priest. She was converted to the Catholic Faith by one of the servants in her house, and dedicated herself to Jesus as a virgin for life. Her father drove her out of his house. She then became a shepherdess on a hillside. Later, she was captured and brought back, and ordered to marry a pagan. She refused, and after many tortures, her head was cut off by the sword. She is one of the fourteen Holy Helpers, and is invoked for kidney diseases.

21. Saint Laurence of Brindisi (1619). He was an Italian Capuchin, born at Brindisi in Italy. He died at Lisbon in Portugal. He converted thousands of heretics back to the Catholic Faith. He made countless thousands of sinners do penance and amend their lives. He was a brilliant, simple and childlike preacher. Pope John XXIII made him a Doctor of the Church on the Feast of Saint Joseph, March 19, 1959. Saint Laurence of Brindisi is the thirtieth Doctor of the Catholic Church.

22. Saint Mary Magdalen (77). After Our Blessed Mother, the Virgin Mary, whose Child was God, no one has more beautifully or nobly borne the name Mary than Saint Mary Magdalen, the sister of Saint Lazarus and Saint Martha. She is called innocently "the Penitent." She was given the name Magdalen because, though a Jewish girl, she lived in a Gentile town called Magdala, in northern Galilee,

Saint Vincent de Paul

and her culture and all her manners were those of a Gentile. As referred to in Holy Scripture, she is, "Mary the Penitent," "Mary the sinner" and "Mary, the sister of Martha and Lazarus." Fourteen years after Our Lord's death, Saint Mary Magdalen was put by the Jews in a boat without sails or oars—along with her brother and sister, Saint Lazarus and Saint Martha, and Saint Maximin, who baptized her, and Saint Sidonious, "the man born blind," and her maid, Sara, and the body of Saint Anne, the mother of the Mother of God—and sent drifting out to sea.

The boat landed on the southern shore of France. Saint Mary Magdalen lived the whole rest of her life in France, as a contemplative in a cave known as Sainte-Baume, near a little town named Saint Maximin. Every day the angels carried her up into the air to hear their choirs singing. Every day she was given the Blessed Eucharist to be her only Food. Saint Mary Magdalen died when she was seventy-two years old. This was the same age as was Our Blessed Lady when she died.

23. Saint Apollinaris of Ravenna (79). He was a disciple of Saint Peter the Apostle. He came with Saint Peter from Antioch to Rome. Saint Peter consecrated him the first Bishop of Ravenna, in eastern Italy. He performed great miracles there, and converted multitudes to the Catholic Faith. He was seized, imprisoned and beaten by his pagan enemies until he died. A beautiful church has been built on the spot where he was martyred.

Saint Christina

24. Saint Christina (295).

She was a little martyr, ten years old. She was born in a town then called Tiro, on the borders of Lake Bolsena, in central Italy. Her father was a Roman nobleman. She took the name Christina because she had been converted to the teachings of Christ. Her father was furious when he heard she had become a Christian. He asked her servants to beat her and throw her into a dungeon. Angels came and healed her wounds. Saint Christina was then thrown into a lake with a millstone tied around her neck. Angels again rescued her, and bore her safely to land. She was then thrown into a burning furnace and stayed there for five days, singing God's praises, and left totally unharmed. She was brought to the Temple of Apollo and asked to sacrifice to the pagan gods. When she stood before the idol of Apollo, it fell and crashed to the ground. Her father died at that moment of a heart attack. But her enemies still persisted. They cut out her tongue, but she still continued to sing. She was shut up in a room with snakes, and at last, shot with arrows, she died. The Cathedral of Bolsena is dedicated to Saint Christina. She is the patroness of the Venetian States, this glorious little ten-year-old girl, a virgin, a confessor and a martyr!

25. Saint James the Greater (42). Saint James the Greater, called *Greater* because he was larger in size than Saint James the Less, was the brother of Saint John the Evangelist and the son of Saint Mary Salome. He was the first Apostle to die. He was beheaded by the Jews in Jerusalem. He was the great Apostle of Spain. Our Lady appeared to him there on a pillar in the year 36, in the town of Saragossa, holding her Divine Child in her arms, and letting Saint James know what a great country for the Catholic Faith Spain would one day be. It was on a visit to Jerusalem that Saint James was martyred. After his death, his body was carried back to Spain. It was buried there, at Compostella, where it still remains. Saint James is the patron saint of Spain. The story of his beheading is told in Chapter 12 of the Acts of the Apostles.

Saint Christopher (250). Saint Christopher was converted to the Catholic Faith in Antioch, where the Chair of Saint Peter was before Saint Peter went to Rome. Saint Christopher was baptized by a saint, Saint Babylas. He was put to death under the cruel Emperor Decius. Saint Christopher is one of the fourteen Holy Helpers. He was a strong and vigorous man. In his charity, he used to carry frail people and little ones across the river, which had no bridge. One day, he carried a child, and found that the child he was carrying was Christ Jesus Himself. And so his name, which means Christ-bearer, beautifully blended that day with his work. Saint Christopher is the patron saint of all travelers.

26. Saint Anne (3 B.C.). "Good Saint Anne" is the loving way many Catholics address the mother of the Virgin Mary, the Mother of God. Mary, the Mother of God, was the only child of Saint Anne and of Saint Joachim, her husband. Mary, the child of Saint Anne, was born fifteen years, three months and seventeen days before the birth of Jesus. Fifty years after Saint Anne's death, Saint Anne's body was brought to France by Saint Mary Magdalen and her companions in the year 47. Countless churches have been dedicated to Saint Anne all over the world. Canada is particularly devoted to her, and has a beautiful shrine named for her there, called "Saint Anne de Beaupré," to which people come from everywhere.

Simplicity is the secret by which we gain Saint Anne's love, her intercession and her protection. Saint Anne taught her little daughter to read the Holy Scriptures. Mary was the fulfillment of all its prophecies. Sensing her daughter's immaculate and incomparable holiness, beauty and brilliance, Saint Anne and Saint Joachim presented Mary in the Temple when she was three years old, and gave her to God and to us forever. The Feast of this Presentation is November 21.

Blessed Titus Brandsma (1942). Blessed Titus, a Dutch Carmelite, was born Anno Sjoerd Brandsma in the Netherlands in 1881. Three of his four sisters became nuns and his only brother became a priest. Titus entered the Carmelite Order, and at the age of twenty-four he was ordained. He earned a doctorate in philosophy in Rome and taught philosophy and the history of mysticism at the Catholic University of Nijmegen. Blessed Titus often said, "Whoever wants to win the world for Christ must have the courage to come in conflict with it." A professional journalist, Titus was appointed ecclesiastic advisor and spiritual director to the Catholic Press in the Netherlands in 1935.

In 1941 the Nazi public relations bureau ordered the Catholic Press to publish its news articles and ads. Titus made a tour of all the Catholic newspapers in the country to insist that they not print Nazi propaganda. Discovering his mission, the Gestapo arrested him in January of 1942. Nazi officials judged him too "dangerous" to their work to be allowed to be free, so he was sent out of the country and imprisoned at Dachau.

There, Blessed Titus was a consolation and example to all the prisoners by his kindness and generosity to everyone. He lasted only five weeks at Dachau. Camp officials considered him a burden because his health was failing rapidly so he was made the subject of "medical experimentation" and finally killed by lethal injection on July 26, 1942.

27. Saint Celestine I (432).

He was the great Pope of the Council of Ephesus, which took place the year before he died. This was the Council which condemned Nestorius, the bishop and heretic who denied the Divine Maternity of the Blessed Virgin Mary. Nestorius claimed that there were two persons in Jesus, and Mary was the Mother of one, and God the Father in eternity the Father of the other. This is blasphemous heresy. There is only one Person in Jesus. That one Divine Person is both the Son of God the Father and the Child of Mary the Virgin. It was Saint Celestine, the Pope, who sent Saint Patrick to be the great apostle of Ireland in 432.

Saint Pantaleon

Saint Pantaleon (305).

He was a physician to Emperor Maximin and a Christian. He associated with bad companions and fell into sin and then abandoned the Faith. The zealous priest Hermolaus, exhorted Pantaleon to repent of his sins and leave his sinful companions. In reparation for his sinfulness Pantaleon devoted himself to the spiritual and temporal welfare of his neighbor. He was brought before the Emperor and accused of being Christian by his early heathen companions. He was ordered to sacrifice to the idols, but Pantaleon called on the God he adored, Jesus Christ, for strength. Pantaleon suffered every conceivable torture then was nailed to a tree, and beheaded. He is one of the fourteen Holy Helpers and is invoked against lung diseases.

Saint Lilian (852).

Saint Lilian (Liliosa) was a glorious martyr who suffered at Cordova in Spain with her husband, Saint Felix. They were killed by the Mohammedans.

28. Saint Nazarius and Saint Celsus (68).

These were two heroic martyrs beheaded at Milan under the Emperor Nero. This was one year after the martyrdom of Saint Peter and Saint Paul. The mother of Saint Nazarius was Saint Perpetua, a spiritual daughter of Saint Peter. The bodies of Saint Nazarius and Saint Celsus were discovered at Milan by the great Saint Ambrose, bishop of that city, in 395, two years before he died. Beside the body of Saint Nazarius was a phial of his blood, as fresh as when he was alive.

29. Saint Martha (80). Saint Martha was the sister of Saint Lazarus and Saint Mary Magdalen. She was often hostess to Jesus in her house in Bethany. Fourteen years after the death of Jesus, Saint Martha, with her sister and brother, and others were put in a boat without sails and oars and pushed out to sea. Saint Martha and her companions landed in France. Saint Martha started a beautiful religious community at Marseilles. Saint Martha might well be called, "the mother of all active French nuns." Her sister, Saint Mary Magdalen, could be called, "the mother of all contemplative nuns."

Saint Olaf (1030). He was a prince, son of a king of Norway, who was baptized as a Catholic when he was fifteen. When he finally became king he called missionaries to Norway to make it a Catholic country. He was driven from his kingdom and martyred.

30. Saint Abdon and Saint Sennen (250). These were two Persian noblemen who were brought as captives to Rome by the Emperor Decius, whose purpose it was to keep the Catholic Faith from extending into Persia. Saint Abdon and Saint Sennen gloriously professed the Catholic Faith in the presence of the Emperor Decius. They were then brought into the great Roman amphitheater, where, before thousands of people, they were torn to pieces by wild beasts.

31. Saint Ignatius of Loyola (1556). Saint Ignatius of Loyola, in Spain, was the founder of the Society of Jesus. He was born in 1491, one year before America was discovered. He died in 1556, at the age of sixty-five. He was at first a page at a royal court in Spain. He was then a soldier and was wounded in battle. When he recovered, because of his reading of the lives of the saints while in bed, he decided to dedicate himself to becoming a soldier of the Catholic Faith. His most astounding literary work is his book, *The Spiritual Exercises*, which has been the food and nourishment of countless souls since his time. There are over one hundred and forty members of the Society of Jesus who have been declared blessed by the Holy See. There are forty-six members of the Society of Jesus, including Saint Ignatius, who have been canonized as saints. Their names are: Saint Ignatius of Loyola, Saint Francis Xavier, Saint Francis Borgia, Saint Francis Hieronomo, Saint John Francis Regis, Saint Peter Canisius, Saint Robert Bellarmine, Saint John Berchmans, Saint Stanislaus Kostka, Saint Aloysius Gonzaga, Saint Alphonsus Rodriguez, Saint Peter Claver, Saint Paul Miki, Saint James Kisai, Saint John de Goto, Saint Isaac Jogues, Saint John de Brébeuf, Saint René Goupil, Saint Noel Chabanel, Saint Charles Garnier, Saint Anthony Daniel, Saint John de Lalande, Saint Gabriel Lalemant, Saint Andrew Bobola, Saint Bernardine Realino, Saint John de Britto, Saint Joseph Mary Pignatelli, Saint Edmund Campion, Saint Alexander Briant, Saint Robert Southwell, Saint Henry Morse, Saint Nicholas Owen, Saint Thomas Garnet, Saint Henry Walpole, Saint Edmund Arrowsmith, Saint Philip Evans, Saint David Lewis, Saint John Ogilvie, Saint Roch Gonzales, Saint Alfonso Rodriguez, Saint John del Castillo, Saint Claude de la Columbiére, Saint Marek Krizin, Saint Stefan Pongracz and Saint Melichar Grodziecky.

August

The Month of the Immaculate Heart of Mary

1. Saint Samona and Her Seven Sons (168 B.C.). This is the feast of the heroic mother of the Machabees, and her seven sons who were cruelly martyred one by one and encouraged to die by their mother for the true faith of Israel and the belief in the Messias to come. Their story is dramatically told in the Second Book of the Machabees, Chapter 7. Their relics were brought to Constantinople by Saint Helena, the mother of the Emperor Constantine, and later translated to the Church of S. Peter in Chains in Rome.

Saint Faith, Saint Hope and Saint Charity (120). These heroic little sisters, aged twelve, ten and nine, were martyred for the Catholic Faith in the early days of the Church. Saint Sophia, their mother, died three days after her little daughters were killed. She died of grief, and they by the shedding of their blood for Jesus. Saint Sophia's feast is September 30.

Saint Alphonsus Maria de Liguori

2. Saint Alphonsus Maria de Liguori (1787). He was born in 1696. He was in his ninety-first year when he died. He founded the Redemptorist Order in 1732. He became a Doctor of the Church by constantly preaching and writing about the Holy Eucharist and about the Virgin Mary. No saint is more complete or superlative in the praise of the virginal Mother of God than he. So far three members of the Redemptorist Order have been canonized saints, thanks to the prayers and example of their father and founder, Saint Alphonsus Maria. These three saints are: Saint John Neumann, whose feast day is January 5, Saint Gerard Majella, whose feast day is October 16, and Saint Clement Mary Hofbauer, whose feast day is March 15, along with Blessed Peter Donders, Blessed Gaspar Stangassinger.

Here are a few of the Catholic men saints who have taken the name Mary: Saint Alphonsus Maria de Liguori (August 2), Saint Anthony Mary Gianelli (June 7), Saint Anthony Mary Claret (October 23), Saint Anthony Mary Zaccaria (July 5), Saint Clement Mary Hofbauer (March 15), Saint John Marie Vianney (August 8), Saint Joseph Mary Pignatelli (November 28), Saint Louis Marie de Montfort (April 28), Saint Peter Louis Marie Chanel (April 28), Saint Vincent Mary Strambi (January 1), Saint Francis Xavier Maria Bianchi (January 31).

Our Lady of the Angels.

We know in simple, childlike faith that the Blessed Virgin Mary is, in flesh and blood, holier, more beautiful, more powerful and closer to God in divine union than all the choirs and hierarchies of angels put together. Mary is the Queen of Angels. The angels obey her slightest command with royal, angelic love. A little ruined church, belonging to the Benedictines of Subasio, about a mile from Assisi and called the Portiuncula, which Saint Francis of Assisi repaired in 1207 and which had been named for Our Lady of the Angels, gave us the first feast of Our Lady under this title. It was on the feast of Our Lady, Queen of Angels, August 2, 1492, that Christopher Columbus, knowing there was a plenary indulgence granted to all who received Holy Communion on that day, went with all his crew to Mass, received Holy Communion, finished packing his boat—called the *Santa Maria*, the Holy Mary—and set sail for the New World. It took Columbus seventy-two days to cross the ocean. The day of his landing in America was a special feast of Our Lady, October 12, and we will speak of that day when it comes. There is a church called Our Lady of the Angels in Rome, dedicated to the Mother of God by Pope Pius IV in the year 1561. This was to secure her protection for Catholics against the horrors of the heresies that were beginning in that century.

The Stoning of Saint Stephen

3. The Finding of the Body of Saint Stephen (415).

Saint Stephen, the protomartyr of the Catholic Church, was stoned to death by the Jews in the year 36. He was buried twenty miles from Jerusalem, on the estate of Saint Gamaliel. The precious relics of Saint Stephen were discovered there in the year 415. Their finding is commemorated on August 3, and their translation to Rome on May 7. The body of Saint Stephen was placed beside the body of Saint Laurence, in Rome. When it was put there, Saint Laurence's body miraculously moved to one side, while he extended to Saint Stephen his hand, welcoming the body of Saint Stephen to rest beside his own. The Italian Catholics call Saint Laurence, because of this kindness, "the courteous Spaniard."

Saint Lydia (First Century). Saint Lydia was Saint Paul's first convert on his second missionary journey. Later on, he stayed at her house, as we are told by Saint Luke in the Acts of the Apostles. Her home was at Thyatira, a city of Asia Minor.

Saint Peter Julian Eymard (1868). He was a French priest who founded a beautiful Religious Order known as "the Priests of the Blessed Sacrament." He was a great advocate of early Communion for Catholic children. "A Catholic youth who has never made his First Communion," he said, "may be regarded as lost to the church." He was a great friend of Saint John Marie Vianney, the Curé of Ars. After a long period of suffering from sickness and other trials, and completely broken in health, Saint Peter Julian Eymard died in his native village at the age of fifty-seven.

4. Saint Dominic (1221).
He was the founder of the great Dominican Order known as the Order of Preachers. He was born in 1170 in Spain and died when he was only fifty-one years old. His mother, also a saint—Blessed Jane of Aza (August 8)—had had two sons who became priests, and wanted a third son who would be her heir. She prayed to Saint Dominic of Silos, whose holy death occurred in 1073 and whose feast day is December 20, and by his intercession her son was born. That is why he was called Dominic. She also saw at once that her son was meant to be God's heir and not her own.

Saint Dominic had his Order approved in 1216. Saint Dominic's full name was Dominic de Guzman. The great apostolate of Saint Dominic was that of the most Holy Rosary. Saint Dominic was given the Holy Rosary by the Blessed Virgin Mary herself, in Toulouse, in France. Every time any Catholic says the rosary it is somehow an honor to the great Saint Dominic. Saint Dominic raised the dead to life and rescued Christians from the Albigenses.

Nearly three hundred members of the Dominicans have been declared blessed by the Catholic Church. There are seventy Dominican canonized Saints, sixty-two men and eight women. There were three popes, sixteen bishops, and three Doctors of the Church. Here are some of their names: Saint Dominic, Saint Raymond of Pennafort, Saint Thomas Aquinas, Saint Albertus Magnus, Saint Peter the Martyr, Saint Peter Gonzalez, Saint Hyacinth, Saint Vincent Ferrer, Saint Antoninus, Saint Pius V, Saint John of Gorkum, Saint Louis Bertrand, Saint Martin de Porres, Saint Catherine of Siena, Saint Catherine de Ricci, Saint Rose of Lima, Saint Agnes of Montepulciano, Saint Margaret of Hungary and Saint Magdalena of Nagasaki.

5. Our Lady of the Snows (355-366).
During the night of August 4 in the year 355, in the middle of summer, snow fell on the Esquiline Hill in Rome, on the exact spot where Our Lady wanted a church to be built in her honor. She let a nobleman named John, and his wife, and also the Holy Father, Pope Liberius, know that that was her will. It took eleven years to build this lovely church of Our Lady in Rome. In the year 435, after it had been defined in the Council of Ephesus dogmatically that Our Lady was the Mother of God, this great church of Our Lady in the Eternal City was rebuilt by Pope Sixtus III.

Our Lady's favorite church in Rome is on the Esquiline Hill. It was first called the Church of Our Lady of the Snows. It was also called the Liberian Basilica. But its prevailing name, and the name which it now holds, is the Church of Saint Mary Major. Sometimes it is referred to as the Church of Saint Mary of the Crib because the crib in which Our Lord was placed when He was born in Bethlehem is kept in this church. The body of Saint Jerome is also buried there, and the relics of Saint Matthias, the Apostle, who took the place of Judas among the Twelve. Saint Jerome died with his head in the crib where Jesus was born.

6. The Transfiguration (32). The Transfiguration of Our Lord occurred on a mountain in Galilee, one year before He died. Three Apostles were with Jesus at the time. They were Peter, James and John. This was a glorious mystery. The same three Apostles were with Jesus in the joyful mystery of the raising of the daughter of Jairus to life from her bed after she had died, and in the sorrowful mystery of the Agony in the Garden, when Jesus sweat blood, the night before He died.

On the mountain of the Transfiguration, the body of Jesus shone, radiant with light. Moses, the greatest writing prophet, and Elias, the greatest speaking prophet, of the Old Testament, came and stood beside Him there. It was at this moment that the voice of God the Father, the First Person of the Blessed Trinity—to show us the divine and adorable dignity of Jesus, true God and true Man, and transcending the majesty of any other being that ever had been in this world—said, "This is My Beloved Son, in Whom I am well pleased. Hear ye Him." The three Apostles fell on their faces on the ground. When they looked up, there was no Moses and no Elias. There was only Jesus, standing humbly beside them and telling them, as Mary's Child, that they had nothing to fear.

7. Saint Cajetan (1547). He was a saint in northern Italy who did valiant work to protect the Holy Catholic Faith there against the heresies and hatreds of the Protestant Reformation. He refused all ecclesiastical dignities. He devoted his life to the service of the sick and the poor. He founded an order called the Theatines, named after a town in Italy. He died in southern Italy, in Naples, when he was sixty-seven years old.

Saint John Marie Vianney

8. Saint Cyriacus (Fourth Century). He was a deacon of the Church of Rome and was imprisoned, tortured and finally beheaded along with several others. He is one of the fourteen Holy Helpers and is invoked against eye diseases. March 16 was the day on which he died, but his body was enshrined on the eighth of August.

Saint John Marie Vianney (1859). This glorious parish priest was born in eastern France, three years before the French Revolution broke out. He was a simple farmer's boy. He received his first Holy Communion secretly in a barn when he was thirteen years of age. He later began studies for the priesthood. Because of the simple innocence of his mind, he found it very hard to pass the seminary examinations. His great devotions were to the Blessed Sacrament and to Our Blessed Lady. After months of prayer to Our Blessed Lady, he finally obtained the favor of being ordained a priest in 1815. He got encouragement to pursue his vocation to the priesthood at the tomb of Saint John Francis Regis. He was first made an assistant pastor at Ecully, and later a pastor at the little village of Ars. He stayed there for forty-one years, until he died. He is always referred to as the Curé of Ars. So great was his sanctity that people from all over Europe came to see him. He used to spend from sixteen to eighteen hours in the confessional every day. Heads of the State, army officers, university professors, bishops and priests, all went to him for direction. Toward the end of his life, nearly 20,000 pilgrims visited him every year. Pope Pius XI proclaimed him the patron of all parish priests. He was one of the most loved priests in the history of the Catholic Church. Everyone remembers him either as sitting in the confessional or kneeling before the Blessed Sacrament or before an image of Our Blessed Mother, always with the rosary beads in his hand.

His favorite saint was a young girl named Saint Philomena who died in 304, and

Saint Laurence

whose relics were found on the twenty-fifth of May, 1802, and whose feast day is in the same month of the Curé of Ars. Saint Philomena's feast is August 11.

9. Vigil of Saint Laurence.

Saint Romanus (258).

He was a Roman soldier who witnessed the torments of Saint Laurence and was thereby converted. Saint Laurence baptized him while in prison and Saint Romanus also became a martyr.

Saint Edith Stein (1942).

Saint Edith was a brilliant Jewish girl from Germany. She earned a doctorate in philosophy and eventually became an avowed atheist. After reading the life of Saint Teresa of Avila she knew that she had found the truth and must become a Catholic. She was received into the Church a few months later, in January of 1922, and then taught in a Dominican high school for several years. Twelve years after her conversion she entered the Carmelite Order at Cologne, Germany and took the name Sister Teresa Benedicta of the Cross.

During the Nazi persecution of the Jews which began in 1938 she was moved to a Carmel in Holland. Here she asked permission of her superiors "to offer [herself] to the Sacred Heart of Jesus as a sacrificial expiation for the sake of true peace…." She and her sister Rosa, also a convert to the Catholic Faith, were taken to Auschwitz in July of 1942. In the terrifying atmosphere of the concentration camp she was calm and prayerful and took especial care of the children. Sister Teresa and Rosa died there in Auschwitz.

10. Saint Laurence (258). Saint Laurence was an archdeacon to Pope Saint Sixtus II. He was martyred three days after Saint Sixtus because he would not tell the pagans where the treasures were concealed for the Holy Father's support of the parishes, the priests and the poor of Rome. Saint Laurence was martyred. He is buried in Rome in a church named for him. It is one of the seven great churches of Rome. Saint Stephen, the protomartyr, is buried beside Saint Laurence there. When Saint Stephen's body was brought to the tomb of Saint Laurence, Saint Laurence's lifeless body moved aside and extended a hand to welcome the body of Saint Stephen. Saint Laurence was a Spaniard by birth and is very greatly honored in Spain. His name is mentioned every day in the Canon of the Mass. It is also recited in the Litany of the Saints.

11. Saint Philomena (304). One of the glories of the 19th century was the discovery in 1802 of the relics of a

Saint Clare of Assisi

young girl, a martyr, who had been buried centuries before in the tomb of Saint Priscilla. Her name, inscribed upon her tomb, was Philomena, which means *beloved.* Her relics have worked so many miracles that the cult of her as a saint has grown enormously in our own day. Her most ardent devotee has been Saint John Marie Vianney, the parish priest of Ars, who died in 1859. Saint Philomena was martyred by the cruel Emperor Diocletian who wanted to marry her. Saint Philomena, the Catholic virgin, refused. And her blood was shed, after many tortures.

Saint Susanna (295). Saint Susanna, also known as Saint Susan, was a beautiful Roman maiden who was the niece of a Pope, Saint Caius. The cruel Emperor Diocletian martyred her because she refused to marry his pagan son-in-law. A beautiful church stands dedicated to her in Rome.

Blessed Peter Faber (1546). He was the first of the companions of Saint Ignatius Loyola to be admitted to the Society of Jesus by the founder of that great society. Blessed Peter Faber labored all his life against the Protestant heretics of the sixteenth century. It was due to his influence that Saint Ignatius was able to win Saint Francis Xavier for the Society of Jesus. Saint Francis Borgia and Saint Peter Canisius both admit that they owe their vocations to his example. Whenever Blessed Peter Faber entered a town to preach, he always invoked his Guardian Angel. He also invoked the Guardian Angel of every person he spoke to. He was a great lover of obedience, and a great apostle of the Guardian Angels. He died when he was in his fortieth year, burned up with fever and consumed with love.

12. Saint Clare (1253).

She was the beautiful nun who took the veil from Saint Francis of Assisi when she was eighteen years old, and under his direction established the Religious Order of nuns known as the Poor Clares. She was born in 1193, and died when she was exactly sixty years old. Two years after she died she was canonized a saint. So radiant and childlike was her evangelical wisdom that Popes, cardinals and bishops all consulted her about their problems. Her sister, Saint Agnes of Assisi, five years younger than she—and whose feast is November 16—was with her when she died, and died three months after her. Saint Clare's devotion to the Blessed Sacrament was so extraordinary that one day, when the Saracens were besieging Assisi and trying to enter the Convent of Saint Damian where she and her nuns lived, she lifted up a monstrance in which the Blessed Sacrament had been placed and called upon Jesus to put the Saracens to flight. They trembled before Jesus in the Blessed Sacrament, and all of them fled in fright and never returned.

13. The Death of Our Lady (58).

Saint John Berchmans

This feast is more lovingly called "the Dormition" (the Sleep) of Our Lady. For although she really and truly died, Mary's death lasted for only forty hours, the same length of time as Our Lord's death. Then, with her body incorrupt, Mary was restored to life and was assumed, body and soul, into Heaven. The Apostles, with the exception of Saint James who had died, and of Saint Thomas who was brought later, were miraculously transported from the parts of the world where they were preaching to attend the death of Our Lady in Jerusalem, when she gave up her immaculate and spotless soul to God. Saint Timothy, Saint Denis the Areopagite and Saint Hierotheus, his friend, were also brought miraculously to our Lady's bedside. Jesus Himself came down from Heaven to assist at Our Lady's death. Just before Mary died, Jesus gave her the Blessed Eucharist, the Body and Blood which she had given to Him when she conceived Him at Nazareth. Our Lady was buried reverently by the Apostles at the foot of the Mount of Olives, just below the place where Our Lord had sweat blood on the eve of His Passion. It was not far from the grave where Saint Lazarus had been buried and was raised from the dead by Jesus.

Mary's soul, during the interval when her Virginal body lay dead, was able to visit the souls in Purgatory so as to comfort and to release them, just as Our Lord's soul, during the three days He lay dead, went to comfort the souls in the Limbo of the Just. Our Lady was seventy-two years old when she died.

Saint John Berchmans (1621). He was a young Belgian who entered the Society of Jesus when he was seventeen. He was one of the most brilliant and noble young members this Order has ever had. Sensing that he would not live long, he would say, "If I do not

FR. MAXIMILIAN KOLBE

Saint Maximilian Kolbe

become a saint when I am young, I shall never be one." His obedience to his superior was perfect. He declared, "May I die rather than violate deliberately the slightest order or rule." His companions in the Society of Jesus called him "the cheerful brother," for his very presence dispelled all gloom and darkness. His three great loves were: Jesus, Mary and the Rules of Saint Ignatius. He died holding his crucifix, his rosary and his rule book in his hands, saying, "These three things are most dear to me, and with these I die." Saint John Berchmans was only twenty-two years old at his death. His great joy was to serve Mass. He has been declared the patron saint of all altar boys.

14. Saint Athanasia (860). She was a Greek woman who turned her house into a convent where many courageous Catholic girls went and lived as nuns. They called Saint Athanasia their abbess. She was an adviser to the royalty, including an empress, Theodora. The name Athansaia means *immortal*. Saint Athanasia is immortal in the love and veneration of the Catholic Church.

Saint Maximilian Kolbe (1941). He was a Polish Franciscan priest, completely dedicated to Our Lady, who founded the Militia of the Immaculata to convert sinners, heretics and especially enemies of the Church. The Marytown friary he set up in Poland and devoted to publishing grew to be the largest in the world. Saint Maximilian was an apostle of the Miraculous Medal of Our Lady. He died in the concentration camp at Auschwitz on August 14, 1941, having voluntarily taken the place of a prisoner who was condemned to death. He once said, "One day, you will see the statue of the Immaculata in the center of Moscow atop the Kremlin."

15. The Assumption of the Blessed Virgin Mary into Heaven (58). This is the day on which the body of the Blessed Virgin Mary, which did not know any corruption despite her death, was reunited with her soul. She was on this day taken in full personality into the Beatific Vision of God, past all the choirs of angels and archangels, to the absolute heights of God's love. To summarize how tremendous this event was to the angels in Heaven and to the souls of the Just who were there in the Beatific Vision, and to Our Lord and to Saint Joseph who were both there in body and in soul waiting for her to come, the Holy Scripture tells us that at the moment of Mary's entrance into Heaven, *"There was silence in Heaven, as it were, for half an hour."* (Apoc 8:1) Eternity almost stopped being eternity so as to receive into itself forever the supreme gift of all time, the Immaculate and ever-blessed Virgin Mary, the Mother of God, the sole reason for which God created all angels and all men.

Saint Rocco

Saint Tarsicius (255). He was a noble young Christian killed while carrying the Blessed Sacrament to be given to Christians in Roman prisons. He died rather than let the Blessed Eucharist be violated by the crowd which attacked him. The angels protected Our Lord in the Eucharist from these heathens after his death.

16. Saint Joachim (4 B.C.). Saint Joachim was the father of the Blessed Virgin Mary. He has his feast on the day after her Assumption. This is by way of a beautiful privilege and a great tribute to this saintly man. Saint Joachim's name is sometimes contracted into Heli or Eliacim. His name means *God has judged.* God judged him to be worthy to be the father of the greatest of all God's creatures. Saint Joachim's wife was Saint Anne. Saint Joachim was let known before his death that his child was to be the Mother of God. Mary was the only child of Joachim and Anne. Saint Joachim died when Mary was a consecrated virgin in the Temple of Jerusalem. She sent angels to guard her father in his last agony. Saint Joachim's feast was first celebrated on September 9, the day after Our Lady's birthday. Later, it was celebrated on March 20, the day after the feast of Saint Joseph. But now it is solemnly kept on August 16, the day after the glorious Assumption of his daughter into Heaven.

When Mary was born on September 8, Saint Joachim knelt beside her for three whole days, looking upon her with awe and love and admiration. On September 12, he was inspired by God—as was Saint Anne, her mother—to give her the name Mary, which means both *Lady* and *Star of the Sea.* It was on September 15, the octave of Our Lady's nativity, that Saint Joachim called his daughter Mary.

Saint Rocco (1327). He was the son of a French governor at Montpellier in France. His father and mother died when he was twenty. Though the heir to much wealth and fame, he renounced them all, gave his money to the poor and set off as a pilgrim to Rome, dressed as a beggar. Saint Rocco's great devotion was to the Sign of the Cross. He cured countless people who were sick simply by making the Sign of the Cross over them. Once when he himself was sick, he withdrew to a cave, and while there a dog used to bring him his food miraculously. He spent the last five years of his life in a prison, completely forgotten by the world. Saint Rocco died when he was only thirty-two years old. When his body was found, the Sign of the Cross, which was miraculously printed on his breast from birth, revealed who he was. The city of Rome and, indeed, all Italians and numberless French, have great devotion to this young victim of God's love.

Saint Hyacinth

17. Saint Hyacinth (1257).

Saint Hyacinth—called Saint Jacek in his native country—was one of the great saints of Poland. He has been called "the apostle of the North." He traveled, preaching the Catholic Faith and bringing back to the Sacraments the peoples of Poland, Denmark, Sweden, Norway and Russia. He even went over to China and converted some of the Chinese. He was a Dominican priest and is lovingly commemorated by all northern Christians. He was a direct disciple of Saint Dominic. He is the brother of Saint Ceslas whose feastday is on July 17.

18. Saint Helena (330).

There is no more loved or remembered royal woman among the saints than Saint Helena (also called Helen, Eleanor, Ellen, Eileen, Elaine) who was an empress and the mother of Constantine the Great. She became a Christian in 313. It was Saint Helena who discovered the True Cross in Jerusalem in 326, four year before she died. She built churches on Mount Calvary, at Bethlehem, and in the little town of Fostat in Egypt where the Holy Family went in flight when Jesus was a Child.

19. Saint John Eudes (1680).

He was the founder of the Sisters of Charity of Refuge. He was the first great promoter of devotion to the Hearts of Jesus and Mary. He dedicated himself by vow to the Blessed Virgin when he was a young boy of fourteen. He became a priest at twenty-four. He has been called one of the greatest missionaries France has ever known. Thousands of people came to listen to Saint John Eudes preach, and thousands were converted. It was due to his influence that the Good Shepherd nuns were founded, patterned after the Sisters of Our Lady of Refuge.

20. Saint Bernard (1153).

Saint Bernard of Clairvaux was a Frenchman. He was born in the year 1091. When he was twenty-two years old, he joined the Cistercian Order at Citeaux. He brought with him thirty companions, among whom were his father, his uncle and four of his brothers. His mother was dead. A short time later, he was sent to be the abbot and founder of a monastery at Clairvaux. He founded one hundred and sixty-three houses of his Order. He preached the Second Crusade to send Christians out to fight as soldiers against the Turks and stop the horrible things they were doing to Christian lands and Christian shrines and Christian customs and Christian peoples.

It is said of Saint Bernard of Clairvaux that he "carried the twelfth century on his shoulders." His great and intense devotion was to the Blessed Virgin Mary, the Mother of God. Saint Bernard wrote the lovely prayer to Our Lady called the *Memorare*, which begins, "Remember, O most gracious Virgin Mary, that never was it known that anyone who fled to thy protection, implored thy help, or sought thy intercession, was left unaided." It was Saint Bernard who added to the prayer, "Hail, holy Queen," the invocation, "O clement, O loving, O sweet Virgin Mary!"

Saint Bernard calls Our Lady, "Mother of Life" and "Mother of Salvation." He says that as through her we received God, so through her God must receive us. As Saint Benedict, in his humility, refused ever to become a priest, so Saint Bernard, in his humility, refused ever to become a bishop. He was offered three bishoprics, each of which he declined. He is often portrayed in art with three mitres at his feet.

21. Saint Jane Frances de Chantal (1641).

In her early years, Jane Frances Frémyot married the Baron de Chantal. After his death, under the spiritual guidance of Saint Francis de Sales, she founded the Sisters of the Visitation, one of the greatest Orders of nuns in the Catholic Church. This was in the year 1610. At the time of her death there were eighty-six convents of this Order in France alone. Saint Francis de Sales called Saint Jane Frances de Chantal "the perfect woman." One of the great admirers and supporters of Saint Jane Frances de Chantal was Saint Vincent de Paul.

Our Lady of Knock (1879).

On August 21, 1879, in the little village of Knock, in County Mayo, in Ireland, Our Lady appeared to a group of fifteen simple Irish peasants, grown-ups and children. Our Lady wanted to bring to the Irish people by this childlike approach a full appreciation of the mystery of her glorious Assumption and her Crowning as Queen of Heaven. She also wanted to renew in the Irish a great love for Saint Joseph, her virginal husband, and for Saint John the Evangelist, her virginal adopted son who both appeared with her. This apparition at Knock was one of a series of many apparitions of Our Lady that occurred in the 19th century so as to let us know that the Age of Mary has arrived.

Our Lady appeared to Catherine Labouré, a little novice nun in Paris, in 1830. Our Lady appeared to two children at La Salette in France, in 1846, wanting them to guard and protect the Holy Name of Jesus and to keep Sunday a sacred day. Our Lady appeared to Marie Bernadette, a fourteen-year-old child, at Lourdes in France, in 1858, four years after the dogma of her Immaculate Conception had been defined by the saintly Pope, Pius IX.

22. The Immaculate Heart of Mary. This is the feast of that beautiful heart which is the abyss of all mysteries. By way of showing us that we are now living in the Age of Our Lady, this feast, first instituted in 1644, was given to the entire Catholic Church in 1944, by Pope Pius XII. The Immaculate Heart of Mary is of such spotless purity that it lives in contemplation and love of God alone. It is called by one of the saints, "the Furnace of Divine Love." Mary's is also the heart that is full of tenderness and love toward us, and is eager to give divine things to all those who greet it as Immaculate, and love it with all their hearts. Numberless saints have spread devotion to the Immaculate Heart of Mary. Two great priests deserve especially to be remembered in this crusade. They are Saint John Eudes (August 19), and Saint Louis Marie de Montfort (April 28). The authors of this book love to call themselves the Slaves of the Immaculate Heart of Mary. They would be slaves to no one else in this world. They consider being Slaves of the Immaculate Heart of Mary to be the greatest of all freedoms.

The Immaculate Heart of Mary

23. Saint Philip Benizi (1285). Saint Philip Benizi was a member of the Servite Order, known better as the Servants of the Blessed Virgin Mary. He wanted to give his whole life to God as a lay brother, but was forced by his superiors to become a priest. He became a General of his Order. He had to go away and hide himself to keep from being elected Pope. He assisted at the famous Second Council of Lyons in 1274, and had the gift of tongues there. He was one of the many well-known saints who raised the dead to life. He was only fifty-two years old when he died.

24. Saint Bartholomew (72). Saint Bartholomew was one of the Twelve Apostles. He was the one Apostle of noble birth. That is why he is called Bartholomew, which means *son of Tolmai*. His name is also Nathanael. He was brought by Saint Philip to meet Our Lord. In the Holy Gospel of Saint John, Saint Bartholomew is called "an Israelite in whom there is not guile." He lived in the town of Cana in Galilee, where Our Lord changed water into wine at the marriage feast. After Our Lord's Ascension, Saint Bartholomew went as far as India, and then came back to Asia Minor; and then went to Armenia, where he was skinned alive and beheaded for the Catholic Faith. His major relics are now on a little island in the River Tiber, near Rome, where there is a church dedicated to him in perpetual love and memory.

Our Lady, Health of the Sick. This is a movable feast, but August 24 is the earliest it can occur. The feast itself is the Saturday before the last Sunday of August, the month of the Seven Joys of Our Lady and of her Immaculate Heart. All our physical ailments, sicknesses or weaknesses should be brought to Our Blessed Lady, Health of the Sick, for healing. If we do this, our health will be protected better than it ever could be otherwise. If we have consulted a doctor, Our Lady will help him to help us. It is wrong, and indeed ungrateful, for any Catholic to call Our Lady, "Health of the Sick," as we do in the Litany of Loreto, and not go to her for aid when any sickness assails us.

Saint Louis of France

25. Saint Louis of France (1270).
He is the glorious King of France who was born at Poissy in 1215. He died fighting in one of the crusades to regain the Holy Land for Christians when he was only fifty-five years old. Saint Louis is the king who started the custom of genuflecting during the Mass when the priest says of the Son of God in the Creed: *Et Homo factus est* (And [He] was made Man). Saint Louis fought in two crusades, the last two. He redeemed the Crown of Thorns of Our Lord from the Venetians and built a beautiful chapel for it in Paris, called *Sainte Chapelle*. All of Saint Louis' relics were destroyed during the French Revolution. But his memory will never die in France, or in the whole Catholic Church. The city of Saint Louis, Missouri, was named for him by early American Catholics who came from France.

Saint Genesius (300).
He was an actor in Rome who, while taking part in a performance that ridiculed Christian Baptism, suddenly sensed the meaning of this sacred and beautiful liturgy and was sacramentally baptized. He was then martyred under Diocletian. Another noted actor who died under the same circumstances was Saint Porphyry, whose feast is September 15, and who was martyred in 362 by Julian the Apostate.

Saint Patricia (655).
She was a beautiful little virgin of Constantinople, a member of a royal family. By way of consecrating herself to God, she ran away from home, went to Jerusalem, and then to Rome, where she became a nun. She died in Naples, and has become one of the patron saints of that city.

26. Saint Zephyrinus (217).
He was the sixteenth Pope. He ruled the Catholic Church as Christ's Vicar for fourteen years. He did beautiful work in taking care of the burying grounds of the Christian martyrs of the early centuries. There were eleven

million of these martyrs in less than three hundred years. Saint Zephyrinus is responsible for the use of metal and, indeed, gold-lined, chalices at Mass to hold the Precious Blood of Jesus.

27. Saint Joseph Calasanctius (1648).
He was a Spaniard who went to Rome after being ordained a priest. There he beautifully took care of the education of young boys and girls. This was his great apostolate. For this purpose he founded the Order of Clerks Regular of the Pious Schools, also called the Piarists. The fruit of his work in central Europe and in Spain and Italy can never be measured. Saint Joseph was called "a second Job." Every day for fifty years he visited each of the seven churches of Rome. Saint Joseph Calasanctius was ninety-two years old when he died.

The Seven Joys of Our Lady.
Seven is a mystical number. Our Lady's Sorrows are seven and are celebrated twice during the year—on the Friday before Good Friday and on September 15. Our Lady's Joys are also seven and are celebrated within the octave of the feast of her Immaculate Heart. The Seven Joys of Our Lady are: (1) The Annunciation; (2) the Visitation; (3) the Birth of Our Lord; (4) the Adoration of Jesus by the Magi; (5) the Finding of the Child Jesus in the Temple; (6) the Resurrection of Our Lord; (7) the Assumption of Mary in body and in soul into Heaven. The feast of The Seven Joys of Our Lady is a very special feast of the Franciscan Order and they recite in its honor the Franciscan Crown, which consists of a seven-decade rosary—seven *Our Fathers* and seventy *Hail Marys*, to which are added two *Hail Marys* because Our Lady was seventy-two when she died and was assumed into Heaven.

28. Saint Augustine (430).
Saint Augustine of Hippo, Doctor of the Church, was born at Tagaste in northern Africa. His early life was spent in wicked ways. But thanks to the prayers of his holy mother, Saint Monica, at the age of thirty-three Saint Augustine was baptized a Catholic, in Milan, by Saint Ambrose. He returned to Africa and was made Bishop of Hippo. He died at the age of seventy-six. His two great works, the *Confessions* and *The City of God*, are among the most notable writings of all Catholic teachers. The body of Saint Augustine now rests at Pavia, in Italy. There is a church dedicated to him in Rome where his mother's body now rests. Any one of the sayings of Saint Augustine lets us know the golden quality of his brilliant mind. He says that, "the heavenly ladder by which God came into the world was the humility of the Blessed Virgin Mary." Saint Augustine composed, along with Saint Ambrose, the beautiful hymn known as the *Te Deum*, which has twenty-nine verses, and which is recited in the Office of Catholic priests and often sung in Catholic choirs.

29. The Beheading of Saint John the Baptist (32).
Saint John the Baptist was six months older than Jesus, but died one year before Him. Saint John the Baptist's head was cut off by the wicked Jewish tetrarch, Herod Antipas, at the order of a horrid woman named Herodias. The head of Saint John the Baptist was given to Herodias by her daughter Salome, and served on a dish to her and her guests at table. Herodias took a bodkin and stabbed, again and again, the tongue that had rebuked her for her viciousness and impurity. This was the tongue that had greeted Our Lord with the salutation, "Behold the Lamb of God Who takest away the sins of the world."

"He must increase and I must decrease," said Saint John the Baptist, referring to Our Lord. By ways of a symbol of this truth, Our Lord increased in death by being raised on a Cross on the hill of Calvary. Saint John decreased by being decapitated. Our Lord was six months younger than Saint John the Baptist, but lived six months longer than he did. Our Lord was crucified, and Saint John the Baptist beheaded, on the same day—March 25—one year apart.

30. Saint Rose of Lima (1617). Saint Rose of Lima, in Peru, the patroness of South America and the Philippines, was the first saint canonized who was born in the New World. Her great model was Saint Catherine of Siena. Her baptismal name was Isabel, but because of a miraculous rose seen over her head one day and because of the beautiful and flower-like charm of her face, she was called Rose. And her bishop, at her Confirmation, gave her that name. Her full name, religiously, was Rose of Saint Mary, a name miraculously given her by Our Blessed Lady one day as she prayed. Saint Rose of Lima was a Dominican of the Third Order. She died when she was only thirty-one years old. Through her intercession a dead person was raised to life. Five wonderful Catholic saints lived in Lima, in Peru, in the first half of the seventeenth century. They are (and their feast days

Saint Rose of Lima

and the year they died): Saint Rose of Lima, August 30, 1617; Saint Turibius, her bishop, March 23, 1606; Saint Francis Solano, July 14, 1610; Saint Martin de Porres, November 3, 1639; and Saint John Massias, September 18, 1645.

Saint Fiacre (670). He was an Irishman who went to Meaux in France where he built a hermitage and eventually a monastery. So many pilgrims had visited his shrine in France that a taxicab was nicknamed a *fiacre* in consequence of the constant use of taxis in conveying people there. He is a patron of gardeners and is often depicted with a shovel.

Blessed Jeanne Jugan (1879). She founded the Little Sisters of the Poor to care for the elderly. She was born in Brittany, France in 1792 and grew up during the chaos of the French Revolution. When she refused an offer of marriage, she explained to her mother, "God wants me for Himself. He is keeping me for a work which is not known, a work which is not yet begun." One winter night Jeanne took an old half-paralyzed woman into her home and placed the woman in her own bed. The French Revolution had left many elderly destitute, so she rented a large home and cared for them there. Three young women came to help her and they began to live a religious life, choosing Jeanne as their Superior. Her Sisters serve the poor in thirty countries on five continents.

31. Saint Raymond Nonnatus (1240). He joined the Order of Our Lady for the Redemption of Captives (the Mercedarians), and succeeded Saint Peter Nolasco as its General. He gave away all his possessions so as to free Catholic slaves from Mohammedans. He was called Nonnatus, which means *not born* because he was taken from his mother's body shortly after she had died. He was only forty years old when he died himself and was born into eternity.

September

The Month of Our Lady of Sorrows

1. Saint Anna the Prophetess (First Century). Saint Anna the Prophetess was the daughter of a man named Phanuel who was of the tribe of Aser, one of the Twelve Tribes of Israel. She was one of the very, very few faithful Jewish girls who believed with all her heart in the revelations of God in the Old Testament, and who awaited their fulfillment in the New Testament. Saint Anna was married when she was fourteen. She became a widow at twenty-one. She was the one in charge of the Blessed Virgin Mary from the time Mary was presented in the Temple at the age of three until she was betrothed at the age of fourteen. Saint Anna was seventy-two years old when she first met Our Lady. She was eighty-four years old when Mary presented Jesus in the Temple. All other Jewish women in the Temple at that time ignored Jesus. Only Anna greeted Him. All the Jewish priests ignored Jesus. Only Simeon greeted Him and held Him in his arms, and declared while Anna was listening, "Now Thou dost dismiss Thy servant, O Lord, according to Thy word in peace."

Anna was the name of Mary's mother. Anna was the name of Mary's teacher in the Temple. The name Anna means *grace*. Mary was not only full of grace, but was companioned by grace all during her childhood.

Saint Aegidius (Giles) (712). Saint Aegidius, known in Italian as Egidio and in English as Giles, was a Benedictine monk and abbot. In his early life, he lived as a hermit in France. He is one of the fourteen Holy Helpers and is invoked for the cure of cripples.

2. Saint Stephen (1038). Saint Stephen was the great King of Hungary, after whom the famous Cathedral in Vienna, known as Stefandom, is named. Saint Stephen was crowned King of Hungary by command of Pope Sylvester II, in the year 1000. He dedicated the whole of his country to the patronage of the Mother of God. His son, Emeric, is a saint. Saint Emeric died in 1031 and his feast day is November 4. Saint Stephen filled his country with Catholic churches and monasteries. He was a royal and noble and saintly ruler who punished severely such crimes as blasphemy, murder, theft, adultery and the missing of Mass on Sunday. His great patrons in Heaven were Saint Martin of Tours and Saint George.

3. Saint Pius X (1914). The glorious Saint Pius X died in 1914, at the beginning of the First World War after having been Pope for eleven years. There has been no more saintly, courageous or beloved saint of modern times than Pope Saint Pius X. He was the vigorous opponent of all the Liberalism that has been trying in modern times to make its way into the Catholic Church, to water down its dogmas and to tie up Catholics with false brotherhoods that have no relationship to Jesus or to the Divine Maternity of Mary. Saint Pius X was the Pope of daily Communion for all, and of early Communion for children. No political influences could make him alter his assignment as Vicar of Christ on earth and the sole ruler of the world in all things that directly pertain to God. Saint Pius X approached the papacy by every simple step a priest could take. He was born in Riese, in Italy; he was a curate at Tombolo; a parish priest at Salzano; a canon at Treviso, and a spiritual director of the seminary there; he was Bishop of Mantua; Patriarch of Venice; and Pope of Rome. His name was Giuseppe Sarto. The only credentials he offered for all he did were these: "I am a simple priest."

Our Lady, Mother of the Good Shepherd. The Good Shepherd, Who is Jesus Christ Our Lord, will feed His lambs and His sheep just as His Mother tells Him to. He will care for them when she wants it and give them what favors she desires Him to give. Jesus as a Child, was the One, Whom Mary the Shepherdess, cared for as a little Lamb. Now that He is the Divine Shepherd, He retains all her ways, all her manners and style of doing things in caring for His flock. There is nothing more lovely than a girl tending sheep. Such was Joan of Arc, the great heroine of France. And such was Lucy, the eldest of the Fatima children, who became Carmelite nun in Portugal, named Sister Mary of the Immaculate Heart, to whom Our Lady appeared six times in 1917.

A beautiful title of the Blessed Virgin Mary, and one that could be and should be given to her, is the Divine Shepherdess. Mary, who is willing to be our Shepherdess if we will be her lambs and her sheep, has already had the experience of having Almighty God as her first little Lamb: "The Lamb of God Who takest away the sins of the world.

4. Saint Rose of Viterbo (1252). Saint Rose of Viterbo was a little peasant girl who wanted to become a Poor Clare nun, but was not received in any of their convents. She died when she was only eighteen years old. After her death, she was buried in a Poor Clare convent by order of the Pope. She raised a dead person to life.

Saint Rosalia (1160).
There are three noted girl saints from three separate towns in the island of Sicily, right off the coast of southern Italy. They are: Saint Agatha from Catania, Saint Lucy from Syracuse and Saint Rosalia from Palermo. Saint Rosalia lived a religious life in a cave on a mountain, three miles from her home, though her family was wealthy and prosperous. Her relics were

Saint Rosalia

discovered in 1624. The town of Palermo calls her its special patroness and prays to her in all its needs.

Saint Moses (Fifteenth Century B.C.). He was the great patriarch and lawgiver of the Old Testament who wrote the first five books of the Bible. He is not called *Saint Moses* when referred to scripturally, but only on September 4, his feast day. The life of Moses was divided into three periods of forty years. He was forty years in Egypt, a little child picked up near a river bank and educated and trained in the court of Pharao. He was then forty years in the Madianite country, south of the Holy Land. And then he was forty years with the Hebrews, in the desert on their way to the Promised Land. Moses died before the Israelites reached the Promised Land. He died on Mount Nebo at the age of one hundred and twenty. His sister Miriam is a great and noble woman of the Old Testament. His brother Aaron, whose feast day is July 1, was the first high priest of the Jews.

5. Saint Laurence Justinian (1456). He was the first Patriarch of Venice. He wrote beautifully, clearly and courageously about the truths of the Catholic Faith. He died when he was seventy-four years old. At his death, all the people of Venice wept bitter tears.

6. Saint Eleutherius (585). He was a Benedictine monk and a great supporter of the future Saint Gregory the Great who was Pope from 590 to 604. Saint Eleutherius, although an abbot at the monastery of Saint Mark near Spoleto, retired to Saint Gregory's abbey in Rome where he lived as the simplest monk. Because of his humility, God gave him great powers to work miracles, including the raising of a dead man to life.

7. Saint Cloud (560). He was the grandson of King Clovis and of Saint Clotilde, the Queen. His uncles, so as to stop his accession to the throne of France, murdered his two brothers, and would have murdered him if he had not been taken into safety. He gave up all idea of becoming a king. He became a simple priest, a hermit—and later an abbot and founder of a beautiful monastery near Versailles.

Saint Regina (250). Saint Regina was a noble little girl who lived in France and was made a Catholic by the instruction of her nurse, and was baptized by her. In an immediate surrender to her Faith, Regina dedicated herself to God in a vow of virginity in honor of the Blessed Virgin Mary. She then went to live as a little shepherdess in the hills. The Prefect of Gaul, named Olybrius, was riding by the field where she was with her sheep. He saw her beauty, sensed her nobility and was annoyed by her holiness. He sent for her and asked her to deny her Faith as a Catholic. When she refused to do so, her clear, pure eyes challenged his lewdness and lasciviousness and, when she refused to violate her vow of virginity and would not sacrifice to idols, he had her beaten, burned with red-hot plates, pincers and iron combs. He finally had her throat cut. So did this little child with the queenly name enter the Kingdom of Heaven.

8. The Birthday of the Blessed Virgin Mary (16 B.C.). Mary was born fifteen years, three months and seventeen days before the birth of Jesus. She was born in a house in which, fourteen years, six months and seventeen days later, the great Angel Gabriel, sent by God, would come and kneel before her and with bowed head say: "Hail, full of grace, the Lord is with thee."

Mary was three years, two months and thirteen days old when she was presented by her parents to God in the Temple. She was just fourteen years old when she was espoused to Joseph. She was fourteen years, four months and fifteen days old when her espousals to Saint Joseph was solemnized. She was in her forty-eighth year when Our Lord died and rose from the dead and ascended into Heaven, in the year 33. And Mary was seventy-two years old when she herself died, and was three days later assumed into Heaven, in the year 58.

Blessed Alan de la Roche (1475). He was a Dominican who was one of the great apostles for spreading the Holy Rosary. He died when he was forty-seven.

9. Saint Peter Claver (1654).

Saint Peter Claver was a Spaniard who joined the Society of Jesus in 1609. Under the inspiration of Saint Alphonsus Rodriguez, a holy lay brother of the Society of Jesus, Saint Peter Claver was moved with the desire to become a missionary and work for the conversion of poor Black slaves in Central and South America. He labored there for forty years. He was not interested in the Blacks sociologically. He was interested in the salvation of their immortal souls. He loved them and cared for them with the tenderness of a father. He worked many miracles. He raised a dead man to life. He baptized three hundred thousand Blacks with his own hands.

10. Saint Pulcheria (453).

Saint Pulcheria, the granddaughter of Theodosius the Great, was an empress and a saint. She was baptized by Saint John Chrysostom and made a vow of virginity as a child. She guided her younger brother Theodosius II so wisely in ruling the Empire, that never before had the Empire enjoyed such tranquility and peace as during his reign. Pulcheria was later exiled by her jealous sister-in-law. Theodosius II was deceived into sheltering two heretics: Eutyches, who denied that Our Lord has both a human and a Divine nature, and Nestorius, who denied that Mary was the Mother of God. The Empire lost this peace and tranquility by harboring these heretics. Pope Saint Leo the Great begged Pulcheria to come out of exile in order to help the Church. Her reappearance caused her brother to renounce the heresiarchs and led eventually to the formal condemnation of their errors by the Council of Chalcedon. At the death of Theodosius II, Pulcheria married General Marcian, who respected her vow of virginity. Under her reign the followers of Eutyches and Nestorius were put to flight, as was Attila the Hun. Saint Pulcheria is praised as a valiant woman and protector of Christendom.

Saint Nicholas of Tolentino (1306).

He was a member of the Order of Saint Augustine. For thirty years he preached ev-

The Child Mary

ery day in the streets of Tolentino to the poor, the lowly, the sick and the abandoned. He was one of the great apostles of the souls in purgatory. Four great apostles of the souls in purgatory are: Saint Odilo, Saint Catherine of Genoa, Saint Nicholas of Tolentino and Blessed John Massias. Saint Nicholas of Tolentino died when he was sixty years old.

11. Saint Paphnutius (356). He was a noble bishop from Egypt. He took part in the Council of Nicea in 325, to defend the Divinity of Jesus against the Arian heretics. Under the Emperor Galerius he was tortured for the Catholic Faith. One of his eyes was plucked out and one of his legs mutilated. Later, Saint Paphnutius became a monk, and a great friend and associate of Saint Anthony of the Desert, and was consecrated a bishop in the Upper Thebaid in Egypt.

Saint John-Gabriel Perboyre (1840). He was born in Cohors, France, was the first martyr of China. His martyrdom is said to have resembled the Passion of Our Lord. He joined the Congregation of the Mission at the age of 16, where he was

Saint Helena

later a seminary professor and Director of Novices. After years of pleading to go to the missions, he was sent to China. He wrote to his Father, "If we have to suffer martyrdom it would be a great grace given us by God." Three years later a persecution of Christians erupted in China. John-Gabriel was betrayed by one of his own converts, mocked, hung up by his thumbs and beaten so severely that "his poor body was one great bleeding wound." He was finally condemned to strangulation on a cross. When his martyrdom began, black clouds blotted out the sun, and as he rendered his soul to God a luminous cross lit up the sky.

12. The Holy Name of Mary. Eight days after the birth of the Blessed Virgin, her holy parents, Saint Joachim and Saint Anne, inspired by God, gave her the name of Mary. The name Mary means *Lady*, and also *Star of the Sea*. Just to say her holy name is a prayer. It gives everyone who does so favor with God and power over the devil. Blessed Pope Innocent XI set up the feast of the Holy Name of Mary in 1683, to thank her for the victory which the Catholic army under John Sobieski, King of Poland, gained over the Turks (Mohammedans), who were trying to sack Vienna and move in and conquer all the Catholics of the West. Mary's name occurs in the first part and in the second part of the *Hail Mary*. In the middle of the *Hail Mary*, one speaks the Holy Name of

Jesus. Great apostles of the Holy Name of Mary have been: Saint Anthony of Padua and Saint Bernard of Clairvaux. Saint Bernard of Clairvaux says, "O most holy Virgin Mary, your name is so sweet and admirable that one cannot say it without becoming inflamed with love toward God and toward you."

13. Saint Eulogius (608). He was a Syrian and became a monk when he was a young man. He was one of the greatest glories of his century. The Holy Scriptures and the Traditions of the Church were the subject matter of all his studies. He became a priest and then a patriarch of Alexandria. He was a great supporter and friend of Saint Gregory the Great.

14. The Exaltation of the Holy Cross (629). The Holy Cross on which Our Lord was crucified was first discovered by Saint Helena in the year 326. A Roman emperor, Hadrian, about two hundred years before, in order to stop Christians from venerating the mount of Calvary where Jesus was crucified, had raised a large mound of earth over it and dedicated a temple there to the goddess Venus. When Saint Helena arrived in Jerusalem, with the help of Saint Macarius, Bishop of that city, she had the

Our Sorrowful Mother

Temple of Venus destroyed. She hired two hundred workmen and one hundred soldiers to dig into the ground, and they found Our Lord's Cross. It was identified miraculously by the instantaneous cure of a little boy with a crippled arm and of a woman who was dying.

A large part of the Cross was placed in a church in Jerusalem. It was stolen in 615 by Chosroes, a king of the Persians. After many prayers and fasts, and a battle to recover it, the Emperor Heraclius defeated Chosroes and brought back the Holy Cross to Jerusalem, fourteen years after it was stolen. This was in the year 629. Part of the Cross was kept in Jerusalem, but a great part of it was brought to the Church of the Holy Cross in Jerusalem in Rome, one of the seven great

churches of the Holy City. Along with the finding of the True Cross, Saint Helena also found the nails and the inscription placed above Our Lord's head on the Cross. The nails are kept in churches in Europe. One of them is in the Iron Crown of Lombardy. The spear which pierced Our Lord's side is kept in one of the pillars in Saint Peter's in Rome. The inscription over Our Lord's sacred head is kept in the Church of the Holy Cross in Jerusalem in Rome, along with four other major relics; one of sacred nails, one of the thorns from Our Lord's crown, a finger from Saint Thomas the Apostle, and the cross of Saint Dismas (the good thief).

Saint Maternus (First Century). Saint Maternus was the son of the widow of Naim whom Jesus raised from the dead, as we are told in the seventh chapter of Saint

Pope Saint Cornelius

Luke. He became an ardent disciple of Saint Peter. He was named by Saint Peter to be the first Bishop of Cologne. A saint very devoted to Saint Maternus, centuries later, was Saint Peter Canisius who labored in Cologne and is one of the two members of the Society of Jesus who are Doctors of the Church. Saint Peter Canisius clearly identifies Saint Maternus as the widow of Naim's son.

15. Our Lady of Sorrows. This is the permanent feast dedicated to the mysteries of Our Lady's sorrows. There is also a movable feast of Our Lady's Sorrows commemorated on the sixth Friday of every Lent. The feast of today was extended to the whole Church in 1817 by Pope Pius VII to try to make atonement to the Blessed Mother of God for the horrors inflicted on all those she loved by the Masons and the Jews of the French Revolution. It was also raised to a solemn feast by Pope Saint Pius X in 1908 when he saw the outrages that were coming to the world with the approach of the First World War.

No heart ever burned with love of God or was united with Him more intimately in grief than was the heart of Mary. Simeon in prophecy told Our Lady when she presented Jesus in the Temple how complete and absolute her grief would be. He said to her, "Thine own soul a sword shall pierce." The Seven Sorrows of Our Lady, as we commemorate them in loving and mystical remembrance, are: (1) the prophecy of Simeon, (2) the flight into Egypt, (3) the losing of Jesus in the Temple when He was twelve years old, (4) Mary's meeting with Jesus on the way to Calvary—the Fourth Station of the Cross, (5) the Crucifixion and Death of Jesus—the Twelfth Station of the Cross, (6) the taking down of the Body of Jesus from the Cross and the placing of it in Mary's arms—the Thirteenth Station of the Cross, (7) the burial of Jesus in the tomb of Joseph of Arimathea on the afternoon of the first Good Friday—the Fourteenth and last Station of the Cross.

16. Saint Cornelius and Saint Cyprian (253 and 258). Saint Cornelius was the twenty-second Pope. Saint Cyprian was a bishop of Carthage in Africa. This Pope and this bishop are commemorated on the same day because Saint Cyprian died on the day that the body of Saint Cornelius was brought to Rome for veneration. This is how loving the Catholic Church is toward the precious remains of her holy saints. Saint Cornelius and Saint Cyprian are mentioned by name together every day by every Catholic priest in the Canon of the Mass.

17. The Stigmata of Saint Francis of Assisi (1224). Two years before the great Saint Francis of Assisi died, he went off to a lonely mountain called Mount Alvernia, to prepare himself by forty days of fasting and prayer for the feast of Saint Michael, the greatest of God's angels. On the feast of the Exaltation of the Holy Cross on September 14, Saint Francis received in his hands, feet and side, the Sacred Wounds from Our Lord's own body. Never was a saint more beautifully loved by Jesus than Saint Francis of Assisi. The wounds Jesus gave him continually bled for two more years, until he died in 1226. So that this beautiful event might have a feast day for itself the Stigmata of Saint Francis is commemorated today. The simple liturgy of this holy saint's life might be put this way: the crib in 1223, and the Cross in 1224.

Saint Hildegarde

Saint Hildegarde (1179). She was a nun who became an abbess, first on Mount Disibode and then on Mount Rupert in Germany. She was greatly admired and praised by Saint Bernard of Clairvaux. She wrote the lives of the two saints on whose mountains she lived: Saint Disibode and Saint Rupert.

18. Saint Joseph of Cupertino (1663). He was a Franciscan, a man of simple and innocent mind, who was first admitted and then dismissed by the Capuchins and later accepted by the Conventuals. Through sheer childlike simplicity he managed to learn enough theology to be ordained a priest. His love for God was so great that the mere mention of the name of Jesus would put him into an ecstasy. At Mass he was seen dozens of times floating in mid-air, in rapture. After a life of great humiliations, he finally departed from this world at the age of sixty.

Saint John Massias (1645). He was a Dominican lay brother who came from Spain and lived a humble life as a doorkeeper in a priory in Lima, in Peru. He was one of the great apostles of the souls in purgatory, and was sixty years old when he died. His special patron was Saint John the Evangelist who often appeared to him and miraculously transported him from place to place in his travels. He was a dear friend of another Dominican lay brother who lived at the same time and in a neighboring Dominican priory in Lima, Saint Martin de Porres.

19. Saint Januarius (304). Noted in the world everywhere, the great Saint Januarius was martyred for the Catholic Faith under the Emperor Diocletian. His body is now enshrined in the Cathedral of Saint Januarius in Naples. There are two vials of his blood there, which liquefy eighteen times every year, on three occasions.

It liquefies on the first Sunday in May, his feast day, September 19, and then on December 16, to commemorate the stopping of the eruption of the volcanic mountain, Mount Vesuvius, which occured in 1631. Millions of visitors have seen this liquefaction of Saint Januarius' blood. This miracle is a childlike tribute to the preciousness of the blood of every martyr who shed it for the truth of the one, holy and apostolic Church, founded by Jesus Christ for the salvation of all men.

20. Saint Eustace (118). He was a Roman general under the Emperor Trajan. He shed his blood for the Catholic Faith along with his beloved wife, Theopista, and his two sons, Agapitus and Theopistus. One day, when he was hunting, a stag with a cross between its horns faced him and told him to embrace the Catholic Faith. The same voice was heard, and the same apparition seen, by his wife. They were converted and immediately persecuted, and divided as a family. Saint Eustace was recalled to Rome by Emperor Hadrian because he was such a brilliant general. He was restored to his position in the Roman Army. But when, after a great victory he had scored in a battle, he and his family refused to sacrifice to pagan gods, they were all thrown into a brazen bull and slowly roasted to death. Saint Eustace is one of the fourteen Holy Helpers. He is invoked for protection against fire.

Saint Andrew Kim Taegon, Saint Paul Chong Hasang and 111 Companions (1839-1867). During the 1800's more than 10,000 Korean Catholics and their missionaries were martyred for the Faith in Korea. One hundred and thirteen were canonized in 1984. Among these martyrs were 3 bishops and 7 priests of the Paris Foreign Mission Society, the first native Korean priest—Saint Andrew Kim—and 102 lay Koreans. Saint Andrew was ordained secretly in China. Just before his martyrdom he wrote his fellow Christians to accept persecution as God's providence, the necessary ingredient to extend Christ's Church. Saint Paul Chong was a Catholic lay apostle who was instrumental in rallying and supporting Korean Catholics. His repeated petitions to Beijing and the Holy See for priests resulted in the arrival of missionary priests from France. He himself was studying for the priesthood when at age forty-five he was martyred.

Korea is unique in the annals of Church history because the Catholic Faith was brought to that country not by foreign priests but by lay Koreans. Korea was called the hermit nation and allowed its people no contact with other countries. Only once or twice a year were embassies sent to China. About 1773, during one of these trips, scholars acquired books on Christianity and became convinced of the truth of the Faith. They taught others Christianity but, without priests, the only sacrament the neophyte Church had was baptism. In 1784 Father Chu Mun-mo from China was smuggled into the country. One hundred years of persecution followed which ended in 1886 when Korea sought treaties with France and the United States.

21. Saint Matthew (65). Saint Matthew's name was originally Levi. He gathered taxes for the Romans in the town of Capharnaum. His vocation to be an Apostle of Jesus Christ is one of the most remarkable ever told. Jesus met Matthew, and had only to say to him, "Follow Me." Without hearing any sermon or seeing any miracles worked, Matthew immediately became a disciple of Our Lord. Just the look of the eyes of Jesus and the sound of His voice gave Matthew his vocation. Saint Matthew was given his name by Our Lord Himself. Matthew means *Gift of God*. Saint Matthew was the author of the first Gospel. This Gospel is in many ways the most glorious revelation ever made by God. Saint Matthew went to Africa to preach the word of God to Gentile pagans. In Ethiopia he raised from the dead the daughter of the king there. Her name was Iphigenia. Because of this outstanding miracle he converted the King, his whole family and many of his subjects to the Catholic Faith.

Saint Matthew dedicated Iphigenia to God as a virgin. She, too, was to become a saint, and her feast is the same as Saint Matthew's. When her father died, his successor, a king named Hirtacus, wished to marry Iphigenia. But, because, under Saint Matthew's direction, she had made a vow of virginity, she refused. She was a girl of admirable holiness and beauty. Saint Matthew wanted her wholly given to Jesus. Because of this, the King ordered Saint Matthew to be killed. He was martyred while celebrating Mass. Saint Matthew's body was later taken to the town of Salerno in Italy. It is kept there now in a church dedicated to his name.

22. Saint Thomas of Villanova (1555). He was an Augustinian friar who was Archbishop of Valencia in Spain. His great apostolate was among the poor. He was a consolation to the Catholic Church in the century of the Protestant Reformation. He was a great guardian of the truths that Protestants were trying, through Luther, Calvin and others, to destroy.

Saint Maurice and the Theban Legion (286). Saint Maurice was the commander of a legion in the Roman Army, called the Theban Legion because it was stationed in the Thebaid in upper Egypt. This Legion was composed of 6,666 men, every one of whom was Catholic. They were noble, holy and devout soldiers. They were ordered by the Roman Emperor Maximian to sacrifice to pagan gods. They all refused. The Emperor first killed every tenth man. But still the Legion would not give in. Again, he killed every tenth man. But the valiant regiment held out. Finally, when asked once more to sacrifice to the gods, Maurice in the name of his soldiers, replied, "O Caesar, we are your soldiers. But we are also the soldiers of Jesus Christ. From you, we receive our pay. But from Him, we receive eternal life. To you, we owe service. But to Him, we owe obedience. We are ready to follow you against the barbarians, but we are also ready to suffer death rather than renounce our Faith." They were then all slaughtered. Saint Maurice, their commander, knelt down and was beheaded.

23. Saint Linus (79). Saint Linus was the Second Pope of the Catholic Church. He ruled from the year 67 to the year 79, a period of twelve years. He was a Gentile. He shed his blood for the Faith, which Saint Peter preached. After he was martyred he was buried beside Saint Peter in Rome. His name is mentioned every day in the Canon of the Mass. He raised a dead man to life. He made the rule that women should wear veils or, at least, a head covering in church.

Saint Thecla (117). She was a young girl of eighteen who lived in Iconium, in Lycaonia. She was converted by Saint Paul. She then became one of his disciples and followed him on several of his missionary journeys. She was submitted to all sorts of suffering for her Faith. She was thrown to wild beasts in the amphitheater. She was thrown into a furnace of fire. She was cast out into the wilderness. Though she still lived, she is given, because of these sufferings, the title of martyr. Her name is invoked in the prayers for the dying. She was seventy-two years a Christian. She was ninety years old when she died.

Padre Pio (1968). Born Francisco Forgione in Pietrelcina, Southern Italy, at the age of 5 he consecrated himself to God in the spirit of Saint Francis of Assisi. He joined the Capuchin Friars at the age of 15 and given the name Fra (Brother) Pio, he

was ordained a priest in 1910. Eight years later on September 20, 1918 he received the stigmata, the five visible marks of the Our Lord's crucifixion. Padre Pio was the first priest ever to receive this gift. Innumerable souls flocked to him in the confessional for spiritual direction. His physical suffering from the stigmata was accompanied by great spiritual suffering. His personal letters reveal this as well as his intense union with God, love for the Blessed Sacrament, devotion to Mary and to the holy souls in Purgatory. He once said, referring to the Holy Sacrifice of the Mass that, "It would be easier for the earth to carry on without the sun than without Holy Mass." Padre Pio was given permission in February 1965 to continue saying the Traditional Latin Mass. Up to the time of his death on September 23, the wounds of the stigmata were still bleeding.

24. Our Lady of Ransom (1218).
This feast commemorates the founding of a Order dedicated to the Immaculate Mother of God in the year 1218, and fully established in the year 1223. Its founders were a saint named Peter Nolasco, a saint named Raymond of Pennafort (a General of the Dominican Order), and a king named James of Aragon. Its purpose was to rescue Catholics from captivity, from the Moors, by the help and protection and intercession of the powerful Mother of God. Prayers are especially said on this day in the Catholic Church to rescue England from the hands of the heretics who are still keeping the lovely people of that country from the true Faith and from the love of the Mother of God. England was once known as "Our Lady's Dowry."

25. Saint Cleophas (First Century).
Saint Cleophas was one of the greatest brothers and husbands and fathers and grandfathers who have ever been in the history of the world. His brother was Saint Joseph, the virginal spouse of the Blessed Virgin Mary. His wife was Saint Mary of Cleophas, whose feast day is April 9. Three of his sons, Saint Simon, Saint James the Less and Saint Jude—and two of his grandsons, Saint James the Greater and Saint John—were Apostles of Jesus. They are called in Holy Scripture, "the brethren of Our Lord." His daughter, Mary Salome, the mother of Saint James the Greater and Saint John, is also a saint. Her feast day is October 22. Still another son, Joseph Barsabas, who is called in Holy Scripture, "the Just," and who was one of the two nominated to take the place of the traitorous Judas Iscariot, is a saint and has a feast day on July 20. Saint Cleophas was one of the two disciples Our Lord met on the road to Emmaus on the day of His Resurrection, as we are told in the Gospel of Saint Luke, Chapter 24.

Our Lord stopped to have supper with these two disciples. At the end of the meal Jesus blessed bread and gave them His Sacred Body to eat. And Saint Luke tells us "they knew Him in the breaking of bread." Saint Cleophas was murdered in the very house in which he had been host to Our Lord on the first Easter Sunday.

Blessed Herman the Cripple (1054).
He was a Benedictine monk called "the Cripple" because of a deformity of his body. He entered the Benedictines when he was a child of seven. He became one of the great religious poets of the Church. It was Blessed Herman the Cripple who wrote the *Salve Regina* (the *Hail, Holy Queen*), which is recited at the end of Low Mass in the Catholic Church, and at the end of the rosary.

26. The Eight North American Martyrs (1642, 1646, 1648, 1649).
The eight North American martyrs were six priests and two lay brothers. They were heroic members of the Society of Jesus who were martyred in North America to bring the Faith that is necessary for salvation to the Huron, the Iroquois and the

Mohawk Indians. Five of the eight North American martyrs were put to death in what is now Canada, and three of them in New York State. There is a shrine to the United States' martyrs at Auriesville in New York State. There is a shrine to the Canadian martyrs at Fort Saint Mary near Midland, Ontario. The names of the eight North American martyrs are: Saint René Goupil, a lay brother martyred in 1642 in New York State; Saint Isaac Jogues, a priest, and Saint John de Lalande, a lay brother, both martyred in 1646 in New York State; Saint Anthony Daniel, a priest, martyred in Canada in 1648; Saint John de Brébeuf, Saint Charles Garnier, Saint Noel Chabanel and Saint Gabriel Lalemant, all priests, and all martyred in Canada in 1649.

Saint Michael the Archangel

Saint Isaac Jogues, after thirteen months' imprisonment by the Mohawks, had several fingers cut off his hand. He went back to Europe, but returned again to North America and was killed by tomahawk blows at Ossernenon, now called Auriesville, in New York State. Saint John de Brébeuf declared before he died, "I have a strong desire to suffer for Jesus Christ." He was tortured terribly, and a burning torch was put into his mouth, which strangled him.

Saint René Goupil said, "Jesus, Jesus, Jesus!" as he died. Saint John de Lalande, eighteen, was the youngest of the martyrs. Saint Noel Chabanel was thirty-six. Saint Isaac Jogues and Saint Gabriel Lalemant were thirty-nine. The oldest of the eight North American martyrs, Saint John de Brébeuf, was fifty-six when the Indians killed him.

27. Saint Cosmas and Saint Damian (303).

Saint Cosmas and Saint Damian were twins. They were Arabs. Both were physicians by profession. So much did they love those who had been baptized and received Holy Communion that they gave all their medical services to them without any charge. Saint Cosmas and Saint Damian were martyred for declaring that, "there is absolutely no salvation outside the

Catholic Church." Their relics are sacredly guarded in Rome. They are mentioned in the Canon of the Mass every day, and always in the Litany of the Saints.

28. Saint Wenceslaus (935). Saint Wenceslaus was the King of Bohemia who obtained his title from the Emperor Otto I. He was a noble and royal ruler, educated in the Catholic Faith by his grandmother, Saint Ludmilla. His great devotion was to the Blessed Sacrament. His father was a Christian. But his mother, Dragomir, pretending to be a Catholic, was a pagan at heart. She did everything to make him suffer. Saint Wenceslaus was killed before the Blessed Sacrament at midnight, by his brutal brother, Boleslas. Saint Wenceslaus was only thirty-two years old at the time. He had dedicated himself to God by a vow of chastity.

Saint Lawrence (Lorenzo) Ruiz and Companions (1633-1637).

These sixteen martyrs, 9 Dominican priests, 2 consecrated virgins, 2 brothers, and 3 laymen, were killed for their Faith in Nagasaki, Japan in 1633, 1634 and 1637. Saint Lorenzo was the first Filipino saint and martyr. Born in Manila of a Chinese father and a Filipino mother, he had been educated by the Dominicans. He was a married man and father. Accused of involvement in a criminal case, he fled to Japan with some Dominican missionaries to avoid arrest. There they were imprisoned for being Christians, and although they were cruelly tortured none would renounce the Faith.

29. Saint Michael the Archangel. The greatest and most powerful of all God's angels is Saint Michael. His name means *Who is like to God?* This was the challenge he issued to Lucifer when Lucifer offended God and was hurled by Saint Michael out of Heaven and into hell. It was Saint Michael who appeared to Abraham to forbid him to sacrifice his son Isaac. Saint Michael brought the plagues to Egypt. Saint Michael led the Israelites on their journey to the Promised Land and fought with Lucifer for the body of Moses. Saint Michael led Josue into the Promised Land. Saint Michael delivered the three young men from the fiery furnace. Saint Michael sent Habacuc to feed Daniel in the lions' den.

Saint Michael was the one who escorted the Blessed Virgin Mary into Heaven on the day of her Assumption. Saint Michael is the Guardian Angel of the Pope. He is the special protector of the Church. He is the special angel of the Blessed Sacrament. He leads the souls of the Just into Heaven when they die. He is invoked in the *Confiteor* at the beginning of Mass and in the lovely prayer said by the priest at the end of Mass: "Holy Archangel Michael, defend us in battle. Be our protection against the wickedness and snares of the devil...."

Saint Michael is invoked in all Masses for the dead, in the Offertory prayer. His name is mentioned in every solemn high Mass when the priest blesses the incense. He is the first one named after Our Lady in the Litany of the Saints. He is invoked in the prayer for the dying. Saint Michael has two feast days: one on May 8, to commemorate the dedication of a chapel to him at Monte Gargano in Italy, in 525, and one on September 29, to commemorate the dedication of the great church to him in Rome, in 530.

Saint Gregory the Great was the Pope specially devoted to Saint Michael. Saint Michael appeared to Saint Joan of Arc and helped her in her battle against the English. He also appeared in France, in Normandy, in 709. A beautiful shrine was built to him on a hill there, the still famous Mont Saint-Michel. Devotion to Saint Michael went over from Normandy to Ireland, to Scotland, where he has been greatly reverenced and loved. Michael has become an almost total Irish name.

30. Saint Jerome (420). Saint Jerome—who is called in Latin, *Hieronymus,* which means *holy name*—was born in Dalmatia. He was baptized a Catholic when he was eighteen years old. After living as a hermit in Palestine, Saint Jerome came to Rome. Much against his will, because of his great humility, he was ordained a priest. He was the great friend and ally of Saint Damasus, the thirty-ninth Pope. Saint Damasus commissioned him to translate the whole Bible into Latin. It took Saint Jerome fourteen years to make his first version in Latin of the Holy Scripture, in what is known as the *Vulgate.*

Saint Jerome had a great devotion and love for the Blessed Virgin Mary. He went to Bethlehem, and lived near the crib where Our Lord was born. He had two wonderful disciples there, a beautiful noble Roman woman, Saint Paula, and her daughter, Saint Eustochium, who set up three convents for nuns under Saint Jerome's direction. Saint Jerome had a great devotion to the Guardian Angels. He is the Doctor of the Church who assures us—and the Church has completely confirmed this—that each one of us has a Guardian Angel for himself. It was also Saint Jerome who beautifully let us know that Saint Cleophas was the brother of Saint Joseph. This explains why Saint James, Saint Simon and Saint Jude, the sons of Saint Cleophas, and Saint James the Greater and Saint John, his grandsons, are referred to as "the brethren of Our Lord."

Saint Jerome died in Bethlehem, with his head in the manger where Our Lord was born. His body is now kept in the Church of Saint Mary Major in Rome, where Our Lord's crib is also kept. Saint Jerome wrote the lives of two wonderful saints—Saint Paul the Hermit and Saint Paula, the beautiful Roman widow.

Saint Jerome is one of the thirty-three Doctors of the Universal Church. He is one of the eight Doctors who were priests. Two of the Doctors of the Church were Popes, three were cardinals, five were patriarchs, ten were bishops, one was an abbot, one was a deacon, and three were women.

Saint Jerome

October

The Month of the Most Holy Rosary

1. Saint Remigius (Remi) (533). He was the great Bishop of Rheims in France. He baptized King Clovis, King of the Franks, on Christmas Day in the year 496. It was due to this great apostolic achievement that France moved as a nation into the Catholic Church, though there had been many individuals and groups of Catholics there before. Saint Remigius was made Archbishop of Rheims when he was only twenty-two years old. He was bishop there for seventy-four years. He died when he was ninety-six years old.

Saint Remigius

2. The Holy Guardian Angels. The mission of the Guardian Angels is, as Saint Paul tells us, to serve the future heirs of salvation. Every kingdom, country, diocese, church and religious order has its protecting Guardian Angel. So has every person. Each bishop of the Catholic Church has two Guardian Angels. Our Guardian Angel is given us at the moment of our birth, stays with us all through life, comforts us in Purgatory, and escorts us, if we are saved, into Heaven. There is a special angel in each church to record all distractions and irreverences that occur there. The greatest joy any of us can give our Guardian Angel is to receive Holy Communion and make our breast a tabernacle of the Eternal God before Whom this angel can adore. Many of the saints saw their Guardian Angels. Saint Rose of Lima did, and so did Saint Gemma Galgani. And so did Saint Frances of Rome, Saint Margaret of Cortona and Saint Bridget of Sweden. A great Pope, Saint Gregory the Great, was tenderly de-

Guardian Angel

voted to his Guardian Angel. Saint Catherine of Siena saw her Guardian Angel. Saint Francis de Sales had, as one of his special devotions, reverence for the Holy Angels who have charge of the care of the tabernacle in every Catholic Church.

There are nine choirs of angels, and three hierarchies. These choirs and hierarchies are: first hierarchy, Angels, Archangels and Principalities; second hierarchy, Powers, Virtues and Dominions; third hierarchy, Thrones, Cherubim and Seraphim. This is in the order of ascent. It is from the first hierarchy—Angels, Archangels, and Principalities—that guardians are chosen by God for man. Angels are for individuals. Archangels are for parishes, churches and religious communities. And Principalities are for provinces, countries and nations. Saint Augustine says, "Go where we will, our angels are always with us." Saint Jerome says, "So sublime is the dignity of the human soul that from its birth there is appointed to each one a Guardian Angel." And Saint Bernard says, "Make the holy angels your friends. No matter how weak we may be, or lowly our condition, or how great the dangers which surround us, we have nothing to fear under the protection of these guardians." In every difficulty, danger and temptation, Saint Bernard urges us to invoke our Guardian Angel.

3. Saint Thèrése of Lisieux (1897).

This beautiful little girl of the 19th century was called Saint Thèrése of the Child Jesus and of the Holy Face. She is now one of the best-known saints in the whole world. She became a Carmelite nun when she was fifteen years old. She died of consumption when she was only twenty-four. In nine short years as a nun, she shed the luster of her love so that all might know it by her prayers, her works and her simple and innocent writing. Her prayers were especially for priests and the foreign missions. She has been united with Saint Francis Xavier and made one of the great patrons of all missionary work done by Catholic priests.

Saint Thèrése called herself the "Little Flower of Jesus," and by that name she is known everywhere. Her great devotions were to the Blessed Sacrament and to Our Lady, who once appeared to her in a grave sickness. Even when daily Communion was not in practice, a holy priest, sensing her love of the Blessed Eucharist, for a time gave her Communion every day. It is in no small way due to Saint Thèrése of Lisieux that daily Communion was restored by Saint Pius X, the holy Pope who loved the Little Flower so much. She was declared a Doctor of the Church on Mission Sunday, October 19, 1997.

Blessed Columba Marmion (1923). Joseph Aloysius Marmion was born in Dublin, Ireland on Holy Thursday, April 1, 1858. Although he dreamed of missionary work, after his ordination in 1881 he became a parish priest. Five years later he entered the newly-founded Benedictine Abbey of Maredsous in Belgium, taking the name Columba. Dom Columba had a reputation for holiness and joy, accuracy of doctrine and clarity of style. Laughter was one of his hallmarks. "Joy is the echo of God's life in us," he wrote. He gained renown for his spiritual direction and retreats for various communities, especially Carmelite nuns. On several occasions he manifested the gift of prophecy concerning souls. Elected Abbot of Maredsous, he aided the Anglican Monks of Caldey Abbey to recognize the supreme authority of the pope and convert to the one, true Faith. His three classic spiritual works are, *Christ, the Life of the Soul, Christ in His Mysteries* and *Christ, the Ideal of the Monk*. His last words were "My God, my mercy."

4. Saint Francis of Assisi (1226).

Francis of Assisi was called by Pope Benedict XV the "greatest image of Our Lord that has ever been." He was born in 1182. His name was John Bernardone. His father was a rich cloth merchant who had to travel frequently to France and who spoke French fluently. His son John (Giovanni) learned to speak French so well that he was called, in Italy, "Francesco," which means *the Frenchman*. When he became a religious he gave up his family name and took his nickname for his title.

Saint Francis of Assisi, in imitation of Jesus with His Twelve Apostles, chose twelve companions with which to begin his Religious Order of the Friars Minor. His Order was approved in 1215. He made a journey to foreign lands so as to be martyred for the Catholic Faith. But he came back unharmed by way of Palestine. Saint Francis of Assisi built the first Christmas crib in

Saint Francis of Assisi

1223. He was given the stigmata, the five wounds of Jesus, in his hands and feet and side, when he was praying on a mountain in 1224. This was when he was making a forty-day crusade of prayer and fasting to Saint Michael, the great Archangel who protects the Catholic Church from its enemies. Along with Saint Clare of Assisi, a beautiful and radiant young girl who joined him when she was eighteen, Saint Francis founded the Poor Clares, an Order for women under the Franciscan Rule. He also founded a Third Order of Saint Francis for the sanctification of lay people who want to practice some of the works of humility and poverty for which the Franciscans are noted. There are various branches of the first Order of Saint Francis, including the Friars Minor, the Capuchins and the Conventuals. The Franciscan order has given the Catholic Church more than one hundred canonized saints.

5. Saint Placid (541). This was the notable Benedictine monk who, two years before the death of Saint Benedict himself, along with his two brothers, Saint Eutychius and Saint Victorinus, and his sister, Saint Flavia, and thirty Benedictine monks, was martyred on the Island of Sicily, in the town of Messina. These are the Benedictine protomartyrs. Saint Benedict was so proud of them that he spoke of these martyrs constantly during the two years he lived after them, until he himself went to Heaven.

Saint Bruno

Blessed Raymond of Capua (1399). He was the Dominican friar who was the spiritual director of Saint Catherine of Siena. He wrote the life of Saint Catherine of Siena and also the life of Saint Agnes of Montepulciano. He became General of the Dominican Order. He did much to promote and preserve its greatness.

Saint Faustina Kowalska (1938). She was born in Poland in 1905 and even in her childhood was noted for her holiness. She entered the Congregation of the Sisters of Our Lady of Mercy in Warsaw when she was 20 years old. Our Lord showed Faustina how pleasing to Him menial work is when done for love of Him by giving her a vision of potatoes changed into roses. During her whole religious life she had deep mystical experiences. She frequently suffered the pains of Our Lord's Passion as a victim soul for the conversion of sinners. Our Lord entrusted to her the mission of teaching the world of His Divine Mercy, saying, "My daughter, tell the whole world about My inconceivable mercy." He asked that the first Sunday after Easter be designated as the Feast of Divine Mercy. He said, "On that day are open all the floodgates through which graces flow."

6. Saint Bruno (1101).

Saint Bruno was the founder of the great Carthusian Order. He was born in Cologne, in Germany, in 1030. He later retired to France, to a solitary place known as *Grande Chartreuse*, from which the name Carthusian is derived. His Order is the most contemplative of all the Orders of Monks in the Catholic Church. Saint Bruno believed that in saintly contemplation of the soul along with God, the highest adoration, love and prayer is evoked. A monk in a

Queen of the Most Holy Rosary

small cell for personal prayer, in a simple chapel for common prayer, and in a country garden for work, was his idea of perfect preparation on a mountain for the life that awaits us at death. He promised all true Catholic contemplatives a peace, which this world does not know, the source of which is the Holy Ghost, the Third Person of the Blessed Trinity, with all His Divine Gifts and Fruits.

7. The Most Holy Rosary.

The Holy Rosary is a lovely instrument of prayer. By it we direct our minds and our hearts to God as we move our mouths and our fingers while we pray. The Rosary was given personally to Saint Dominic by Our Blessed Lady in the year 1214, in Toulouse, in France. Saint Dominic was the first great apostle of the Holy Rosary. Our Lady appeared to Saint Dominic many times. Once she came with Saint Catherine of Alexandria and Saint Cecilia as her companions. Mary came with the Divine Infant Jesus in her arms the day she gave Saint Dominic the Holy Rosary. Saint Dominic died in 1221, at the age of fifty-one. The last great apostle of the Holy Rosary was Saint Louis Marie de Montfort, who died in 1716 at the age of forty-three. The great Pope who promoted the cult of the Holy

Rosary was Saint Pius V, who died in 1572. In the year 1571 he set up the feast of the Most Holy Rosary on October 7. The Catholics won a great naval victory that day over the Turks at Lepanto, who were trying to crush them and blot out their Faith. Their protection was the Holy Rosary.

Another great victory of the Catholics over the Turks because of the Holy Rosary was in 1716, in Hungary, the year Saint Louis Marie died. Pope Gregory XIII, in 1573, Pope Clement XI, in 1716, and Pope Leo XIII, in 1888, all did much to make the feast of the Most Holy Rosary on October 7 more and more observed and reverenced in the liturgy of the Church. The Rosary is not only a prayer, it is a weapon. The little beads of love that are strung on the rosary are bullets of destruction against the enemies of the Catholic Faith and the enemies of one's salvation. In a simple chaplet, five decades of the rosary, the Holy Name of Jesus invoked fifty-four times, and the Holy Name of Mary, one hundred and seven times. No Catholic should ever be without the rosary in his possession, night or day. The devil is afraid of these beads as they lie in our pockets or are held in our hands.

8. Saint Bridget of Sweden (1373). She was the noble and saintly woman who, in her widowhood, founded a monastery on the Shore of Lake Wetten in Sweden. Her Order is known as the Bridgettines. One of her daughters is a Saint, Saint Catherine of Sweden, who persuaded the man to whom she was betrothed to join her in a vow of chastity. The year before Saint Bridget died she had constant visions of Our Lord's life and death and passion. She was even shown the humble cave at Bethlehem where Jesus was born, and she saw, at the moment of the Nativity, Our Lady kneel and adore Him, and exclaim, "O welcome, my Lord and my Child!"

9. Saint Denis (95). Saint Denis is called "the Areopagite" because, as a judge, he lived on the hill of Ares in Athens. He was converted to the Catholic Faith by Saint Paul and was soon brought by him to see the Blessed Virgin Mary in Jerusalem. Saint Denis said, when he beheld the Mother of Jesus, that if he had not been prevented from doing so, so outstanding was Mary's beauty, he would have fallen on his face and adored her as God. Saint Denis was the first Bishop of Athens in Greece. He later became the first Bishop of Paris in France. He was transported with the Apostles miraculously to Jerusalem to witness the death and burial of Our Blessed Lady, as were also Saint

Saint Bridget of Sweden

Timothy, and Saint Hierotheus of Athens, teacher and friend of Saint Denis. Saint Denis was beheaded under the Roman Emperor Domitian. He is the patron saint of France. He is one of the fourteen Holy Helpers, and is invoked against demons.

Saint Abraham (2000 B.C.). The great patriarch of pre-Christian times was Abraham, who lived two thousand years before the coming of Christ. He was first called Abram, which means *father*. His name was later changed by God to Abraham, which means *great father*, father of a multitude. Abraham was a type of God the Father's generosity in sacrificing His Divine Son for our salvation. Abraham was asked by God to sacrifice his son Isaac. Abraham agreed to do so because it was God's request. But God stopped Abraham, and Abraham sacrificed a ram instead. Abraham's name is mentioned everyday by every Catholic priest in the Canon of the Mass, in the second prayer after the consecration of the Most Precious Blood. Mary, the Mother of God, uses Abraham's name in her beautiful canticle, the *Magnificat.* Mary calls those who fully acknowledge her Divine Maternity and share its fruits, "the seed of Abraham forever." Abraham was one hundred and seventy-five years old when he died.

10. Saint Francis Borgia (1572). Saint Francis Borgia was the Duke of Gandia and Viceroy of Catalonia, and intimate and trusted friend of the King and Queen of Spain. When his wife died, he distributed his vast estates and titles among his children and became a religious. He joined the Society of Jesus and was its third General. He was one of the great opponents of the rise of Protestantism in the sixteenth century. Saint Francis Borgia died in 1572, the same year as his great friend, Saint Pius V, who gave us the feast of the Most Holy Rosary. Saint Francis Borgia's last words as he was dying were, "I long for Jesus."

11. The Divine Maternity of Our Lady. This glorious feast was established as a commemoration of the Third Ecumenical Council of the Church at Ephesus, in 431. It was set up for our own time in 1931 by Pope Pius XI, fifteen hundred years after the Council of Ephesus. The Catholic Church infallibly declares and defines the Divine Maternity of Our Lady. The Catholic Church tells us that in order to be saved we must believe with our full hearts that the same Person Who is the Son of God the Eternal Father in His Divine nature is also the Child of Mary the Virgin in His human nature. Anyone who refuses or hesitiates to call Mary the Mother of God will never be saved. Saint Elizabeth, the cousin of Our Lady, cried out for joy in her doorway when Mary came to visit her after the Annunciation and said, "And whence is this to me that the Mother of my Lord should come to me!" (Luke 1:43). Saint Paul clearly tells us in the Epistle to the Galatians, Chapter 4, verse 4, "God sent His Son born of a woman." The dignity of the Mother of God transcends anything that can ever be imagined. It is God giving Himself in fullness to a creature in relationship and in love. Now that God has become man, the Second Person of the Blessed Trinity through all eternity must call God the Father His Father and Mary the Virgin His Mother. What God the Father is to the Second Person of the Blessed Trinity by nature, Mary the Virgin is to Him by grace. At the command of Mary, God must now obey. The two loveliest prayers a Catholic can say are the *Our Father, Who art in Heaven*, and the *Hail, Mary, full of grace.* It was the Council of Ephesus, which gave us the end of the *Hail Mary:* "Holy Mary, Mother of God, pray for us sinners." And through Catholic love and reverence there was added the phrase, "now and at the hour of our death, Amen."

Saint Alexander Sauli (1592). Once as a youth he had pushed his way to the front of a crowd of people who were being entertained by acrobats and tumblers and, waving a crucifix in the air, warned them to be aware of the dangers of frivolous entertainment and pleasure-seeking. As a young man he joined the order of Barnabites and was ordained. He quickly became known as a great preacher and was the spiritual director of Saint Charles Borromeo. Firm and zealous in implementing the reforms of Pope Saint Pius V as a means of halting the inroads of Protestantism into the True Faith, Saint Alexander was appointed Bishop of Corsica. So wisely did he rule that he received the surname of Apostle of Corsica. Saint Philip Neri, his close friend, called him a model bishop. This saint of the Catholic Reformation is known to have performed many miracles such as calming a stormy sea and prophesying the future.

12. Our Lady of the Pillar (36).

This feast commemorates the apparition of the Mother of God during her own lifetime to Saint James, the great apostle of Spain, in the year 36, in the town of Saragossa in Spain. This was to encourage Saint James to be the apostle to the great country of Spain, which by its valiant Catholicism and its many saints was to mean so much to the one true Faith in the centuries to come. The feast of Our Lady of the Pillar has a very important significance to us Americans. Christopher Columbus packed his boat to sail from Spain to America on August 2, 1492, the feast of Our Lady of the Angels. Columbus and his men sailed all the rest of August and the whole of September without sighting the land they were looking for. And then October approached. Columbus said if he did not see land on October 12, the feast of Our Lady of the Pillar, he would turn and go back to Spain. By the special providence of Our Lady, it was on October 12 that Columbus first saw land. Columbus did not choose this day because it was October 12 simply. He chose it because it was the feast of Our Lady the Pillar. In childlike innocence, every one of us must admit that it was because of the protection of the Blessed Virgin Mary, the Mother of God, that America was discovered. The whole New World was meant to belong to her.

On the second voyage of Columbus to America in 1493, he put his whole expedition under the protection of the Immaculate Conception. He called the boat on which he sailed on this second voyage, Gracious Mary. Columbus had called the island on which he first landed in the New World on his first voyage, San Salvador, which means Holy Saviour. Enemies of the Catholic Faith, of the Blessed Virgin, of all true history and, of course, of Columbus himself, have changed the name of that island to Watling Island.

On his second voyage to America, Columbus saw a group of Islands south of San Salvador. He called these islands the Virgin Islands, in honor of the 11,010 virgins who were martyred with Saint Ursula in Cologne, in 383.

13. Saint Edward the Confessor (1066).

Saint Edward the Confessor, known as Good King Edward, was raised to the throne of England when he was forty years old, on Easter Sunday in 1042. To satisfy his nobles and his people, and so that England might have a queen, he married a noblewoman named Edith, but he lived with her as a brother with a sister because he had already vowed himself to the Blessed Virgin in chastity. He had a great devotion to the poor, especially to beggars and to lepers. God gave him the power of working miracles to heal diseases. During his twenty-four years as king, England prospered as almost never before. Saint Edward rebuilt all the ruined churches he could find. His greatest and noblest work by way of restoring a church was Westminster Abbey, which it took him nearly sixteen years to construct. It was completed just before he died. His saintly body was buried in it. It remains there even to this day, unfortunately now in the possession of Anglican heretics. Saint John the Evangelist, to whom Saint Edward had a great devotion, came to escort him to Heaven when he died.

Saint Gerald (909). He was a Count of Aurillac in France. He led a life of great and heroic virtue. He founded a Benedictine Abbey right on his own estate. He made it one of the most beautiful religious houses of his day. His great devotion was to the poor.

14. Saint Callistus (222). He

was the seventeenth Pope and reigned for five years. He built a beautiful church to Our Lady called "Holy Mary beyond the Tiber." He was martyred for the Faith.

15. Saint Teresa of Avila (1582). She is the radiant

Carmelite nun and prioress who was born at the beginning of the sixteenth century and died at the age of sixty-seven in the year 1582. Saint Teresa of Avila was one of twelve children. From reading the lives of the saints, when she was seven years old, she wanted to go and be martyred by the Moors. Her mother died when she was twelve. When she was eighteen she became a Carmelite. She has often been called "the greatest woman of Christendom." She wrote three wonderful spiritual books: her *Autobiography*, telling of her visions and revelations; the *Way of Perfection*, for the direction of her nuns; and *The Interior Castle,* a study in mystical theology.

It was reading Saint Jerome that gave her her vocation. And

Saint Teresa of Avila

after she became a Carmelite, it was reading Saint Augustine that drove her to the heights of perfection. She suffered dreadfully from physical sicknesses, and was constantly attacked by the devil. Our Lord once appeared to her, and asked her who she was. She replied, "I am Teresa of Jesus." Our Lord then said to her, "I am Jesus of Teresa." In the year 1558 her heart was pierced by the lance of an angel, which left her with a consuming love of God. Saint Teresa's special patron in Heaven was Saint

Joseph, the virginal spouse of Mary. Her spiritual friends and directors among the saints were: Saint Peter of Alcántara, a Franciscan, Saint Francis Borgia, a member of the Society of Jesus, Saint John of the Cross, a Carmelite, and Saint Louis Bertrand, a Dominican. She was also indebted for spiritual direction to a townsman of her own, Blessed John of Avila, a very humble and worthy priest.

When Our Lord once appeared to Saint Teresa and told her to carry out a certain work, she asked Our Lord why He did not tell some learned theologian to do this. Our Lord replied to her: "Theologians will do nothing to enter into personal communication with Me. Repulsed by them, I must choose women to open to them My Heart and speak of My affairs."

Saint Teresa's motto was, "To suffer or to die." She craved for martyrdom so that she could see God in the Beatific Vision. When she was dying, and Holy Viaticum was brought to her, she said, "O God, it is about time that we see each other." The day she died, by dramatic arrangement, Pope Gregory XIII changed the calendar to

make allowance for the proper insertion of Leap-year day. Ten days were dropped out of the calendar to commemorate one thing in one way, but to commemorate the going to God of the great Teresa of Avila in another, and though she died on October 4, her feast is on October 15. The day Saint Teresa died, she was welcomed into Heaven by the ten thousand martyrs of Mount Ararat, who were crucified there in 138 A.D., and to whom she had a great devotion all her life. These martyrs came to welcome her and escort her to the Beatific Vision. She was declared the first woman Doctor of the Church.

16. Saint Gerard Majella (1755). He was a poor boy of Southern Italy. His great loves were the Blessed Sacrament, Our Lady and the crucifix. He used to say, "Suffer only for God and your suffering will

Saint Hedwig

bring you Heaven on earth." He tried to become a Capuchin friar but was refused on account of his ill health. The Redemptorists took him when he was twenty-three. He lived with them as a lay brother. His obedience to his superiors was the most exemplary in the history of that congregation. Every moment not given to work he spent in adoration of the Most Blessed Sacrament. He was, by his prayers, a great missioner and converted hundreds of sinners to repentance. Saint Gerard Majella died at the age of twenty-nine. He is one of the seven saints of the Redemptorist Congregation.

Saint Marguerite d'Youville (1755). Marie Marguerite Lajemmerais was born in Quebec, Canada in 1701 and educated by the Ursulines. She married Francois d'Youville in 1722, who proved to be a difficult and dishonest man. She was widowed with two boys eight years later and had her husband's debts to pay, but she still found time to devote herself to the poor and infirm. In 1737 she and three other women founded the Grey Nuns, or Sisters of Charity, to work in hospitals. Before Saint Marguerite died at the age of seventy she had the pleasure of seeing both her sons become priests. The Grey Nuns run schools, hospitals and orphanages from Canada to South America.

Saint Hedwig (1243).

Saint Hedwig was the aunt of Saint Elizabeth of Hungary. She was a queen. She did much to foster convents for the consecration to Jesus and Mary of young Catholic girls. She herself became a nun in her widowhood. She was canonized twenty-three years after her death.

17. Saint Margaret Mary (1690).

Saint Margaret Mary Alacoque was a Visitation nun who, in the year 1675, received

Saint Margaret Mary

from Our Lord, Who appeared to her out of the depths of the Blessed Sacrament, the assignment to be the great apostle of the public veneration of his Most Sacred Heart. Her spiritual supporter and director was a saintly priest of the Society of Jesus, Saint Claude de la Colombiére. He died eight years before her. Our Lord told Saint Margaret Mary that He received in the Blessed Eucharist only irreverence and ingratitude. It was to her that Our Lord made the request that the Friday after the octave of Corpus Christi be set aside as a special feast in honor of the Sacred Heart. It was to Saint Margaret Mary that Jesus made the request that Catholics receive Him in Holy Communion on each first Friday of the month, and keep the Holy Hour on the night before the first Friday with the Blessed Sacrament exposed.

The great apostles of the feast of Corpus Christi and the feast of the Sacred Heart were girls; both were nuns. It was Saint Juliana of Cornillon, an Augustinian nun who died in 1258 in Belgium, who was chosen by God to work for the institution of the feast of Corpus Christi. It was Saint Margaret Mary, a Visitation nun who died in 1690, who was chosen by God to work for the institution of the feast of the Most Sacred Heart.

18. Saint Luke (84).

Saint Luke the Evangelist was a doctor of medicine in Antioch in Syria. He was converted to Christianity and became a disciple of Saint Paul. He is the one Gentile who wrote books in the New Testament. His two books are the third Gospel and the Acts of the Apostles. All we know about the Incarnation,

Saint Peter of Alcántara

birth and childhood of Our Lord comes to us from Saint Luke. He was a great painter. He painted a most beautiful picture of the Blessed Virgin Mary, to whom his whole life was devoted. Saint Luke was martyred for the Catholic Faith.

19. Saint Peter of Alcántara (1562).

He was a Franciscan. He was a great friend and encourager of the great Saint Teresa of Avila. He was the son of the Governor of Alcántara. At sixteen years of age, he distributed all his fortune to the poor so as to become a Franciscan. Though given high offices in his Order, Saint Peter resigned from them. He went to live in the mountains of Portugal as a hermit. He instituted the Alcantarine reform in the Franciscan Order and led with his friars a life of the utmost austerity and poverty. He ate only every third day. He lived in a cell so small he could never lie down to sleep. He died when he was sixty-three years old.

20. Saint John Cantius (1473).

He was born at Kenty in Poland. Its Latin name is Cantius, and that is why he is called Saint John Cantius. He became a student and eventually a professor and a preacher at Cracow. He strengthened and brightened the Catholic Faith in the lovely country of Poland by his brilliant, childlike and apostolic teaching. He made many pilgrimages to Rome, on foot and all alone. His devotion to the Passion of Our Lord was so great that he walked all the way to Jerusalem to see where Jesus died, hoping to be martyred there by the Turks. A notable story told about Saint John Cantius is that once, on his way to Rome, some robbers beat him and took from him all his money. He had some gold pieces sewed up in his clothes when he told the robbers he had no more money. He had forgotten these gold pieces were there. When he discovered them, he ran after the robbers and gave them the money. The robbers were so impressed by this simplicity and innocence that they threw themselves at his feet, gave him back all they had stolen from him and begged his forgiveness.

Saint Irene (653). She was a Portuguese nun who was martyred in defense of her chastity. Her body was thrown into the river and then miraculously recovered. So many miracles were worked at her tomb that she was canonized as a saint. Her shrine, which is at "Santarem" (Saint Irene), has been in no small part responsible for the beautiful quality of the Catholic Faith which the Portuguese people have kept even to this day.

21. Saint Ursula (383). When the pagan Saxons started to invade England in the fourth century, with the intention of destroying the Catholic Faith and the purity of all young English virgins, a great group of English girls, numbering ten friends of Saint Ursula, and each having a thousand companions—which made their number in all, 11,011—fled from England to the Continent. In the year 383, Saint Ursula and her 11,010 companions were all slaughtered for their purity and their Faith. This great martyrdom occurred in Cologne, in Germany. A shrine has been erected to them there, containing as many of their bones as could be rescued. A Religious Order of nuns in the Catholic Church in honor of Saint Ursula was established by Saint Angela Merici in the year 1535. They are known as the Ursulines.

22. Saint Mary Salome (First Century). Saint Mary Salome, a daughter of Saint Mary of Cleophas, was first called simply, Salome. She added Mary to her name in honor of the Blessed Virgin. Her father and her mother both were saints. She was the wife of Zebedee, who was not a saint. But she was the mother of Saint John and Saint James the Greater. And her brothers were Saint Simon, Saint James the Less and Saint Jude, Apostles, and Saint Joseph Barsabas, a disciple of Our Lord.

Saint Mary Salome was one of the "three Marys" who stood by the Cross of Jesus when He died, and to whom He appeared on the first Easter Sunday. She and her mother, and Saint Mary Magdalen, Saint Martha and companions, were put on a boat which had no sails and no oars, during a persecution by the Jews in the year 47, and were pushed out to sea. The boat miraculously floated unharmed to the south of France. Saint Mary Salome died in France. She is still venerated there with great love and devotion.

Saint Mary Dominic Mazzarello (1881). She was one of the Daughters of Mary, Help of Christians, a branch of nuns affiliated with the Order of Salesians and founded by Saint John Bosco. Her great apostolate was among motherless girls. She became superioress of her Order. She governed it with great wisdom until she died. She looked on Saint John Bosco as the very mouthpiece of God. She sought his guidance in all things. Her Order, now known as the Salesian Sisters, is spread all over the world. The great devotions of Saint Mary Dominic Mazzarello were to Our Lord in the Blessed Sacrament and to the Blessed Mother of God. "Trust Our Lady," she said. "She will help you in all things." Saint Mary Dominic died when she was only forty-four years old, the same age as Saint Francis of Assisi. Every time she heard the clock strike, she said, "One hour less here. One hour nearer to eternity." Her feast day is also celebrated on May 14.

23. Saint Anthony Mary Claret (1870). He was born in Catalonia, in Spain, in 1807. He was ordained a priest in 1835. He was a missioner in his own country and in the Canary Islands, which are just off the northwest coast of Africa. He formed a group of priests into an order known as the Missionary Sons of the Immaculate Heart of Mary—also known as the Claretians. He was made Archbishop of Santiago in Cuba, in 1851. He was recalled to Spain in 1857. He was exiled with his queen in the revolution there of 1868. Many attempts were made on his life. He is the one saint so far canonized who was present at the Vatican Council of 1869-1870.

Saint Ignatius of Constantinople (877). He was the son of a Byzantine emperor. He was first a monk, then an abbot, and then a patriarch of Constantinople.

He suffered much from the horrible Photius, who was the father of the Greek Schism that eventually led to the so-called Greek Orthodox Church, which divided people from unity with the Holy Roman Catholic Church, outside of which no one can be saved.

24. Saint Raphael. There are seven special angels who stand before the throne of God. We know the names of three of them. They are: Saint Michael, whose name is a challenge and means *Who is like to God?*; Saint Gabriel, whose name is a message and means *Strength of God* (God going the limit by way of grace); and Saint Raphael, whose name is a comfort and means *Healer of God* or *Medicine of God.* In some loving ways, Saint Michael is the angel of Saint Joseph, Saint Gabriel is the angel of Our Lady and Saint Raphael is the angel of Our Lord.

Tobias and the Archangel Raphael

Saint Raphael was the angel who came to console Our Lord in His bitter agony in the Garden of Olives, when Jesus had sweat blood. Saint Raphael's name is mentioned in Catholic prayers, including the Litany of the Saints. He is one of our special helpers in times of sickness and the hardships that go with it. His story in the Old Testament makes up nearly all of the Book of Tobias.

25. This is the earliest day that the feast of **Christ the King** (the last Sunday in October) can occur. The latest day on which it can fall is October 31.

Saint Crispin and Saint Crispinian (285). They were shoemakers by trade who, because of the simple holiness and innocence of their lives, were known to be Catholics. They courageously refused to yield to the persecutors of their Faith who wanted them to apostatize. At the beginning of the reign of Diocletian they were both beheaded. They are the patrons saints of Catholic cobblers.

Saint Isidore the Farmer (1170). Saint Isidore was born in Madrid, in Spain. He worked all his life in the field. He is a patron saint of Madrid. His wife, too, was a saint. Her name is Saint Mary de la Cabeza. He is the patron saint of farmers.

26. Saint Evaristus (121). He was the sixth Pope of the Catholic Church. He succeeded Saint Anacletus in the year 112. He was the Pope who divided Rome into its parishes and set up the dignity of cardinal priests. Saint Evaristus was martyred for the Catholic Faith. He was buried near the tomb of Saint Peter.

27. Saint Frumentius (380). He was born in Tyre near the Holy Land. He knew Saint Athanasius and was appointed by him Bishop of Ethiopia in Africa. He went there with his brother, Saint Aedesius, and brought thousands of Africans into the one true Faith. His great patron was Saint Matthew, the Evangelist, who was martyred in Ethiopia in the year 65.

28. Saint Simon and Saint Jude (67). They were Apostles of Our Lord and were brothers. We are let known what eager and ardent apostles of the Faith Saint Simon and Saint Jude were first, by the distance they traveled to preach the Gospel (they went eventually as far as Persia), and also by the names given to them. Saint Simon is called the Zealot, both to distinguish him from Simon Peter and to show his ardor in preaching the true Faith. Saint Jude is called Thaddeus, which means *bighearted.*

Saint Simon was martyred by being crucified. Saint Jude was martyred by being clubbed to death. Both were killed in the same year. Their relics were brought back and were placed near those of Saint Peter and Saint Paul in the Vatican, in Rome. Saint Jude is the author of one of the Epistles in the New Testament. "Keep yourselves in the love of God, waiting for the mercy of Our Lord Jesus Christ unto life everlasting," Saint Jude writes in his holy Epistle.

29. Saint Narcissus (222). Saint Narcissus was the Bishop of Jerusalem. He died when he was one hundred and sixteen years old. He was eighty years old when he was made Bishop of Jerusalem. He was a wonderful and paternal pastor of souls. Once, he miraculously changed water into oil to make lights for the lamps of the church on the vigil of Easter. Once, three men who made false witness against him were struck dead.

30. Saint Alphonsus Rodriquez (1617). The lifelong devotion of Saint Alphonsus Rodriquez was to Our Lady. He married a very holy young woman. But his wife died four years after their wedding, when he was thirty-one years old. He then applied for admission to the Society of Jesus. The superior of that Order kept refusing him because he thought he was a little too old. But finally, the Provincial of the Society of Jesus said, "Let us receive him on account of his holiness." He became a lay brother in the Society of Jesus and was made porter at the College of Montesión on the Island of Majorca, just east of Spain, in the Mediterranean. Prayer and mortification were what Saint Alphonsus called "the two wings" by which he would go to God. One of his disciples was the great Saint Peter Claver whom he urged to become the apostle of the Negroes in South America. His last word was a loud and lingering utterance of the Holy Name of Jesus.

31. This is the latest day on which the feast of **Christ the King** can occur.

Saint Wolfgang (994). He was a native of Swabia in Germany. He was educated by the Benedictines and joined that Order when he was forty years old. He was raised to the priesthood, and sent with a group of monks as missionaries to the Magyars and eventually was made Bishop of Ratisbon. He was tutor to the Emperor Henry II. He restored many of the Benedictine abbeys of his day, raised the standard of education and was so devoted to the poor that he became known as the Great Benefactor for those who were without material possessions. Saint Wolfgang's pupil, Emperor Henry II, became a saint. Saint Henry's feast day is July 15.

November

1. All Saints. This is the feast, not only of all saints who have been canonized, but of all saints who have not been canonized and are in Heaven. It is, in a generous way, the feast of all those who are still on earth and are trying to be saints. No one can be a saint without love for and protection by and devotion to the Blessed Virgin Mary. She is Queen of All Saints. She is abundantly called so in the Litany of Loreto, where she is greeted as Queen of Angels, Queen of Patriarchs, Queen of Prophets, Queen of Apostles, Queen of Martyrs, Queen of Confessors, Queen of Virgins, Queen of All Saints, Queen Conceived without Original Sin, Queen Assumed into Heaven, Queen of the Most Holy Rosary, Queen of the Family, Queen of Peace.

Saint Paul tells us that the will of God is not merely for our salvation, but also for our sanctification. Everyone is called to be a saint. Anyone who does not become a saint has no one but himself to blame. Our Lady holds her greatest bounties and generosities in store for those who are starting to be saints.

2. All Souls. On this day every priest in the Catholic Church is allowed to say three Masses for the souls in Purgatory. The first saint who started the celebration on this day of the feast of All Souls was Saint Odilo, whose feast day is January 1. This was in 998. All prayers for the souls in Purgatory are most efficacious when put under the protection of the Blessed Virgin Mary.

Saturday is Our Lady's special day during the week. Our Lady visits Purgatory every Saturday to release the souls there who have died during the week and who have worn the brown scapular of Our Lady of Mount Carmel. When Our Lady was assumed into Heaven on August 15, she undoubtedly took countless souls from Purgatory with her, perhaps all of them that were then there. Our Lady's promise to those who wear the brown scapular is this: "Whosoever dies in this scapular shall not suffer eternal fire. On Saturday, as many as I shall find in Purgatory, I shall free." Saint Claude de la Colombiére says that, "of all the forms of our love for the blessed Virgin and its various modes of expression, the scapular is the most favored." The prophecy of Ezechiel declares, "The gate of the inner court that looks toward the East shall be shut for six days, but on the sabbath day it shall be opened." This prophecy is read in the Saturday Mass in honor of Our Lady of Mount Carmel. The "inner court" means Purgatory, and the "sabbath day" means Saturday, the day when Our Lady abundantly releases souls from Purgatory and brings them to Heaven.

3. Saint Martin de Porres (1639). He was a South American, born of a Spanish father and an Indian mother. He lived at Lima in Peru. He became a lay brother in the Dominican Order. So great was his holiness that his light shone all through the New World. His memory will never be forgotten. So great was his power of prayer that he raised a dead man to life. He was seventy years old when he died.

Saint Malachy O'More (1148). He was a noble Irish saint who was born at Armagh in the year 1095. He was the Primate of Armagh in his day. Armagh was the first see established in Ireland by Saint Patrick. On a pilgrimage he made to Rome, Saint Malachy stopped at the Abbey of Clairvaux, and died in the arms of Saint Bernard, its abbot. Saint Bernard wrote the life of Saint Malachy. Saint Bernard and Saint Malachy were buried in the same grave. Saint Malachy O'More is well known for his famous prophecies concerning the nearness of the end of the world.

Saint Sylvia (572). Saint Sylvia was the mother of Saint Gregory the Great, Pope and Doctor of the Universal Church. She was one of the most beautiful widows Rome has ever known. Saint Gregory's sanctity and intellectual brilliance are in no small way due to this precious mother. A chapel has been built on the Caelian Hill in Rome on the spot where her house was when she lived there.

Saint Winifred (650). She was a niece of Saint Beuno, a bishop of Wales. She was murdered and her head cut off by Caradog of Hawarden who wanted to vio-late her purity. The spot where her head fell on the ground caused the rising of a holy well, called Saint Winifred's Well. It still pours forth nine and one-half million gallons of water every day, and miracles still occur there. Saint Beuno wrapped Saint Winifred's body and severed head in his cloak, and laid them at the foot of the altar where he was to say Mass. When the Mass was ended, Saint Winifred was restored to life again, with her head rejoined to her body. She is perhaps the greatest glory of Wales. She is certainly the clearest remembrance of the truth Wales once had when it was a Catholic country.

Saint Hubert (727). He was a French saint and a noble-man who before he was con-verted was a worldling and a lover of pleasure. His chief pas-sion was for hunting, to which he devoted nearly all his time. On Good Friday morning, when the faithful were going to the churches, Hubert mounted his horse for the woods. As he was pursuing a magnificent stag, the animal turned to look at his pur-

Saint Hubert the Hunter

suer, and Hubert saw a crucifix between its antlers, then heard a voice saying, "Hubert, unless you turn to the Lord, and lead a holy life, you will quickly go down into Hell." Hubert dismounted and prostrating himself said, "Lord, what would You have me do?" He received the answer, "Go and seek Lambert, and he will instruct you." He found the holy Saint Lambert and was instructed in the faith. At the death of his wife, Hubert became a cleric. He is the patron saint of hunters.

4. Saint Charles Borromeo (1584). He was the nephew of Pope Pius IV. He was "the soul of the Council of Trent," which protected the Catholic Faith in the sixteenth century against the inroads of the Protestant Reformation. Saint Charles Borromeo wrote the following prayer to his Guardian Angel: "O beloved angel, who has been given me as a protector by the Divine Majesty, I desire to die in the Faith which the Holy, Roman and Apostolic Church adheres to and defends, in which all the saints of the New Testament have died, and outside of which there is no salvation." Saint Charles Borromeo gave Saint Aloysius his first Holy Communion.

Saint Charles Borromeo

5. Saint Zachary and Saint Elizabeth (First Century). Saint Zachary and Saint Elizabeth were the father and the mother of Saint John the Baptist, the last and the greatest of the prophets and the precursor of Our Lord. Saint Zachary's story is beautifully told in the first chapter of Saint Luke. Saint Zachary spoke one of the three canticles of the New Testament, which is known as the *Benedictus*. It is constantly recited in the prayers of all priests as part of their liturgical worship. Saint Zachary was inspired by God through an angel to give Saint John the Baptist his name. Saint Zachary was martyred in the Temple of Jerusalem by the Jews. The martyrs of the Old Testament run from A to Z, from Abel, the son of Adam and the first martyr that ever was, to Zachary, the father of John the Baptist and the last martyr of the Old Testament.

Saint Elizabeth was the cousin of the Blessed Virgin Mary. It was to her that Mary went in haste after she had conceived her Child, and after she learned that Elizabeth had conceived hers. The second phrase in the *Hail Mary*, "Blessed art thou among women and blessed is the fruit of thy womb," was given us by Saint Elizabeth. And so, her memory is beautifully kept in the Rosary, where this phrase is mentioned fifty-three times. Saint Elizabeth's first greeting to Our Lady, when she saw her standing in her doorway, was: "Whence is this to me that the Mother of my

Lord should come to me!" This was a sheer and unequivocal way of proclaiming Mary, her own cousin, to be the Mother of God.

With Elizabeth's as the central greeting, the Angel Gabriel's as the first and that of the Council of Ephesus as the last, this is the full *Hail Mary*:

Hail, Mary, full of grace; the Lord is with thee; blessed art thou among women, and blessed is the fruit of thy womb, Jesus. Holy Mary, Mother of God, pray for us sinners, now and at the hour of our death. Amen.

The Holy Relics. The Catholic Church, having celebrated in November the feast of All Saints and the feast of All Souls, on this day honors all the holy relics of their bodies, which will remain on earth until the day of the last resurrection. Veneration for the bodies of the saints is a belief in the resurrection of the body. The dead bodies of the saints are precious to every Catholic because all Catholics believe that these bodies will one day rise in glory and be with the souls of the saints to whom they belong, in complete personality, for all eternity. Irreverence shown to the bodies of the saints is a sacrilege.

6. Saint Leonard of Limoges (559).
He was a nobleman at the court of Clovis, the first Catholic King of France. King Clovis was his godfather. Saint Leonard was even more noted for his sanctity than for his nobility. He has been kept in loving remembrance by French Catholics from his day to ours.

Saint Leonard of Reresby (Thirteenth Century).
He was an English saint who fought gloriously in the crusades to take the Holy Land away from the Mohammedans. He was imprisoned by them, but escaped miraculously and returned to his home in Yorkshire. Leonard is a noted English, a noted French and a noted Italian name.

7. Saint Willibrord (739).
He was born in England. He was trained in Ireland to be a missionary. He then went to what is now Holland, and Belgium and Denmark, accompanied by eleven other English monks. He was made Bishop of Utrecht. Much of the Faith of the Dutch and the Belgians and the Danes, who have been in many ways such beautiful Catholic people, is due to this English-born, Irish-trained saint.

Saint Willibrord

Saint Ernest (1148). He was a Benedictine abbot from Germany who joined the second crusade. He was tortured and killed at Mecca for refusing to embrace Islam.

8. Saint Godfrey (Geoffrey) (1115).

He was a French saint who became a monk when he was five years old. He spent nearly all of his time, night and day, in prayer. He was Benedictine. When made a bishop, he lived in his palace just like a monk. He fed people with his own hands. He constantly visited the hospitals where the sick, and even the lepers, were kept. He was a great opponent of the greed and laxity of the clergy of his day.

Blessed John Duns Scotus (1308). Blessed Duns Scotus, born in Scotland, entered the Franciscans when very young where he was outstanding for humility and obedience. He found the study of philosophy so difficult that he prayed to God and to Our Blessed Lady for wisdom and knowledge. Our Lady appeared to him and said that his prayer would be heard. In return he promised to devote his life to her service and to her honor.

At the age of nineteen he became a Professor and Doctor of Theology at the University of Oxford. When the doctrine of the Immaculate Conception was attacked, he defended it so brilliantly that the University of Paris gave him the honorary title of Doctor of the Immaculate Conception and forbade that any contrary doctrine be ever taught there.

9. The Basilica of the Holy Saviour (324).

This marks the day, in 324, when the great Pope Sylvester consecrated this church to Our Lord. It is one of the seven great churches of Rome. Since the twelfth century it has been called the Basilica of Saint John Lateran because it has been also especially dedicated to Saint John the Baptist, under whose patronage the baptistry of this church was placed. It is the major church of the Holy Father, the Pope. The heads of Saint Peter and Saint Paul are kept in it. It is called in an inscription on its walls, "The Mother and the Head of All Churches of this City and the World."

10. Saint Andrew Avellino (1608).

He was a member of the Theatines, or Clerks Regular of Saint Paul at Naples. On account of his great devotion to the Cross, he took the name in religion of Andrew because he so lovingly remembered the crucifixion of Saint Andrew the Apostle, who hung for two days on the cross, preaching to his enemies. Saint Andrew Avellino's name in the world was Lancelot. He was born in Sicily. Saint Andrew was a great friend of Saint Charles Borromeo. He was eighty-eight years old when he died. He dropped dead at the foot of the altar just as he was about to say Mass.

11. Saint Martin of Tours (397).

Saint Martin of Tours was a great saint whose life was written by Saint Gregory of Tours. He is called, "the glory of Gaul." Saint Martin was born in Hungary. He was educated in Italy. He became a Christian in France. His father was in the military and transferred to Italy. It was in Italy that Martin learned of the Catholic Faith, and became a catechumen. At 15 he was forced to join the military and while on duty one day in winter he noticed a poorly clad man begging for alms at the city gate. Martin having nothing to give the poor old man took the woolen cloak from his back and cut it into two pieces, giving one half to the beggar, and wrapped himself in the other. That night in his sleep, Martin saw Jesus, surrounded by angels and wrapped in his woolen cloak. On rising, Martin "flew to be baptized."

Saint Martin of Tours

He was the uncle of Saint Patrick, the great apostle of Ireland. He was the staunch friend and ally of Saint Hilary of Poitiers, the first Doctor of the Church to die. In France there are four thousand churches and five hundred villages named for Saint Martin of Tours.

Saint Martin of Tours worked many miracles while on earth, including the raising of the dead. Among other saints who have raised the dead to life, we may mention: Saint Peter, Saint Paul, Saint John, Saint Matthew, Saint Patrick, Saint Benedict, Saint Dominic, Saint Anthony of Padua, Saint Vincent Ferrer, Saint Francis Xavier, Saint John of the Cross, Saint Peter Claver, Saint Philip Neri, Saint Francis of Paula, Saint Philip Benizi, Saint Nicholas of Bari, Saint Eleutherius, Saint Linus, Saint Stanislaus of Cracow, Saint John Bosco, Saint Martin de Porres, Saint Hilary, Saint Julian of Antioch, Saint Macarius the Elder, Saint Beuno, Saint Germanus of Auxerre, Saint Hyacinth, Saint Abundius of Como, Saint Catherine of Siena, Saint Teresa of Avila, Saint Joan of Arc, Saint Rose of Viterbo and Saint Agnes of Montepulciano.

12. Saint Martin the Pope (655). Saint Martin I was Pope for six years. He was the great opponent of the heretics known as the Monothelites. These heretics tried to destroy the full human nature of Jesus by denying Him a human will. In Jesus, there is one Person, a Divine Person; and there are two natures—the nature of God and the nature of man. Jesus has a full human nature, body and soul; He has a human body, a human mind and a human will. He has the same Divine nature as His Father and the Holy Ghost. In Jesus, there is only one Person, the same Person Who proceeds from the Eternal Father. And from the Father and the Son proceeds the Holy Ghost.

Saint Martin was imprisoned by the cruel enemies of the Faith. He was taken to the

Saint Martin the Pope

Island of the Chersonese, and left there to die.

Saint Roy (Rufus) (200). The name Roy is a form of Rufus. Saint Roy was the first Bishop of Avignon, in the south of France. Avignon was the city that the Popes were exiled, seven of them, from the year 1309 to 1377. The seven Popes there were: Clement V, John XXII, Benedict XII, Clement VI, Innocent VI, Blessed Urban V and Gregory XI. It was not the place where the Popes should have been. Rome is the Eternal City, and where the head of the Catholic Church must always reside. The years of the stay of the Pontiffs in the city of Avignon is known, and rightly so, as the Avignon Captivity. Part of the protection of the Popes while they were at Avignon was the prayers of Saint Rufus, first bishop of that city. The Avignon Captivity is also known as the Babylonian Captivity, because it lasted almost seventy years, the number of years the Jews of the Old Testament were kept in captivity at Babylon, away from Jerusalem—from 606 B.C. to 536 B.C.

13. Saint Stanislaus Kostka (1568). He was born in Poland. He entered the Society of Jesus when he was eighteen years old. He died within ten months, famous for his angelic innocence and sanctity. He died on the feast of the Assumption of Our Lady, as he had predicted. His great friends in the Society of Jesus were Saint Peter Canisius, who sent him to Rome, and Saint Francis Borgia, who received him into the Order of Saint Ignatius. Saint Stanislaus Kostka is one of the twenty-seven canonized saints of the Society of Jesus. The Blessed Eucharist was the center of his life. Every morning he heard two Masses. Before his entrance into the Society of Jesus, twice the angels brought him Holy Communion when he was being persecuted by his own family. Our Lady appeared to him and placed the Infant Jesus in his arms. It was Our Lady who told him to become a member of the Society of Jesus.

Saint Frances Xavier Cabrini (1917). The first saint ever to die in the United States of America as an American citizen was named Frances. She is Saint Frances Xavier Cabrini, who was born in 1850, and who died in 1917 at the age of sixty-seven. She came to this country from Italy in an effort to keep her beloved Italian Catholics from being perverted in their Faith by those in this country who plotted against it. She became an American citizen a few years before she died. She died in Chicago. Her body is now in New York. She is the namesake of that notable saint called Frances of Rome, who died in 1440, and who is remembered on her feast day on March 9. Saint Frances Xavier Cabrini added Xavier to her name because she wished to make the great apostle of the Society of Jesus, Saint Frances Xavier, the patron of her crusade for the Faith in the United States.

14. Saint Laurence O'Toole (1180). Saint Laurence O'Toole was born in Leinster in Ireland. He became an Augustinian when he was a little boy of twelve. He was made Abbot of Glendalough when he was twenty-five. Eight years later he was made Archbishop of Dublin. At the tomb of Saint Laurence O'Toole seven dead persons were raised to life. He was canonized in 1226, the year Saint Francis of Assisi died.

15. Saint Albertus Magnus (1280). Saint Albertus Magnus (Albert the Great) was a Dominican. He was a teacher of Saint Thomas Aquinas. He is one of the greatest theologians of the Catholic Church. He studied all the sciences, and knew and saw and declared how shallow they were for all purposes of eternal wisdom. His great devotion was to the Blessed Sacrament and to Our Blessed Lady. He was seventy-four years old when he died. Saint Albert the Great is one of the thirty-three Doctors of the Catholic Church.

16. Saint Gertrude the Great (1302). Saint Gertrude, who is called the Great, was a brilliant and holy little German girl who entered religion at the age of five. She was born in the town of Eisleben, which later gave the world the heretic, Martin Luther. The Order she joined was the Benedictines. She was so brilliant in her earliest years that all the simple and clear truths of Divine Revelation became part of her thoughts and her speech. Though capable of learning all secular sciences, Our Lord appeared to her and told her to love no other books but the Bible and the works of the Fathers of the Church. Saint Gertrude was the first great apostle of devotion to the Sacred Heart of Jesus. On the feast of Saint John the Evangelist, she was taken by him to Jesus and permitted to rest her head on His Sacred Heart. Saint Gertrude was forty-six years old when she died, on the Wednesday after Easter Sunday. Two saints especially devoted to Saint Gertrude were Saint Teresa of Avila and Saint Francis de Sales.

Saint Stanislaus Kostka

17. Saint Gregory Thaumaturgus (Wonderworker) (268). He was born of pagan parents in Neo-Caesarea. He went to Caesarea to attend law school but instead became the pupil of Origen, who recognized in Gregory a great love of truth. After his conversion to the Catholic Faith, Saint Gregory returned to his birthplace and was appointed bishop of the seventeen Christians living there. His fame grew because of his gift of miracles: he had power over evil spirits and once dried up a lake that was the cause of a dispute. He likewise altered the course of two rivers. Most of his miracles involved curing the sick, which also brought about the conversion of their souls. Shortly before his death he inquired about the number of infidels that yet remained in his See and, discovering it to be only seventeen. He thanked God for his great mercy, because on coming to that city there were only seventeen Christians; now he left but seventeen idolaters.

Saint Hugh of Lincoln (1200).

Saint Hugh of Lincoln, though born in France, became a Carthusian monk at the age of twenty and went to England. He was sixty years old when he died. So great was his holiness that kings and nobles carried his coffin to the grave. He was canonized twenty years after his death.

Saint Rose Philippine Duchesne (1852).

She was a French girl born at Grenoble who became a Visitation nun. After her Order had been violently attacked and dispersed during the French Revolution, she incorporated her community into the Madams of the Sacred Heart under the guidance of Saint Madeleine Sophie Barat.

Saint Gertrude the Great

Saint Rose Philippine's great desire was to go and labor in foreign missions. When she was forty-nine years old, she set sail for America. She landed at New Orleans, and then went north to Saint Charles, not far from Saint Louis, Missouri. She later worked among the Indians at Sugar Creek. The Indians called her "the woman who prays always." It is one of the glories of the United States that the body of this saintly nun is still kept in our country. She died when she was eighty-three years old. She is buried at Saint Charles, Missouri.

18. The Basilicas of Saint Peter and Saint Paul.

The Basilica of Saint Peter, the Apostle and first Pope, was built at the foot of Vatican Hill in Rome by Pope Saint Cletus. It has since grown to be the greatest and most impressive church in the world. Fifty thousand people can be accommodated in it. The feast of November 18 commemorates the solemn consecration of the new basilica there by Pope Urban VIII, in 1626. It is on the spot where Saint Peter was crucified upside down in the year 67.

Pope Saint Cletus also built a church over the tomb of Saint Paul-outside-the-Walls, on the road to Ostia. This church has been made larger and larger through the years. A great fire destroyed it in 1823. It was rebuilt, and its final structure, as we see it today, was consecrated by Pope Pius IX in 1854, two days after he had defined the dogma of the Immaculate Conception. Saint Paul's great devotion, after his conversion, was to the Blessed Virgin Mary. His disciple, Saint Luke, wrote the Gospel of the Blessed Virgin Mary, the third Gospel. Whenever Saint Paul made a journey he always wanted to return to Jerusalem to see the Blessed Virgin Mary. He spent his whole life in sorrow over the persecution he had inflicted upon Christians in the early days. Saint Paul loved Mary, the Mother of God, with all the ardor of his heart once he had been converted to the true Faith. It was her inspiration which made him the Apostle of the Gentiles, the people who would love her, and took him away from the Jews, the people who would not love her.

19. Saint Elizabeth of Hungary (1231). Saint Elizabeth was a princess of Hungary. She married Louis of Thuringia, and had three children. After his death, she became a Franciscan. She is the patron saint of the Third Order of Saint Francis. She died when only twenty-four years old, the same age as the Little Flower of Jesus, Saint Casimir of Poland and Saint Gabriel of the Most Sorrowful Virgin. Four years after her death, Saint Elizabeth of Hungary was canonized. The dead have been raised to life when brought to her tomb.

20. Saint Felix of Valois (1212). Saint Felix of Valois, when seventy years old, along with Saint John of Matha, founded in France, in 1197, a Religious Order known as the Trinitarians. The purpose of this Order was to take captive Christian slaves away from the Mohammedans in Spain and in North Africa. So pleased was the Blessed Virgin Mary with this Order of Trinitarians, that when Saint Felix was dying, she appeared to him wearing the habit of his Order. Saint Felix Valois was eighty-five years old when he died.

Blessed Angeles de San Jose Lloret and Sixteen Companions

(1936). These Spanish Sisters were members of the Congregation of the Sisters of Christian Doctrine. Under the guidance of Blessed Angeles, their Superior General, the Sisters dedicated their lives to teaching Catholic doctrine. Arrested during the Spanish Civil War, they continued even in prison to teach the Catholic Faith. They were martyred together in the autumn of 1936.

Saint Elizabeth of Hungary

The Communists, with the help of Russia, usurped the government of Spain in the 1930's. During the civil war that ensued more than 7,500 priests and nuns and thousands of lay people were martyred because of their fidelity to their Catholic Faith. Under the leadership of Francisco Franco, the Spanish people finally regained control of their country.

21. The Presentation of the Blessed Virgin Mary. (13 B.C.). Saint Joachim and Saint Anne, the father and the mother of the Blessed Virgin Mary, presented her to God in the Temple, to live there and to belong to God forever, when she was three years, two months and thirteen days old. Saint Joachim and Saint Anne sensed in the Blessed Virgin Mary from the moment of her birth that she was divinely great, and belonged to God and not to them. When her father and her mother brought Mary to the Temple of Jerusalem and presented her there, Saint Zachary, a priest of the Temple and the father of Saint John the Baptist and the husband of Saint Elizabeth, received her. He took her by the hand and led her into the cloister of virgins who dwelt in the Temple. There she stayed, adored God and prayed until she was fourteen years old. Then her first espousals to Saint Joseph were miraculously arranged by God, so as to give her a virginal husband to protect her in her virginal motherhood when she conceived her Divine Child and brought God into this world.

22. Saint Cecilia (230). Saint Cecilia is one of the most venerated virgin martyrs of the Church. Her name is mentioned every day in the Canon of the Mass and always in the Litany of the Saints. She belonged to a noble family of Rome. Her father was a pagan and her mother a Christian. From her early youth she consecrated her virginity to Christ. Her father insisted on her marrying a young pagan nobleman named Valerian. On the evening of her wedding day, she told Valerian that she had an angel guarding her virginity. Valerian said that if he could see the angel, he too would believe in Jesus Christ. Cecilia told Valerian that if he were baptized a Christian he could see the angel. He went and was baptized by Pope Urban I—he and his brother Tiburtius. They returned to Cecilia, and both of them saw a most beautiful angel standing beside her. These two brothers, Valerian and Tiburtius, proclaimed themselves Christians, and were martyred in the year 229, along with their jailer whose name was Maximus. Cecilia buried them. Less than a year later the Roman soldiers broke into Cecilia's house. They tried to suffocate Cecilia in a bath, and when they could not, one soldier struck her three times on the neck with a sword. She lay on the ground for three days before she died. She was buried in the Catacomb of Saint Callistus. She was eighteen years old when she was martyred. There is a church built to Saint Cecilia in Rome, and dedicated to her. At the end of the sixteenth century, her body was found to be incorrupt and as beautiful as the day she died, preserving after thirteen centuries, all its virginal loveliness and modesty.

23. Saint Clement (100). Saint Clement was the fourth Pope. He reigned in the Catholic Church from the year 90 to 100. There were four Popes in the first century. Saint Peter was the first, Saint Linus was the second, Saint Cletus was the third and Saint Clement was the fourth. These four Popes are mentioned every day in the Canon of the Mass, which is one of the greatest honors that ever can be bestowed on a saint. Catholic churches are dedicated to Saint Clement everywhere throughout the world. Saint Clement, as did all the early Popes, shed his blood for the Faith. He died the same year as Saint John the Evangelist.

Blessed Miguel Augustin Pro (1927). Blessed Miguel pro was a Mexican Jesuit martyred during the Masonic-inspired Mexican Revolution. He was born in Guadalupe, Mexico in 1891 and entered the Jesuits in 1911. Because of the religious persecution of the revolution, he was sent to Belgium to complete his studies and then to Spain where he was ordained. He returned to Mexico in 1925, when all the churches were closed and priests were being hunted down. At great peril to his life Blessed Miguel went about in disguise to bring the sacraments to the people. In 1927 he was falsely accused of conspiracy and sentenced to death. At his execution he refused a blindfold as he faced the firing squad with this arms extended in the form of a cross. His last words, spoken in a strong voice, were *"Viva Christo Rey!"*—"Long live Christ the King."

During the first three hundred years of Christianity over eleven million Catholics were killed for the Faith. In the following sixteen centuries, with the Protestant Revolt, the French Revolution and the missionary periods, many thousands more were martyred for their fidelity to Christ's true Church. However, those who study the growing religious persecution in the world today insist that the twentieth century alone has produced more martyrs than did the early ages of the Church—possibly more than all the previous centuries combined.

Blessed Miguel Pro

The primary menaces to Christianity today are Communism and Islam. In countries where these false philosophies prevail there have been and continue to be countless men, women and children killed for their Christianity. During World War II millions of Catholics, especially in the Ukraine, were killed because they remained true to their beliefs. In Communist China alone there are untold numbers of martyrs, and the persecution of Catholics continues.

24. Saint Chrysogonus (304). He was martyred for the Faith at Aquilea in northern Italy during the persecution of Diocletian. His name is mentioned in the Roman Canon of the Mass. He consoled and encouraged the martyr, Saint Anastasia, during her imprisonment.

Saint Flora (856). Saint Flora was the companion of a beautiful Spanish girl named Mary, and their feasts are celebrated together. They were beheaded by the Mohammedans for refusing to deny their Catholic Faith.

Saint John of the Cross (1591). Saint John of the Cross, Doctor of the Church, was a Spanish Carmelite priest. He died when he was only forty-nine years old. He was the great friend and supporter of Saint Teresa of Avila. He has been called the "mystic of mystics." His brilliant works, *The Ascent of Mount Carmel*, *The Dark Night of the Soul*, *The Spiritual Canticle* and *The Living Flame of Love*, are beautiful inspirations for those who wish to be detached from all worldly things and dedicate themselves wholly to God. Saint John suffered great persecutions, even from his own Order. He was once kept in prison for nine months and slandered by everyone. But his motto and his prayer was "to suffer and to be despised." He gloriously lived up to his title, "of the Cross."

Saint Andrew Dung-Lac and Companions, Martyrs of Vietnam (Eighteenth—Nineteenth Century). These one hundred and seventeen saints were martyred at different times but canonized together in 1988. Ninety-six of the martyrs were Vietnamese—fifty-nine lay people and thirty-seven priests. Andrew Dung-Lac (1839) was one of the secular Vietnamese priests. There were six Dominican bishops and five Dominican priests, including Bishops Hieronymys Hermosilla and Valentin Berrio Ochoa, and also two bishops and seven priests from the Paris Foreign Missions society.

Among the martyrs was **Saint Johannes Theophane Venard (1861)**, the missionary whom Saint Thèrése of Lisieux so much admired for his extraordinary simplicity and innocence. His joy and Faith impressed all who knew him—even his persecutors. He was chained in a cage for two months and eventually beheaded for the Faith on February 2, 1861.

Saint Catherine of Alexandria

The period of persecution of Catholics in Vietnam lasted from 1625 to 1886—more than twelve years longer than the persecution of the early Church under the Roman emperors. Fifty-eight bishops and foreign priests, and one hundred and fifty Vietnamese priests, and about 130,000 Vietnamese Catholic lay people were martyred for their Faith.

25. Saint Catherine of Alexandria (307).

There is hardly a more glorious name among Catholic girls who became saints than the name of Catherine. The first and foremost of all the Catherines among the saints is the beautiful, young, eighteen-year-old girl of Alexandria in Egypt who was martyred for her Faith. The intellectuals of her time and place were so upset by the brilliance of her mind that she was called to defend the Catholic truths before fifty pagan philosophers. She completely confounded them with her arguments and her eloquence. They tortured her by means of an engine fitted with a spiked wheel. On this wheel she was rolled, but before it could do harm to her it miraculously fell apart. She was then scourged and thrown into prison and at last beheaded. She is the patroness of philosophers. She is one of the fourteen Holy Helpers, and is invoked in lawsuits. Saint Catherine's body was carried by angels to Mount Sinai, where God gave Moses the Ten Commandments. There, on the top of this sacred hill, her virginal remains await the resurrection on the last day.

26. Saint Leonard of Port Maurice (1751). Saint Leonard of Port Maurice was a most holy Franciscan friar. He lived at the monastery of Saint Bonaventure, in Rome. He was one of the greatest missioners in the history of the Church. He used to preach to thousands in the open square of every city and town where the churches could not hold his listeners. The Immaculate Conception of the Blessed Virgin, the adoration of the Blessed Sacrament, and the veneration of the Sacred Heart of Jesus were his crusades. He was in no small way responsible for the definition of the Immaculate Conception made a little more than a hundred years after his death. But Saint Leonard's most famous work was his devotion to the Stations of the Cross. He is sometimes called the Saint of the Stations of the Cross. So brilliant and holy was his eloquence that once when he gave a two weeks' mission in Rome, the Pope and the College of Cardinals came to hear him. Saint Leonard of Port Maurice also gave us the Divine Praises, which are said at the end of a Low Mass and always at the end of Benediction. He died a most holy death in his seventy-fifth year, after twenty-four years of uninterrupted preaching.

27. The Miraculous Medal of the Blessed Virgin Mary (1830). This is the feast of the lovely medal designed by the Mother of God herself and given to a beautiful nun, Sister Catherine Labouré, now a canonized saint, a Sister of Charity of Saint Vincent de Paul. Our Lady appeared three times to Saint Catherine Labouré in the year 1830. Our Lady told Saint Catherine just how the medals in her honor should be made and designed. On one side of each medal is an image of Mary, with the words, "O Mary conceived without sin, pray for us who have recourse to thee." On the other side is the first letter of the name Mary, placed in the center with twelve stars around it, a cross just above it, and the hearts of Jesus and Mary engraved just below it. These miraculous medals are now called, in simplicity, "Mary medals." By holding them, wearing them, kissing them or showing them to others, countless favors and miracles have been worked everywhere by the powerful intercession of the Mother of God.

Blessed Leonard Kimura (1619). Blessed Leonard Kimura of the Society of Jesus was a descendant of a noble Kimura who was the first Japanese baptized by Saint Francis Xavier. Blessed Leonard Kimura, through humility, became a lay brother in the Society of Jesus. He joined the Society of Jesus at the age of thirteen, and was a catechist for thirty years. Along with thirteen other brave Japanese Catholics, he spent three years in prison. Right in the prison itself—which he turned into a religious house, with regular hours for prayer—he converted ninety-six Japanese to the Catholic Faith. He was burned to death on the hill of Nagasaki. He was forty-three years old when he went to God.

28. Saint Joseph Mary Pignatelli (1811). He was born at Saragossa in Spain. When the Society of Jesus was banished from Spain, he followed his religious

Saint Andrew

brethren into exile. It was in no small part due to him that the Society of Jesus, suppressed in 1773, was restored again, three years after his death, in 1814. His feast is also celebrated on November 11, and is now especially commemorated in the Society of Jesus on November 15, the day he died.

Saint James of the Marches. (1476). Born at Montebrandone in Ancona, he studied law and then joined the Franciscans. He studied under Saint Bernardine of Siena, and worked as a missionary with Saint John Capistrano. He and Saint John Capistrano were named inquisitors against the Fraticelli by Pope Saint Martin V. He had the gift of miracles and made countless conversions. For forty years he never let a day go by without giving a sermon or an exhortation.

29. Saint Saturninus (303). He was an aged priest from Carthage in Africa, who fled to Rome with his deacon, Sisinius. He was arrested there and sentenced to hard labor in the building of huge baths for the pagans of Rome. In the midst of his hard work and toil, and despite his age, the light of his Faith was seen by all who met him. Many Roman pagans began to be converted by Saint Saturninus, attracted by the holiness of his looks and encouraged by what he taught and said. He and his deacon were beheaded by order of the pagan Emperor Diocletian.

30. Saint Andrew (61). Saint Andrew was the older brother of Saint Peter. He was the first of the Apostles to be called by Our Lord. He was a disciple of Saint John the Baptist, who pointed out Jesus to him as the Messias. Saint Andrew summoned his brother, Peter, and both became glorious Apostles of Our Lord. Saint Andrew preached the Gospel, after Our Lord's death, in Asia Minor and to the people of Scythia. He then went to Macedonia and to Greece. He was martyred at Patras, in Achaia, by being tied to a cross shaped like the letter X, and ever since called the "Saint Andrew's cross." Saint Andrew made his cross a pulpit. On it, while he bled from scourgings he had received, he preached to the faithful for two days until he died. Part of his body is now in the town Amalfi in southern Italy. His head is in Saint Peter's in the Vatican, in Rome. He is the patron saint of Russia and also of Scotland.

Saint Maura (Fourth Century or earlier). Saint Maura was a young Catholic virgin of Constantinople, cruelly martyred for the Faith. Her memory haunted the haters of the Catholic Faith for years after her death. Even Julian the Apostate, the Roman Emperor who died in 363, was worried about the way in which Saint Maura was venerated. One of the Ionian Islands, between Greece and Italy, was named after her. Her name is a beautiful variant of Mary, the name of the Mother of God.

December

The Month of the Divine Infancy

1. Saint Natalie (311). She was a courageous woman from Nicomedia who took great care of the martyrs there during the persecution of Diocletian.

Saint Edmund Campion (1581). He was born in London in 1540. He went to the University of Oxford where he was perhaps its most brilliant student. Queen Elizabeth, the heretical Queen of the English, met him there on a visit in 1566.

Saint Francis Xavier

She was fascinated by his good looks, his manner and his brilliance of mind. Temporarily, he took the oath of supremacy to her, but when he saw how the Catholic martyrs were being tried in England and the doctrines for which they were willing to shed their blood, he threw aside all his heretical leanings. He went to Douai, in France, and later to Rome, where he entered the Society of Jesus. He returned to England and made an effort to win all Protestants back to the Catholic Faith. He was seized and arrested and brought to the Tower of London. The Queen came to see him. She tried to persuade him to give up his strong stand for the Catholic Church. She made offers to him of every liberty and honor if he would forsake the Catholic Faith. Edmund Campion refused. He was tortured on the rack, and for four long conferences faced the heretics who opposed him and refuted brilliantly every one of their arguments. He was hanged, drawn and quartered on the first day of December. He has been one of the glories of the Society of Jesus ever since.

2. Saint Vivian (Bibiana) (363).

Saint Vivian was a heroic Roman girl, the daughter of a father and mother who were saints. Her sister was also a saint. All four of this family were martyred for the Catholic Faith. Her father, Saint Flavian, has his feast day on December

22. Her sister, Saint Demetria, has her feast day on June 21. And Saint Dafrosa, the mother of Saint Vivian, has her feast day on January 4. This is how this holy little family is scattered through the year in liturgical love. It was Julian the Apostate, in 363, who martyred Saint Vivian. He could not induce her to give up either her Faith or her chastity, even though she was tied to a pillar and scourged with metal ropes. When she died, her body was thrown to the dogs. A Catholic priest rescued it. There is a great church dedicated to Saint Vivian (Saint Bibiana) in Rome. Her mother and her sister are buried with her. Saint Vivian is the patroness of the diocese of Los Angeles in the United States of America.

3. Saint Jason (283). He was the son of the martyr, Saint Claudius, a Roman tribune. Saint Jason was beheaded along with his brother, Saint Maurus. Their mother, Saint Hilaria, buried them. She was arrested while praying at their tomb and was also martyred.

Saint Francis Xavier (1552).

Saint Barbara

Saint Francis Xavier of the Society of Jesus has been the greatest apostle of the Catholic Church since the time of Saint Paul. He is called the second Saint Paul. He entered the Society of Jesus when he was twenty-eight years old. When he was thirty-four years old he set out as a missionary to India and Japan, in the year 1540. He took with him no other book except his breviary. He landed in Goa on May 6, 1542, after a long and most dangerous journey of thirteen months. He went to the Molucca Islands. He was three times shipwrecked. He often spent days without food. The Mohammedans attacked him. After his great work in India, he started off for Japan. The next great country he wished to go to was China, and he almost reached it in 1552, when he landed on the small island of Sancian, near the coast of China. There he was taken ill and died. Saint Francis Xavier baptized three million people. He destroyed forty thousand idols in the pagan East. He built over a hundred churches. He raised about twenty-five people from the dead. His last words were, "Virgin Mother, remember me." Saint Francis Xavier was canonized on March 12, 1622. The Novena of Grace, celebrated in his honor, always ends each year on that day. Saint Francis Xavier was forty-six years old when he died. All his missionary work in the East was done in ten years.

4. Saint Peter Chrysologus (450).
Saint Peter Chrysologus was only forty-four years old when he died. Yet he has been declared one of the Doctors of the Catholic Church. His name Chrysologus means *golden speech*. All his sermons are in the clear, simple, authoritative style of Our Lord when He preached to the Apostles and told them how to preach to others. Saint Peter Chrysologus was the Archbishop of Ravenna in Italy. He was one of the great crusaders for frequent Holy Communion among the faithful.

Saint Barbara (235).
Saint Barbara was born and lived in northern Egypt, in the city of Heliopolis. This was the city through which our Lady and Saint Joseph carried Our Lord on the Flight into Egypt, and where all the pagan idols crashed to the ground when the Holy Family walked through the streets. Saint Barbara was a most beautiful

Saint Nicholas of Bari

girl. Her father kept her locked up in a tower, where she had three windows made, in honor of the Blessed Trinity. She was secretly baptized a Catholic. Her tyrannical father hated her for this. He denounced her. He had her tortured, and then martyred her himself by cutting off her head with a sword. Before her death she had destroyed all the idols in her father's house. Her father was later struck by lightning and killed.

Saint Barbara is one of the fourteen Holy Helpers, and is invoked against lightning.

5. Saint Sabbas (532).
He was an abbot, a most saintly monk who came from Cappadocia in Asia Minor, and lived in the desert land between Jerusalem and the Dead Sea. He finally took charge of all the monasteries in that territory. He was a great fighter to protect the humanity of Jesus Christ from the Monophysite heresy, which denied the human nature of Jesus, thus putting an end to the Sacred Heart of Jesus and to His Most Precious Blood. One of the monasteries built by Saint Sabbas,

not too far from the Garden of Olives where Our Lord sweat blood on the night of His Passion, still remains. It is the second oldest monastery in the history of the Church. The oldest monastery is that of Saint Catherine of Alexandria on Mount Sinai. Saint Sabbas was ninety-three years old when he died. His relics are now in the Church of Saint Mark in Venice.

6. Saint Nicholas of Bari (350). The great Saint Nicholas, whom everybody knows and speaks of, was an Archbishop at Myra in Asia Minor. He has come to be honored as the patron saint of children. His relics were taken by the Italians to Italy in 1087, and are now honored there, at Bari. Saint Nicholas raised three children from the dead. His name has been corrupted from Saint Nicholas into "Santa Claus." Sentimental and unsaintly representations of him in a red coat and trousers and with a white beard are paraded in front of our commercial stores at Christmas time. The true Saint Nicholas is the one who honors those who love and venerate him as a saint, not as an advertisement. Saint Nicholas is the patron saint of Russia.

7. Saint Ambrose (397). Saint Ambrose is one of the four great Doctors of the Western Church. He was a bishop of Milan in Italy. He began by being the governor of northern Italy but when the Bishop of Milan died, because of the voice of a child in the crowd shouting "Ambrose for Bishop!", Saint Ambrose, though only a catechumen at the time, was baptized, confirmed, ordained a priest, and was consecrated a bishop on December 7 in the year 374. Saint Ambrose died when he was only fifty-seven. He died on Good Friday. He was buried by the side of the martyrs, Saint Gervase and Protase, who were the protomartyrs of Milan. It was Saint Ambrose who baptized Saint Augustine on April 24, 387. This was on Holy Saturday, the day before Easter, and the day on which Saint Ambrose and Saint Augustine composed the beautiful hymn known as the *Te Deum*, an indispensable prayer of the Catholic Church. The sayings of Saint Ambrose as a Doctor of the Catholic Church are so profound and clear and noble that any one of them, once listened to or read, can never be forgotten. Saint Ambrose says that the devil keeps an account of our sins, but if we accuse ourselves of these sins before a Catholic priest in confes-

Saint Ambrose

sion, no accuser, not even the devil, will appear before us when we stand at the Judgment Seat of God.

8. The Immaculate Conception of the Blessed Virgin Mary (17 B.C.). This is the mystery of Mary to which our whole country, the United States of America, was dedicated at the Sixth Provincial Council of Baltimore in 1846. The meaning of this mystery is that from the first instant of her conception in the womb of Anna, her mother, Mary was without original sin. Nothing of the guilt which Adam bestowed on the whole human race, because of his sin in the Garden of Paradise, was allowed to touch the perfect soul of the Blessed Virgin Mary. God created the soul of Mary in sheer holiness, full of every grace He could bestow on her. In our own day, which is rightly called "the age of Mary," in 1854,

The Immaculate Conception

on December 8, the courageous and holy Pope, Pius IX, defined the Immaculate Conception of the Blessed Virgin Mary as a dogma of the Catholic Faith. Anyone who does not believe in this dogma can never enter Heaven. Four years after the definition of this dogma, Our Lady, in 1858, in one of her eighteen apparitions to Saint Marie Bernadette of Lourdes, a little fourteen-year-old girl who lived in southern France, said, by way of innocently emphasizing the papal definition of Pius IX and its meaning, not "I was immaculately conceived," but, "I AM the Immaculate Conception." This she said on the feast of the Annunciation, March 25. Mary let us know thereby that she was the very notion of this grace in the mind of God from all eternity. Mary is God's love, His dove, His beautiful one.

9. Saint Leocadia (303). A glorious little virgin martyr, killed for the Catholic Faith in Spain, is Saint Leocadia. Her home was at Toledo. She was thrown over a precipice by haters of her Faith and her purity. She was a beautiful image of the Mother of God. Her precious body was crushed to pieces from falling on rocks.

Saint Juan Diego (1548). Saint Juan was a 57-year-old Aztec Indian to whom the Mother of God appeared in December, 1531 at Guadalupe, Mexico. She said, "Juan Diego, my good and faithful son, know that I am Mary, ever-Virgin, Mother of the True God.... I am the mother of your people...." She also told Juan she wanted a church built where she stood, on Tepeyac Hill. Though it was winter, she had him pick some roses there on the barren hill. She arranged the roses in his tilma, and sent him with them to Bishop Zumarraga as a proof of her appearance. As Juan opened his tilma in the presence of the bishop, the roses tumbled out and the bishop fell to his knees. There, on Juan's rough tilma was a miraculous picture of the Holy Virgin, just as she had appeared to Juan Diego. A church and later a cathedral were built on Tepeyac Hill, where the holy image on the tilma is displayed to this day. Pilgrims come in throngs to see and honor it. Because of her appearance to Juan Diego, nine million Mexican people were converted. Juan spent his last years as a catechist and the guardian of her image.

10. Our Lady of Loreto. This feast commemorates the translation of the holy little house where Mary was conceived and born, and where Jesus, true God and true Man, was conceived. Houses and dwelling places are an important part of Christian love. The beautiful holy house where Mary and Jesus were both conceived, and where Mary was born, was miraculously transported from Nazareth to Dalmatia in the year 1291. In the year 1294, it was again miraculously transported to the little town of Loreto in northeast Italy. One of the greatest privileges a Catholic can ask of God is to visit this holy house, enter its doorway, and see where Jesus and His virginal Mother lived during Our Lord's childhood, young manhood and hidden life, until He was thirty years of age. Numberless saints visited the Holy House of Loreto, and many, many Popes have given it their blessing. A little saint who especially loved it, and nearly died of joy when she visited it, was Saint Thérèse of the Child Jesus and the Holy Face, the Little Flower.

Saint Eulalia of Mérida (304). She was only a child of twelve and hearing of the persecution of her fellow Christians she traveled to the town of Mérida to denounce the persecutor Judge Dacian. Dacian was at first amused at the young girl and attempted to flatter and bribe her, but she saw his deceits and held firm to her belief in the One True God. Dacian then showed her the instruments of torture if she did not yield to offering incense to the idols. Eulalia then spat at the judge. Dacian commanded the executioners to take her to the place of execution. Iron hooks tore her body and lighted torches were applied to her wounds. Fire from the torches ignited her hair and she suffocated in the smoke. Her tomb is in the Cathedral of Oviedo, Italy.

Blesseds Brian and Sidney (1591). Brian was born in Yorkshire in England and was hanged at Tyburn, during the Protestant Reformation, for sheltering his cousin, a priest. Sidney was hanged at Tyburn for protecting Catholic priests in England. His name may be spelled Sydney.

11. Saint Damasus (384). He was the thirty-ninth Pope. He was a Spaniard, born in Rome. He is called by Saint Jerome, "an incomparable man." He was the Pope of the second Ecumenical Council of the Church (the Council of Constantinople I) that defended the Divinity of the Holy Ghost. He was the Pope who assigned Saint Jerome to make the complete Latin version of the Holy Scriptures that has served all true Catholics from that time to this. One of the great devotions of Saint Damasus was to Saint Laurence the martyr who shed his blood in 258.

Saint Daniel Stylites (494). Saint Daniel became a monk in Syria at the age of 12. He visited Saint Simon Stylites who live on a pillar (*stylos* is Greek for "pillar") and decided to emulate him. Saint Daniel set up his own pillar near Constantinople, where he said Mass, cured the sick, prophesied and converted many. He always remained standing, resting at night by leaning on a balustrade. He climbed down from his pillar only once in 38 years, to warn the people against the heresy of the Monophysites who taught that Our Lord had only one nature. Saint Daniel lived to be 80 years old.

12. Our Lady of Guadalupe (1531). Guadalupe is a little town three miles north of Mexico City. There, in the year 1531, thirty-nine years after Columbus discovered America, Our Lady appeared to a simple Indian fifty-five years old, named Juan Diego. Juan Diego had been converted to the Catholic Faith six years before. Our Lady appeared to this simple Indian three times, and to his uncle once. She wanted a shrine built in Guadalupe in her honor. Our Lady saw in the Mexicans a people she could love and beautifully make her children. For the sake of those who doubted that Juan Diego had seen her, on the morning of December 12, 1531, Our Lady told him to gather the roses from the hill and put them in his cloak and carry them to the bishop of his diocese. Juan Diego did so. When he opened his cloak—the Mexicans call it his *tilma*—in the presence of the authorities, there was found imprinted on it one of the most beautiful pictures of the Mother of God that has ever been seen. This picture is called "Our Lady of Guadalupe." Within eight years after

Saint Lucy

the apparition of Our Lady to this simple Mexican Indian, nine million converts among his people were made to the Catholic Faith. Mexicans have beautifully preserved the Catholic Faith through the years in spite of all the opposition of the enemies of Christ. There are great numbers of Mexicans in Heaven.

Saint Abra (361). She was the daughter of Saint Hilary of Poitiers, a Doctor of the Church, born before he was converted to the Catholic Faith and gave up his wife to God. Saint Abra was eighteen years old when she died, and was the greatest glory of her father's heart.

13. Saint Lucy (304). Saint Lucy was a little Sicilian girl who lived in Syracuse, and was martyred when she was twenty-one years old for the Catholic Faith. Her name is mentioned every day in the Canon of the Mass and always in the Litany of the Saints. Wonderful miracles have been worked through her intercession. She refused to marry a pagan. She died a Christian virgin.

14. Saint Nicasius and Saint Eutropia (407). Saint Nicasius was the Bishop of Rheims in France. He was martyred there, along with his holy sister, Saint Eutropia, and a great number of other Christians. This was in the same year that Saint John Chrysostom went to Heaven.

15. Saint Christiana (Nino) (320). She lived in Georgia in southern Russia. Even when enslaved by the haters of the Catholic Faith, Saint Christiana, by her beautiful humility in all her prayers and by her wonderful miracles, converted thousands and thousands to the one true Faith.

16. Saint Ananias, Saint Azarias, and Saint Misael (Seventh Century B.C.). These were the three handsome and royal Jewish boys (their Babylonian names were Sidrach, Abdenago and Misach) who, during the Babylonian Captivity of the Jews, which lasted from 606 B.C. to 536 B.C., as companions of the great prophet Daniel, by command of the King Nabuchodonosor were asked to eat forbidden food and adore a golden statue. When they refused, they were thrown into a fiery furnace, which had no power to destroy them. It was they who composed, while in the midst of the flames, the beautiful canticle found in the third chapter of the prophet Daniel which the Catholic Church still sings and recites, and which begins, "Blessed art Thou, O Lord, the God of our fathers, and worthy to be praised and glorified and exalted above all forever." Saint Ananias, Saint Azarias and Saint Misael are popularly known as "the three young men in the fiery furnace."

Saint Alice (Adelaide) (999). She was the daughter of a king of Burgundy. She married the King of Italy. On his death, she married the Roman Emperor, Otto the Great. Left a widow, she became the ruler of the Empire. Before her death she dedicated herself to God in a convent as a nun. Saint Alice was a princess, a queen, an empress and a nun. She died at the convent she erected to honor the holy Apostles, Peter and Paul in the town of Seltz on the Rhine, when she was sixty-nine years old. Her body remained there until the French Revolution, and was eventually taken to Vienna. But her remains are thought to have been destroyed by the French Calvinists when the church and monastery were burned and the dust of her body was scattered to the winds.

17. Saint Lazarus (First Century). Saint Lazarus was the brother of Saint Mary Magdalen and Saint Martha. He was raised from the dead by Jesus, as we are told in the eleventh chapter of Saint John. He was one of the very first apostles to France. He was driven out of the Holy Land by the Jews and sailed on a boat without sails or

The Raising of Lazarus

Saint Thomas the Apostle

oars, with his two sisters and others, and landed on the coast of southern France. He became the first Bishop of Marseilles. He is one of the most loved of all the saints of the Catholic French people. His name appears in landmarks all over France in the French from, *Saint Lazare.*

18. The Expectation of the Blessed Virgin Mary (1 B.C.). This is the first day of the octave before the birth of Jesus from the womb of Mary. It is the beginning of Our Lady's last novena, awaiting the coming of her Divine Child, Whom she had kept in her womb for nine months. What those last days of expectation before the nativity of Jesus meant to the heart and soul of the Mother of God, anyone with childlike love can somehow imagine, and with the help of God can realize intensely. It is a loving and prayerful prelude to Christmas to remember Our Lady on this day.

19. Blessed Urban V (1370). Blessed Urban V was a Pope in the fourteenth century during the dreadful period when the Popes were living in Avignon, in France, and not in Rome, where they belonged. This was much to the detriment of the good of the Church. Blessed Urban V was the sixth of the seven Popes to rule the Church from Avignon. By the encouragement of a brilliant Catholic woman, Saint Bridget of Sweden, Pope Urban V made plans to return to Rome, and did so. He was forced to return again to France, where he died. But because of his courage, the Avignon Captivity, which lasted from 1309 to 1377, came to an end under his successor, Pope Gregory XI.

20. Saint Dominic of Silos (1073). He was first a shepherd. He later became a priest and lived as a hermit under the Rule of Saint Benedict. He was appointed Abbot of Saint Sebastian's at Silos in Spain. He miraculously delivered more than three hundred prisoners taken by the Mohammedans shortly after his death. It was because of the intercession of Saint Dominic of Silos that Blessed Jane of Aza brought into the world, in 1170, the great Saint Dominic who founded the Order of Friars Preachers. All the queens of Spain used to keep his staff in their room when they were giving birth to a child.

21. Saint Thomas (74). Saint Thomas the Apostle, who is also called Didymus, which means *twin*, was the great and outstanding apostle to the East after the death and resurrection of Our Lord. Persia and India both learned the true message of the Catholic Faith from this heroic and courageous soldier of the truth. It was Saint Thomas who baptized the Magi, in the year 40. In the year 58, he was miraculously transported back to Jerusalem, on the third day after Our Lady's death. It was his love for

Mary and his eagerness to open her grave and see her body that revealed to all the Apostles and those gathered with him that she had been assumed into Heaven. Saint Thomas was martyred by being pierced through with spears. His body is now reverently and lovingly kept in the town of Ortona in Italy.

Saint Thomas was the same age as Our Lord. He was seventy-four years old when he died in the year 74 A.D. Saint John, the youngest of the Apostles, was eighteen when he was called, twelve years younger than Our Lord, and died in the year 100 at the age of eighty-eight. Saint James the Less was the oldest of the Apostles. He was sixty-five when he was called and ninety-six when he died in the year 62.

22. Saint Flavian (362). He was the husband of Saint Dafrosa and the father of Saint Bibiana (Vivian) and Saint Demetria, all of whom were martyred for the Faith under Julian the Apostate. Saint Flavian, who had once been prefect of Rome, was branded on the forehead as a slave and sent into exile, where he died of privations.

23. Saint Yvo of Chartres (1115). Saint Yvo was a member of the Order of Saint Augustine. He was made Bishop of Chartres, and was a consultant to King Philip of France. He is responsible in no small part for the Code of Canon Law in the Catholic Church as we have it today.

24. Saint Adam and Saint Eve (First Age of the world). As we have said elsewhere, Adam and Eve are not called saints in ordinary reference, historical or scriptural. But they may be called saints on their feast day, which is the vigil of Christmas, because we know from sound Catholic tradition that they repented of their great sin, lived lives of holiness and are now in Heaven. Adam is the father of the human race. Eve, his wife, was formed from Adam's body. All of us have descended from these two. Adam was created in a state of paradisal innocence, with no human frailties or weaknesses. Adam sinned by disobeying the command of God not to eat a forbidden fruit. The whole human race inherited original sin because of Adam. Adam personally repented. Adam lived for 930 years. By his sorrow, his contrition, his pleading, and his love, Adam finally won God's full forgiveness for himself. Adam died and went to the Limbo of the Just, which is called "hell" in the Apostles Creed. This was not the hell of the damned. It was the place where the Just had to wait for the coming of Christ. Adam ascended into Heaven in body and in soul with Our Lord on Ascension Thursday, forty days after Easter. Adam's feast is the vigil of Christmas, which is also the feast of Eve, his wife, who is with him in Heaven.

Saint Sharbel Makhlouf (1898). Saint Sharbel was born in a mountain village of Lebanon. At the age of 23 he became a monk at Saint Maron monastery and was ordained when he was 30. In 1875, after nineteen years in community life, he asked permission to live as a hermit. The remainder of his life was spent in solitary prayer, penance, and adoration of Our Lord in the Blessed Sacrament for the salvation of souls. Both during and after his life he was famous for miraculous cures. During the forty nights after he was buried, a bright light shone around his tomb. Because of this phenomenon his body was exhumed a few months later and found to be incorrupt. Saint Sharbel is the patron saint of Lebanon.

25. The Nativity of Our Lord and Savior Jesus Christ (1 A.D.). On December 25, five thousand, one hundred and ninety-nine years after the creation of the world, in a little stable in the town of Bethlehem, six miles southwest of Jerusalem, of a beautiful young virgin, fifteen years, three months and seventeen days old,

The Birth of Jesus Christ

took place the birth of all births in the history of the world. The Eternal and Everlasting God, the Second Person of the Blessed Trinity, generated in the bosom of the Father before all ages, having taken a human nature (a human soul and a human body) came forth like light from the womb of Mary of Nazareth, in the town of Bethlehem in Judea. Mary was a virgin before, during and after the birth of Jesus. The nativity of Jesus did not in any way alter the virginal character of her body. Jesus issued from Mary's womb as light comes through a window. Mary at once wrapped Jesus in swaddling clothes and laid him in the straw of a manger, where an ox and an ass had been eating. Angels at once began to sing on the hilltops, to tell innocent shepherds what had happened. A star that began to shine on March 25, nine months before, was leading Kings from the East to show them where God was born. It was Christmas Day.

The crib in which Our Lord was laid when He was born is now kept in the Church of Saint Mary Major in Rome.

Saint Anastasia (304). Anastasia was a beautiful Roman woman who for the Catholic Faith was tortured and burned alive in Rome. Every priest remembers her daily in the Canon of the Mass by name. She has the great distinction of being commemorated in the Second Mass of Christmas every year because it was in her church in Rome that the Holy Father used to say the second Mass on Christmas Day, the day on which every priest may say three Masses. Saint Anastasia's mother, Fausta, is a saint and is commemorated on December 19, six days before her martyred daughter.

Saint Eugenia (257). She was a noble young virgin who was converted by her slaves, Saint Protus and Saint Hyacinth. Her father was Saint Philip, a former prefect of Egypt, who became a convert and a martyr. Saint Eugenia founded a convent of virgins. After many trials she was beheaded under Valerian.

26. Saint Stephen (36). The name Stephen means *crown*, and this is appropriate when you think of the saints because the first martyr of the Catholic Faith—the protomartyr as he is called—was named Stephen. Saint Stephen was stoned to death by the Jews in the year 36. Saint Paul was present at this martyrdom, and it was a grace that in no small way caused his conversion. Saint Stephen's full story takes up two chapters in the Acts of the Apostles, Chapters 6 and 7. Saint Stephen was one of the first seven deacons. Saint Stephen's name is mentioned every day in the Canon of the Mass. He is the first martyr named in the Litany of the Saints. He is buried in Rome, beside Saint Laurence, and greatly venerated there. Saint Stephen's greatest honor is that his feast is the day after the birth of Our Lord.

27. Saint John (100).

Saint John the Evangelist was the youngest of all the Apostles. He was twelve years younger than Our Lord and eighteen years old when he became a disciple of Jesus. Saint John was the brother of Saint James and the son of Saint Mary Salome. He is called by God's own inspiration, "the disciple whom Jesus loved." On Mount Calvary he was given charge and care of the Blessed Virgin, the day Jesus died. Saint John the Evangelist was the Blessed Virgin Mary's priest. He said Mass for her every day. He gave her Holy Communion every morning. He listened to her say the *Magnificat* every morning after she had received her Divine Son in

Saint Stephen

the Holy Eucharist. He was the priest who put back into the mouth of the Mother of God the Precious Body and Blood which came from her womb, divinized by the Second Person of the Blessed Trinity. Saint John the Evangelist wrote the fourth Gospel, three Epistles and the Apocalypse: one historical book, three doctrinal books and one prophetical book.

After the death of the Blessed Virgin Mary and her Assumption into Heaven, in the year 58 A.D., Saint John went to Ephesus. He preached in Asia Minor with such intensity and with such fruits that a Roman Emperor had him dragged over to Rome. In the year 95, he was tried in Rome and condemned to be thrown into a caldron of boiling oil, which by God's Providence did him no harm. He was then exiled to the island of Patmos, where he wrote the Apocalypse in the year 95. He then returned to Ephesus where he wrote the fourth Gospel in the year 96, and later his three Epistles. He died at Ephesus, in the year 100. He was eighty-eight years old when he died. No relics of him remain. His body was assumed into Heaven with his soul. Saint Robert Bellarmine assures us of this great fact.

Saint Fabiola (400). She was a noble Roman woman. Her life was at first very worldly. But after becoming a widow and performing public penance, she gave all her wealth for the care of the Catholic sick in a hospital in Rome. She was a great friend of Saint Jerome's. Her wish was to become a nun at Bethlehem, but she was needed in Rome to care for the sick. Crowds of admiring Catholic believers attended her funeral when she died.

28. The Holy Innocents (1 A.D.).

These were seventy-two little Jewish boys of two years and under who were killed by the order of King Herod the Great in his effort to get rid of Jesus, once the news of Our Lord's birth had been made manifest. The Catholic Church calls these little boys "the flowers of the martyrs." They were the first little innocents to die for Jesus, the beginning of the millions who would, in the history of the Catholic Church, be killed for the sake of what they were and what they believed. Relics of several of these holy martyrs are venerated at the Basilicas of St. Mary Major and St. Paul-outside-the-Walls.

29. Saint Thomas à Becket (1170).

Saint Thomas à Becket was an archbishop of Canterbury in England. He became archbishop there in 1162. He would not let any

Saint Thomas à Becket

political power in England move in and govern, or destroy, any kind of the God-given liberties of the Catholic Church. He was killed in his own cathedral in Canterbury at the foot of the altar. His brains and his blood were thrown all about the place by those who claimed to be carrying out the orders of the King. His shrine was one of the most famous and revered in all England. Constant pilgrimages to Canterbury were made up to the time of the Protestant Reformation.

Saint David the King (973 B.C.).

David, the great king and prophet of the Old Testament, whom we call Saint David on his feast day, lived a thousand years before Our Lord. He was King of Israel for forty years, from 1013 to 973. He was seventy years old when he died. Despite his human frailty, his will was notably attached to the love and service and praise of God. It was King David who wrote the one hundred and fifty Psalms that the Catholic Church uses in every part of its prayer, in the Mass and in the Divine Office. King David has been called a "a man after God's own Heart."

30. Saint Sabinus (303).

Saint Sabinus was a heroic Catholic bishop who was martyred along with two of

Pope Saint Sylvester

his deacons at Spoleto, in Italy, under the cruel Emperor Diocletian. His death began by having both his hands cut off, those consecrated hands, which a short time before had been holding the Body of Jesus Christ in the Sacrifice of the Mass.

31. Saint Sylvester (335).

Saint Sylvester I was the thirty-fourth Pope. He was elected to the Chair of Saint Peter in 314, the year after the Emperor Constantine had ended the bloody persecution of the Catholic Church. Saint Sylvester was the Pope who instituted the first Roman Martyrology. He was very devoted to Church music. He is responsible for the Nicene Creed in the Mass and also put in the Mass the invocation *Kyrie Eleison*. He was the Pope of the First Ecumenical Council at Nicea in 325, when Arius, a heretic who denied the Divinity of Jesus, was formally condemned.

Saint Catherine Labouré (1876). She was a religious of the Sisters of Charity of Saint Vincent de Paul. She was sent to a convent in Paris where Our Lady appeared to her three times in the year 1830, and gave her the inspiration for the beautiful miraculous Mary medal, which so many Catholics wear today.

Saint Catherine Labouré is the saint of the Mary medal. Saint Dominic is the saint of the Rosary. Saint Simon Stock is the saint of the Brown Scapular. Saint Francis of Assisi is the saint of the Christmas Crib. Saint Bernadine of Siena is the saint of the Holy Name. Saint Leonard of Port Maurice is the saint of the Stations of the Cross. Saint Paschal Baylon is the saint of the Blessed Sacrament. Saint Gaspar del Bufalo is the saint of the Most Precious Blood. Saint Margaret Mary is the saint of the Sacred Heart of Jesus. Saint Louis Marie de Montfort is the saint of slavery to Mary. Saint Teresa of Avila is the saint of Saint Joseph. Saint Jerome is the saint of the Guardian Angels. Saint Thèrése is the saint of the Holy Face.

We could go on and on, remembering the saints of the Catholic Church and what they especially stood for, but it is December 31 and we have come to the end of our book.

Index

Saints to Remember from A to Z

The date given in parentheses after the saint's name is the year of death. The day of the month is the feast day of the saint and the name day of all those who bear that particular name. Included in the list are popular variations and derivatives of various Christian names. Listings that are not bold are here for reference only. There are no biographical sketches for these in the book.

Archibald (Erkonwald) (686) ------------- April 30
Arlene (Charlene), see **Charles**
Armand, see **Herman**
Arnold (1254) ------------------------------- March 14
Arthur Venerable (1643) ------------- December 11
Ascension
    Earliest ------------------------------------ April 30
    Latest ------------------------------------- June 3
Ash Wednesday
    Earliest ------------------------------ February 4
    Latest ------------------------------------- March 10
Assumption (58) ----------------------- August 15
Athanasia (860) ----------------------- August 14
Athanasius (373) ------------------------- May 2
Audifax (270) ------------------------- January 19
Audrey (Etheldrea) (679) --------------- June 23
Augustine (430) ----------------------- August 28
Augustine of Canterbury (604) ---------- May 28
Azarias (7th cent. B.C.) ------------- December 16

— B —

Baldwin (Balduinus) (1140) ---------------- July 15
Balthasar (1st cent.) -------------------- January 6
Baptism of Our Lord (30) ------------- January 6
    Commemoration ----------------------- January 13
Barachisius (327) ----------------------- March 29
Barbara (235) ------------------------- December 4
Barnabas (60) --------------------------- June 11
Barnard, see Bernard
Barry, see Finbar
Bartholomew (72) ---------------------- August 24
Basil (379) ------------------------------- June 14
Basilica of the Holy Saviour (324) November 9
Basilissa (68) -------------------------- April 15
Beatrice (1490) -------------------------- August 16
Bede the Venerable (735) ----------------- May 27
Benedict (543) ------------------------ March 21
Benedict Biscop (690) ------------------ January 12
Benedict Joseph Labre (1783) ---------- April 16
Benedict the Moor (1589) ---------------- April 4
Benjamin (421) ---------------------------- March 13
Bennett, see **Benedict**
Berard (1220) --------------------------- January 16
Bernadette (1879) -------------------- February 18
Bernard (1153) ------------------------- August 20
Bernard of Menthon (1008) ------------- May 28
Bernardine (1444) ----------------------- May 20
Bernice (4th cent.) ---------------------- October 4
Bertha (725) ------------------------------- July 4
Bertrand (623) ---------------------------- June 30
Beuno (630) ---------------------------- April 21
Bianca, see Blanche
Bibiana (Vivian) (363) --------------- December 2
Blaise (316) ----------------------------- February 3
Blanche (5th cent.) ----------------------- July 5
Bonaventure (1274) ----------------------- July 14
Boniface (755) --------------------------- June 5
Boniface of Tarsus (307) ----------------- May 14
Bonnie, see **Bonaventure**

Botolph (680) ------------------------------June 17
Brandon, see **Brendan**
Brendan (578) ----------------------------- May 16
Brian (1591) ------------------------- December 10
Bridget of Kildare (525) --------------- February 1
Bridget of Sweden (1373) -------------- October 8
Bringing Back of the Child Jesus
from Egypt (3 A.D.) -------------------- January 7
Bruce, see Ambrose
Bruno (1101) --------------------------- October 6
Byron (650) ---------------------------- December 3

— C —

Caesar (Caesarius) (543) ----------------- August 27
Caius (296) --------------------------------- April 22
Cajetan (1547) ---------------------------- August 7
Callistus (222) ---------------------------- October 14
Camilla (437) ------------------------------- March 3
Camillus de Lellis (1614) ------------------ July 18
Canute (1086) ------------------------------January 19
Camela, Carmen, see **Mary**
Carmes, Martyrs of the (1792) ---- September 2
Caroline, see **Charles**
Carrie, see **Charles**
Carter (Carterius) (315) ---------------- November 2
Cary, see **Charles**
Casimir (1483) ---------------------------- March 4
Caspar, see **Gaspar**
Catherine Labouré (1876) --------- December 31
Catherine of Alexandria (307) --- November 25
Catherine of Siena (1380) ---------------- April 30
Catherine of Sweden (1381) ----------- March 22
Cecil, (Cecilius) (3rd cent.) ------------------ June 3
Cecilia (230) -------------------------- November 22
Ceferino Jimenez Malla (1936) ----------- May 4
Celeste, Celia, see **Celestine**
Celestine I (432) ----------------------------- July 27
Celestine V, see **Peter Celestine**
Celsus (68) ---------------------------------- July 28
Ceslas (1242) ------------------------------- July 17
Charity (120)------------------------------ August 1
Charles Borromeo (1584) ----------- November 4
Charles Garnier (1649) ----------- September 26
Charles Lwanga
and Companions (1886-1887) ------------- June 3
Charles the Good (1124) ---------------- March 2
Charlotte, see **Charles**
Cherry, see **Charity**
Cheryl, see **Charles**
Chester (Ceslas) (1242) -------------------- July 17
Chinese Martyrs --------------------------July 9
Christ the King
    Earliest ------------------------------- October 25
    Latest --------------------------------- October 31
Christian (1138) ----------------------------- June 12
Christiana (Nino) (320) ------------December 15
Christina (295) --------------------------- July 24
Christopher (250) ------------------------- July 25
Chrysogonus (304) ------------------ November 24

Circumcision (1 A.D.)------------------ January 1
Clara, see **Clare**
Clare (1253) ---------------------------- August 12
Clarence (620) ----------------------------- April 26
Claude de la Colombiére (1682) --- February 15
Claudia (1st cent.) ------------------------ August 7
Claus, see **Nicholas**
Clement (100) ------------------------ November 23
Clement Mary Hofbauer (1820) ------ March 15
Cleophas (1st cent.) ----------------- September 25
Cletus (90) ------------------------------- April 26
Clotilde (545) ------------------------------ June 3
Cloud (560) --------------------------- September 7
Coleen, see **Colette**
Colette (1447) ----------------------------- March 6
Colin, see **Nicholas**
Colman (689) -------------------------------- July 8
Columba, see Columbkille
Columba Marmion (1923) ------------- October 3
Columbkille (597) ------------------------- June 9
Concetta, see **Mary**
Connor, Conor, see **Cornelius**
Conrad (1894) ------------------------------ April 21
Constance (1st cent.) ---------------- September 19
Cora, Cordelia, Cordula, see **Delia**
Cornelius (253) ---------------------- September 16
Cornelius the Centurion (1st cent.) - February 2
Corpus Christi
  Earliest -------------------------------- May 21
  Latest --------------------------------- June 24
Cosmas (303) ------------------------- September 27
Creation, First Day of ------------------ March 20
Crispin (285) ----------------------------- October 25
Crispinian (285) ------------------------ October 25
Crystal, see **Christina**
Cunegunda (1040) ----------------------- March 3
Cynthia (249) ----------------------------- February 8
Cyprian (258) ------------------------- September 16
Cyriacus (4th cent.) --------------------- August 8
Cyril (869) -------------------------------- July 7
Cyril of Alexandria (444) ------------- February 9
Cyril of Jerusalem (386) -------------- March 18
Cyrus (303) ------------------------------- January 31

— D —

Daisy, see **Margaret**
Dafrosa (363) --------------------------- January 4
Damasus (384) ----------------------- December 11
Damian (303) ------------------------- September 27
Damien the Leper (1889) ---------------- May 10
Daniel (5th cent. B.C.) ------------------- July 21
Daniel Stylites (494) ----------------- December 11
Daphne --------------------------------------- July 13
Darlene (Daria) (283) ------------------- October 25
David of Wales (601) ---------------------- March 1
David the King (973 B.C.) --------- December 29
Death of Our Lady (58) --------------- August 13
Deborah (13th cent. B.C.) ------------- September 1
Delbert (Adalbert) (997) ------------------ April 23

Delia (383) -------------------------------- October 22
Delphina, Delphine (1360) --------- September 26
Demetria (363) ----------------------------- June 21
Denis (95) -------------------------------- October 9
Denise (484) ---------------------------- December 6
Dermot O'Hurley (1584) ----------------- June 30
Derrick (Theodoric) (533) ----------------- July 1
Diane (1236) --------------------------------- June 9
Dismas (33) -------------------------------- March 25
Divine Maternity of Our Lady ----- October 11
Dolores, see **Mary**
Dominic (1221) ---------------------------- August 4
Dominic of Silos (1073) ------------- December 20
Dominic Savio (1857) -------------------- March 9
Donald (8th cent.) ------------------------- July 15
Donna (Donata) ---------------------- December 31
Dora, Doreen (Theodora) (132) ----------- April 1
Doris, see **Dorothy**
Dorothy (311) --------------------------- February 6
Drew, see **Andrew**
Duane (Dubhan) (6th cent.) ---------- February 11
Duns Scotus (1308) -------------------- November 8
Dunstan (988) -------------------------------- May 19
Dymphna (7th cent.) ------------------------ May 15

— E —

Earl (Herluin) (1078) ------------------- August 26
Easter (First) ---------------------------- March 27
  Earliest ------------------------------- March 22
  Latest ---------------------------------- April 25
Edgar (975) --------------------------------- July 8
Edith (984) ----------------------------- September 16
Edith Stein (1942) ------------------------ August 9
Edmund Campion (1581) ----------- December 1
Edna (695) ----------------------------------- July 5
Edward the Confessor (1066) ------- October 13
Edwin (633) ----------------------------- October 12
Eileen, see **Helena**
Elaine, see **Helena**
Eleanor, see **Helena**
Eleutherius (585) ------------------------ September 6
Elias (9th cent. B.C.) ---------------------- July 20
Eliseus (9th cent. B.C.) ------------------- June 14
Elizabeth (1st cent.) ----------------- November 5
Elizabeth Ann Seton (1821) ----------- January 4
Elizabeth of Hungary (1231) ----- November 19
Elizabeth of Portugal (1336) -------------- July 8
Ella, see **Helena**
Ellen, see **Helena**
Elliott, see Elias
Elmer (Ermelius) ------------------------- August 25
Elmo, see **Erasmus**
Eloise, see **Louise**
Elsie, see **Elizabeth**
Emil (Emilian) (574) ---------------- November 12
Emily (1852) ------------------------- September 19
Emma (1045) --------------------------------- June 29
Emmanuel (304) ------------------------- March 26
Ephrem (373) ------------------------------- June 18

Harry, see **Henry**
Harvey (575) -------------------------------- June 17
Hedwig (1243) -------------------------- October 16
Heidi (Adelaide), see **Alice**
Helena (330) ------------------------------- August 18
Henry (1024) ------------------------------- July 15
Herbert (687) ----------------------------- March 20
Herman Joseph (1241)--------------------- April 7
Herman the Cripple (1045) ------- September 25
Hermengild (585) -------------------------- April 13
Hesychius (4th cent.) --------------------- October 3
Hilary (468) -------------------------- February 28
Hilary of Poiters (368) ----------------- January 14
Hilda (680) -------------------------- November 17
Hildebrand, see **Gregory VII**
Hildegarde (1179)------------------ September 17
Hippolytus (236) ------------------------- August 13
Holy Family, Sunday within the Octave of the Epiphany
Holy Innocents (1 A.D.) ------------ December 28
Holy Name of Jesus (1 A.D.) ---------- January 2
Holy Name of Mary (16 B.C.) ---- September 12
Holy Relics ---------------------------- November 5
Holy Rosary ------------------------------- October 7
Hope (120) ----------------------------------- August 1
Howard, (Philip Howard) (1595) ----- October 19
Hubert (727) ------------------------------ November 3
Hugh of Cluny (1109) ---------------------- April 29
Hugh of Grenoble (1132)------------------ April 1
Hugh of Lincoln (1200) ------------ November 17
Humphrey, see **Onuphrius**
Hyacinth (1257) ------------------------- August 17
Hyacintha Mariscotti (1640) --------- January 30
Hyginus (158) ---------------------------- January 11

— I —

Ida (1113) ----------------------------------- April 13
Ignatius of Antioch (107) ------------- February 1
Ignatius of Constantinople (877) --- October 23
Ignatius of Loyola (1556) ----------------- July 31
Ilsa, Ilse, see **Alice**
Imelda (1333) ------------------------------- May 12
Immaculate Conception (17 B.C.)   December 8
Immaculate Heart of Mary ----------- August 22
Inez, see **Agnes**
Ingrid (13th cent.) ----------------------------- July 1
Iphigenia (1st cent.) ------------------ September 21
Irenaeus (202) ---------------------------- June 28
Irene (304) ----------------------------------- April 5
Irene of Portugal (653) --------------- October 20
Irish Martyrs (1579-1654) --------------- June 30
Irma (Irmina) (708) ------------------- December 24
Irving (Urban) (230) ------------------------ May 25
Isaac Jogues (1646) ----------------- September 26
Isabel, see **Elizabeth**
Isaias (7th cent. B.C.) ----------------------- July 6
Isidore (636) -------------------------------- April 4
Isidore the Farmer (1170) ----------- October 25
Ita (570) ----------------------------------- January 15

Ivan, see **John**

— J —

Jacinta Marto (1920)----------------- February 20
Jack, see **John**
Jacob (1689 B.C.) ------------------------ August 28
Jacqueline, see **James**
James Duckett (1602) --------------------- April 19
James Kisai (1597) --------------------- February 5
James of the Marches (1476) ----- November 28
James the Greater (42) --------------------- July 25
James the Less (62) ------------------------- May 11
Jane Frances de Chantal (1641) ----- August 21
Janet, see **Jane**
Janice, see **Jane**
Januarius (304) ---------------------- September 19
Jared (1st age) ------------------------------ March 1
Jarvis, see **Gervase**
Jason (283) ------------------------------ December 3
Jasper, see Gaspar
Jean, see **Joan**
Jeanne Jugan (1879) --------------------- August 30
Jeff, see **Godfrey**
Jennifer, see **Jane**
Jeremias (590 B.C.) ------------------------- May 1
Jerome (420) ------------------------- September 30
Jerome Emiliani (1537) ----------------- February 8
Jesse (11th cent. B.C.) ----------------- December 29
Jessica, see **Jane**
Jill, see **Julia**
Jillian, see **Juliana**
Joachim (4 B.C.) ------------------------- August 16
Joan of Arc (1431) -------------------------- May 30
Joanna (1st cent.)------------------------- May 24
Joel (8th cent. B.C.) ------------------------- July 13
John (362) -------------------------------- June 26
John Baptist de la Salle (1719) ---------- May 15
John Baptist de Rossi (1764) ------------- May 23
John Berchmans (1621) --------------- August 13
John Bosco (1888) --------------------- January 31
John Cantius (1473) ------------------- October 20
John Capistrano (1456) --------------- March 28
John Chrysostom (407) ---------------- January 27
John Climacus (605) -------------------- March 30
John Damascene (749) ------------------ March 27
John de Brébeuf (1649) ------------ September 26
John de Goto (1597) -------------------- February 5
John de Lalande (1646) ----------- September 26
John Duns Scotus (1308) ------------- November 8
John Eudes (1680) ---------------------- August 19
John Fisher (1535) ------------------------- July 6
John Francis Regis (1640) --------------- June 16
John-Gabriel Perboyre (1840) --- September 11
John Joseph (1734) ------------------------ March 5
John Leonardi (1609) ------------------- October 9
John Marie Vianney (1859) ----------- August 8
John Massias (1645)----------------- September 18
John Nepomucene (1393) ----------------- May 16
John Neumann (1860) ------------------ January 5

Onesimus (95) ------------------------ February 16
Onuphrius (Humphrey) (400) -------------- June 12
Orestes (304) --------------------------- November 9
Oscar (Ansgar) (865) -------------------- February 3
Oswald (642) --------------------------------- August 5
Otho (1220) ------------------------------- January 16
Our Lady, Health of the Sick -------- August 24
Our Lady, Help of Christians ------------ May 24
Our Lady, Mediatrix of All Graces --- May 31
Our Lady, Mother of the Good Shepherd
-- September 3
Our Lady of Fatima (1917) -------------- May 13
Our Lady of Good Counsel (11ᵗʰ cent.) April 26
Our Lady of Guadalupe (1531) --- December 12
Our Lady of Knock (1879) ----------- August 21
Our Lady of Loreto ----------------- December 10
Our Lady of Lourdes (1858) ------- February 11
Our Lady of Mount Carmel -------------- July 16
Our Lady of Perpetual Help (13ᵗʰ cent.) June 27
Our Lady of Pontmain (1871) ------- January 17
Our Lady of Prompt Succor ---------- January 8
Our Lady of Ransom (1218) ----- September 24
Our Lady of Sorrows ------------- September 15
Our Lady of Victories -------------------- March 2
Our Lady of the Angels ---------------- August 2
Our Lady of the Blessed Sacrament ---- May 13
Our Lady of the Holy Cross of Jer. - March 31
Our Lady of the Pillar (36) ---------- October 12
Our Lady of the Snows (355-366) ----- August 5
Our Lady of the Way -------------------- May 24
Our Lady, Queen of Martyrs ------------ May 13
Our Lady, the Mother of Fair Love ---- May 31
Owen (680) (also see **Nicholas Owen**) --- March 3

— P —

Pachomius (348) --------------------------- May 9
Padre Pio (1968) -------------------- September 23
Pamela, see **Helen**
Pancho, see **Francis**
Pancratius (304) -------------------------- May 12
Pantaleon (305) --------------------------- July 27
Paphnutius (356) -------------------- September 11
Paschal Baylon (1592) -------------------- May 17
Patricia (665) --------------------------- August 25
Patrick (493) --------------------------- March 17
Paul (362) ---------------------------------- June 26
Paul, Apostle (67) ------------------------ June 30
  Basilica ------------------------------ November 18
  Beheading --------------------------------- June 29
  Conversion (36) ---------------------- January 25
Paul Chong Hasang (1839) ------- September 20
Paul Miki (1597) ----------------------- February 5
Paul of the Cross (1775) ----------------- April 28
Paul, the First Hermit (342) ---------- January 15
Paula (404) ------------------------------- January 26
Paulinus (431) --------------------------- June 22
Pearl, see **Margaret**
Peggy, see **Margaret**

Pentecost
  Earliest -------------------------------------- May 10
  Latest -- June 13
Peregrine (1345) ---------------------------- May 1
Perpetua (203) --------------------------- March 6
Peter (67) -------------------------------- June 29
  Basilica---------------------------- November 18
  Chair of (36) (42) -------------------- February 22
Peter (304) ------------------------------------ June 2
Peter Canisius (1597) -------------------- April 27
Peter Celestine V (1296) ------------------ May 19
Peter Chrysologus (450) ------------- December 4
Peter Claver (1654) ------------------- September 9
Peter Damian (1072) ------------------ February 23
Peter Faber (1546) ----------------------- August 11
Peter Julian Eymard (1868) ------------ August 3
Peter Louis Chanel (1841) --------------- April 28
Peter Mavimenus (743) -------------- February 21
Peter Nolasco (1256) ------------------- January 28
Peter of Alcantara (1562) ------------ October 19
Peter of Morocco (1220) --------------- January 16
Peter of Rome (304) ------------------------ June 2
Peter of Verona (1252) ------------------ April 29
Petronilla (1ˢᵗ cent.) ---------------------- May 31
Philip (61) ----------------------------------- May 11
Philip Benizi (1285) -------------------- August 23
Philip Howard (1595) ----------------- October 19
Philip Neri (1595) ------------------------- May 26
Philip of Jesus (1597) ----------------- February 5
Philip the Deacon (1ˢᵗ cent.) --------------- June 6
Philomena (304) ----------------------- August 11
Phoebe (1ˢᵗ cent.) --------------------- September 3
Photina (1ˢᵗ cent.) ------------------------ March 20
Pio, Padre (1968) -------------------- September 23
Pius I (167) --------------------------------- July 11
Pius V (1572)--------------------------------- May 5
Pius IX (1878) ------------------------- February 7
Pius X (1914)-------------------------- September 3
Placid (541) ------------------------------ October 5
Polycarp (166) -------------------------- January 26
Polyeucte (259) ----------------------- February 13
Porphyry (420) ------------------------ February 26
Precious Blood --------------------------------- July 1
Presentation of Mary (13 B.C.) -- November 21
Presentation in the Temple (1 A.D.) - February 2
Prisca (270)---------------------------- January 18
Priscilla (1ˢᵗ cent.) ------------------- January 16
Protase (165) -------------------------------- June 19
Pulcheria (453) ---------------------- September 10
Purificaton (1 A.D.) -------------------- February 2

— Q, R —

Queenship of Mary ------------------------ May 31
Quentin (287) ----------------------------- October 31
Quevedo, Mary Teresa (1950) ----------- April 8

Rachel (18ᵗʰ cent. B.C.) --------------- September 2
Rainier (1160) ----------------------------- June 17
Ralph (700) ----------------------------------May 27

Ralph Milner (1591) ------------------------- July 7
Raphael, Archangel -------------------- October 24
Raymond Nonnatus (1240) ----------- August 31
Raymond of Capua (1399) -------------- October 5
Raymond of Pennafort (1275) ------- January 23
Reba, see Rebecca
Rebecca (3rd cent.) -------------------- September 4
Regina (250) --------------------------- September 7
Reginald (1220) ------------------------- February 1
Relics, see Holy Relics
Remigius (Remi) (533) ------------------ October 1
René Goupil (1642) ----------------- September 26
Resurrection and First Easter (33) -- March 27
Richard (1253) ------------------------------ April 3
Richard, King (720) -------------------- February 7
Rita (Margherita) (1456) ------------------ May 22
Robert Bellarmine (1621) ----------------- May 13
Robert of Newminster (1159) ------------ June 7
Rocco (1327) ----------------------------- August 16
Roderick, Roderigo (857) -------------- March 13
Roger (1367) -------------------------------- March 1
Roger Dickenson (1591) --------------------- July 7
Roland (1386) ------------------------- September 15
Romanus (258) --------------------------- August 9
Romanus (1010) ---------------------------- July 24
Romuald (1027) ------------------------- February 7
Ronald (1158) ---------------------------- August 20
Rosalia (1160) ------------------------ September 4
Rosamond (11th cent.) ----------------------- April 3
Rose of Lima (1617) -------------------- August 30
Rose of Viterbo (1252) -------------- September 4
Rose Philippine Duchesne (1852) November 17
Roy, (Rufus) (200) ------------------ November 12
Rudolph (1066) ------------------------- October 17
Rupert (720) ------------------------------- March 27
Ruth (13th cent. B.C.) ----------------- September 1

— S —

Sabbas (372) ------------------------------- April 12
Sabbas, Abbot (532) ----------------- December 5
Sabina (127) ------------------------------ August 29
Sabinus (303) ------------------------- December 30
Sacred Heart
    Earliest ---------------------------------- May 29
    Latest -------------------------------------- July 2
Sadie, Sally (Sarah) (19th cent. B.C.) - August 19
Salvator (1567) ---------------------------- March 18
Samona and Her Seven Sons (168 B.C.) August 1
Samson, Sampson (565) --------------------- July 28
Samuel (11th cent. B.C.) ----------------- August 20
Sancho (851) --------------------------------- June 5
Sandra, Sanders see Alexander
Saturninus (303) --------------------- November 29
Scholastica (543) ---------------------- February 10
Sebastian (288) -------------------------- January 20
Selma, see Anselm
Sennen (250) ------------------------------- July 30
Septuagesima Sunday
    Earliest -------------------------------- January 18

Latest ----------------------------------- February 21
Serapion (4th cent.) ------------------------ March 21
Sergio (Sergius) (701) ----------------- September 8
Seth (1st age) --------------------------------- March 1
Seven Holy Founders (1233) ------- February 12
Seven Joys of Our Lady --------------- August 27
Shamus, see James
Sharbel Makhlouf (1898) ---------- December 24
Sharon ("Rose of Sharon," title of Our Lady) ---- Sept. 12
Shawn, see John
Sheila, see Cecilia
Sidney (1591) --------------------------- December 10
Sidonius (1st cent.) ----------------------- August 23
Sigmund (Sigismund) (524) ----------------- May 1
Silas (1st cent.) -------------------------------- July 13
Silverius (538) ------------------------------ June 20
Simeon (1st. cent.) ------------------------- October 8
Simeon Stylites (459) --------------------- January 5
Simon (67) --------------------------------- October 28
Simon of Trent (1475) ------------------ March 24
Simon Stock (1265) ------------------------- May 16
Sixtus II (258) ------------------------------- August 7
Solemn Espousals of Our Lady and
Saint Joseph (1 B.C.) ------------------- January 23
Sonya, see Sophia
Sophia (120) ------------------------------ September 30
Sophie, see Madeleine Sophie
Sophronius (639) -------------------------- March 11
Soter (182) ----------------------------------- April 22
Stacy, see Anastasia
Stanislaus Kostka (1568) ---------- November 13
Stanislaus of Cracow (1079) --------------- May 7
Stella, see Mary
Stephanie (1530) ------------------------- January 2
Stephen (36) ------------------------------ December 26
    Finding of body (415) ------------------ August 3
Stephen of Hungary (1038) --------- September 2
Susanna (295) ---------------------------- August 11
Swithin's Day (964) ----------------------- July 15
Sybil (Sibyllina) (1367) ------------------ March 23
Sylvester (335) ------------------------- December 31
Sylvia (572) --------------------------------- November 3

— T —

Tammy, see Thomas
Tanya, see Anthony
Tarsicius (255) --------------------------- August 15
Telesphorus (154) ------------------------ January 5
Terence (1st cent.) ---------------------------- June 21
Terence O'Brien (1651) ------------------ June 30
Teresa Benedicta of the Cross (1942) -- August 9
Teresa of Avila (1582) ---------------- October 15
Teresa of Saint Augustine
and Companions (1794) ------------------ July 17
Teresa of the Andes (1920) --------------- July 13
Terry, see Teresa or Terence
Thaddeus, see Jude
Theban Legion (286) ---------------- September 22
Thecla (117) --------------------------- September 23

Thelma (Anthelmus) (1178) --------------- June 26
Theodora (120) ----------------------------- April 1
Theodore (310) --------------------------------July 4
Theodore (306) -------------------------- February 7
Theophane Venard (1861) -------- November 24
Theopistus (118) --------------------- September 20
Thèrése Couderc (1885) ------------- September 26
Thèrése of Lisieux (1897) -------------- October 3
Thomas (74) -------------------------------December 21
Thomas à Becket (1170) ------------- December 29
Thomas Aquinas (1274) ------------------- March 7
Thomas More (1535) --------------------------July 6
Thomas of Villanova (1555) ------ September 22
Tiffany see **Theophane**
Tillie, see **Matilda**
Timothy (97) ----------------------------- January 24
Timothy of Egypt (286) --------------------- May 3
Tina, see **Christina**
Titus (96) --------------------------------- February 6
Titus Brandsma (1942) -------------------- July 26
Tobias (8th cent. B.C.) --------------- September 13
Tracy, see **Teresa**
Transfiguration (32) --------------------- August 6
Trinity Sunday
    Earliest ------------------------------------- May 17
    Latest --------------------------------------- June 20
Turibius (1606) -------------------------- March 23

— U, V —

Ugandan Martyrs (1886) -------------------- June 3
Una, see **Winifred**
Urban V (1370) ----------------------- December 19
Ursula (383) ----------------------------- October 21

Valentine (269) ----------------------- February 14
Valerian (229) -------------------------------- April 14
Valerie, (Valeria) (2nd cent.) --------------- April 28
Valerius (1st cent.) ---------------------- January 29
Vanessa (Esther) (6th cent. B.C.) ------------July 1
Vera, see **Veronica**
Vernon (Berno) (927) -------------------- January 13
Veronica (1st cent.) ----------------------- July 12
Veronica Giuliani (1727) -------------------- July 9
Vicky, see **Our Lady of Victories**

Victor (1st cent.) --------------------------- March 20
Vida, see **David**
Vincent (304)------------------------------January 22
Vincent de Paul (1660) -------------------- July 19
Vincent Ferrer (1419)---------------------- April 5
Vincent Mary Strambi (1824) -------- January 1
Viola, Violet ----------------------------------- May 3
Virgil (Virgilius) (784) -------------- November 27
Virginia, see **Mary**
Visitation of Our Lady (1 B.C.) -----------July 2
Vitus (303) ---------------------------------- June 15
Vitalis (2nd cent.) ------------------------- April 28
Vivian, see **Bibiana**
Vladimir (1015) ----------------------------- July 15

— W, X, Y, Z—

Walburga (779) ----------------------- February 25
Walter (1099) --------------------------------- April 8
Warren, (Guarinus) (1159) ----------- February 6
Wayne (Dwynan) (2nd cent.) --------------- April 8
Wenceslaus (935) -------------------- September 28
Wendell (Wendelin) (650) ----------- October 21
Werner (1275) -------------------------------- April 19
Wilfred (709) ----------------------------- October 12
William of Norwich (1144) ------------ March 24
William Tirry (1654) --------------------- June 30
William the Abbot (1142) --------------- June 25
Willibald (786) --------------------------------July 7
Willibrord (739) ----------------------- November 7
Winifred (650) ------------------------- November 3
Wolfgang (994) ------------------------- October 31

Xavier, see Francis Xavier

Yolanda (1298) ------------------------------ June 15
Yvo (1115) --------------------------------- December 23
Yvonne (1303)------------------------------- May 19

Zachary (1st cent.) --------------------- November 5
Zachary, Pope (752) --------------------- March 22
Zeno (303) ------------------------------- December 22
Zephyrinus (217)------------------------- August 26
Zita (1278) --------------------------------- April 27
Zoe (140) -------------------------------------- May 2

The Most Common Patron Saints and Intercessors

Abandoned Children ---- Jerome Emiliani
Accountants -------------- Matthew
Actors --------------------- Genesius, Vitus
Advertising -------------- Bernardine of Siena
Air travelers ------------- Joseph Cupertino
Altar boys ---------------- John Berchmans
Anesthetists -------------- René Goupil
Archers ------------------- Sebastian
Architects ----------------- Barbara, Thomas,
                Apostle
Art ------------------------- Catherine of Bologna

Artillerymen ------------- Barbara
Artists --------------------- Luke
Astronomers ------------- Dominic
Athletes ------------------- Sebastian
Authors ------------------- Francis de Sales
Aviators ------------------- Our Lady of Loreto,
                Joseph Cupertino

— B —

Bakers -------------------- Elizabeth of Hungary,
                Nicholas of Myra
Bankers/Bank workers -- Matthew

Picture Credits:

Special thanks to the Salesians for the Cover picture of Our Lady Help of Christians and to Carey Winter for art used on:

p. 13—St. John Bosco

p. 47—Blessed Damien the Leper

p. 91—St. John Marie Vianney

p. 95—St. Maximilian Kolbe

p. 143—Blessed Miguel Pro